中华翻译文摘

2006—2010

Abstracts of
Chinese Translation
Studies

罗选民 主编

中国出版集团
中译出版社

图书在版编目(CIP)数据

中华翻译文摘：汉英对照/罗选民主编．—北京：中译出版社，2019.4
（中译翻译文库）
ISBN 978-7-5001-5908-7

Ⅰ.①中… Ⅱ.①罗… Ⅲ.①翻译理论-文集-汉、英 Ⅳ.①H059-53

中国版本图书馆CIP数据核字（2019）第042637号

出版发行／中译出版社
地　　址／北京市西城区车公庄大街甲4号物华大厦6层
电　　话／(010) 68359827, 68359376（发行部）；53601537（编辑部）
邮　　编／100044
传　　真／(010) 68357870
电子邮箱／book@ctph.com.cn
网　　址／http://www.ctph.com.cn

出 版 人／张高里
总 策 划／贾兵伟
策划编辑／胡晓凯
责任编辑／胡晓凯　范祥镇
封面设计／黄　浩

排　　版／北京竹页文化传媒有限公司
印　　刷／北京玺诚印务有限公司
经　　销／新华书店

规　　格／710毫米×1000毫米　1/16
字　　数／304千字
印　　张／20.5
版　　次／2019年4月第一版
印　　次／2019年4月第一次

ISBN 978-7-5001-5908-7　　定价：59.00元

版权所有　侵权必究
中 译 出 版 社

本书编委会

国际顾问　International Advisory Board
Annie Brisset, University of Ottawa, Canada
Goran Malmqvist, Royal Swedish Academy of Sciences
Howard Goldblatt, University of Colorado, USA
Mona Baker, University of Manchester, UK

主　编　Chief Editor
罗选民　清华大学/广东外语外贸大学
Luo Xuanmin, Tsinghua University/Guangdong University of Foreign Studies

副主编　Associate Editors
莫爱屏　广东外语外贸大学
Mo Aiping, Guangdong University of Foreign Studies
侯　松　广东外语外贸大学
Hou Song, Guangdong University of Foreign Studies

编　委　Editorial Board
陈　琳　同济大学
Chen Lin, Tongji University
黄　勤　华中科技大学

Huang Qin, Huazhong University of Science and Technology

赖慈芸　台湾师范大学
Sharon Tzu-Yun Lai, National Taiwan Normal University

李德凤　澳门大学
Li Defeng, University of Macau

苗　菊　南开大学
Miao Ju, Nankai University

孙艺风　澳门大学
Sun Yifeng, University of Macau

司显柱　北京第二外国语学院
Si Xianzhu, Beijing International Studies University

谭载喜　香港浸会大学
Tan Zaixi, Hong Kong Baptist University

王东风　中山大学
Wang Dongfeng, Sun Yat-sun University

王　宁　清华大学/上海交通大学
Wang Ning, Tsinghua University/Shanghai Jiao Tong University

文　军　北京航空航天大学
Wen Jun, Beihang University

张春柏　华东师范大学
Zhang Chunbai, East China Normal University

张　政　北京师范大学
Zhang Zheng, Beijing Normal University

周领顺　扬州大学
Zhou Lingshun, Yangzhou University

序

《中华翻译文摘》（以下简称《文摘》）（2006—2010）即将付梓。与以往一样，《文摘》（2006—2010）源自中国大陆及港澳台地区的期刊论文和专著，具体包括：CNKI 期刊库、三大文摘（《人大复印资料》《高校社会科学文摘》《新华文摘》）、超星数字图书馆、香港学术期刊网、香港中文大学出版社、香港牛津大学出版社网站、香港台湾各大书店的网上平台、澳门中文期刊论文索引、台湾华艺线上图书馆、华艺学术文献库、台湾师范大学图书馆网站、台湾书目查询系统、台湾大学出版社、联经出版社等著名出版社网站。我们先从中精选 140 篇/年，并按一定的主题进行归类，然后请评审专家剔除其中 30—40 篇，再联系作者修改、拓展其摘要。考虑到一些主客观因素，《文摘》（2006—2010）最终定稿 100 篇左右。必须指出的是，《文摘》所有入选的文章，全以电子邮件寄送给各位编委，在收到他们的反馈意见后，我们又对之进行调整和补充；选材不仅考虑文章的质量，也考虑其代表性。然而，由于种种原因，仍有不少好的文章未能收入，我们将力求今后把遴选的工作做得更细一些。《文摘》（2006—2010）以中英文对照的形式编排，在某些方面做了一些改进，内容更加充实，选材更加宽泛，版式更加美观，特色更加突出。

我们对作者提供的中英文摘要初稿加以审阅，并做了必要的编辑、修改等工作。在编辑过程中，我们得到了诸多方面的支持，首先要感谢广东外语外贸大学对《文摘》重新启动的大力支持，没有这样的支持，我们的工作是很难顺利开展的。

我们对编委会的专家学者也特别感激，他们在百忙之中帮助《文摘》

审阅选稿，其认真负责的态度和精神，可谓是中国翻译学研究事业发展之大幸！此外，广东外语外贸大学高级翻译学院研究生周子淳、严怿洲、周秀能、李志翔，广东外语外贸大学国家级同声传译实验教学中心莫娟老师等做了大量的联络、编排等工作，对他们的辛勤付出也表示由衷的感谢。

我们还要感谢中译出版社，英国 Routledge 出版集团及 Abstracts of Translation Studies 要将英文电子版收入，为我们的《文摘》走出国门、走向世界奠定了基础。由于《文摘》(2006—2010) 编辑过程短，加上中间部分编辑成员易人，书稿留下了一些缺憾。我们期待来自学界更多的关注、批评与指正，也希望得到专家、学者们的关心和扶持。

最后，我们要感谢所有的读者和入选文摘的作者，因为只有他们的大力支持，《文摘》才能越办越好，才能成为译苑中一朵鲜艳的花蕾。

目 录

翻译理论与思想 / 001
Translation Theories / 003

翻译史 / 063
Translation History / 065

翻译文学与文化 / 107
Translated Literature and Culture / 109

语言学与翻译 / 173
Linguistics and Translation / 174

学科与应用翻译研究 / 189
Applied Translation Studies / 190

翻译教学 / 213
Teaching of Translation / 214

语料库、翻译技术与机器（辅助）翻译 / 245
Corpus, Translation Technology and Machine (Aided) Translation / 246

口译研究 / 275
Interpreting Studies / 276

翻译研究专著 / 297
Monographs on Translation Studies / 298

翻译理论与思想

1. 从"忠实于源文本"到"对源语文化负责":也谈翻译规范的重构　刘亚猛
2. "文化转向"核心问题与出路　曾文雄
3. 新史料求证严复的翻译思想——从发展的角度看"信、达、雅"的包容性和解释力　周领顺
4. 传事已尽,尚质而无斫凿;委本从圣,求真务令有失——道安"五失本、三不易"说源流考及现代诠释　祝朝伟
5. 翻译即解释:对翻译的重新界定——哲学诠释学的翻译观　朱健平
6. 重新解读韦努蒂的异化翻译理论——兼与郭建中教授商榷　蒋骁华、张景华
7. 论双语翻译的认知心理研究——对"翻译过程模式"的反思和修正　刘绍龙
8. 译者的职责　孙致礼
9. 当代中西翻译质量评估模式的进展、元评估及发展方向　武光军
10. 译者"思维习惯"——描述翻译学研究新视角　邢杰
11. 论翻译批评空间的构建　刘云虹
12. 文化翻译与全球本土化　孙艺风
13. 翻译能力的构成因素和发展层次研究　王树槐、王若维
14. 试论翻译认知心理学的研究内容与方法　颜林海
15. 翻译、诠释、权力意志　陈佩筠
16. 解构主义翻译理论的论争与接受——以"确当的"翻译为例　韩子满
17. 新历史主义与翻译　蒋骁华
18. 论译文的效度和信度　司显柱、刘利琼
19. 距离合法性视角下译者当译之本的知情选择与情感同构　屠国元、李静
20. 翻译的诗学变脸　杨柳
21. 文本类型理论及其对翻译研究的启示　张美芳

22. 视域差与翻译解释的度——从哲学诠释学视角看翻译的理想与现实　朱健平
23. "翻译诗学观念"：论美国语言诗的诗学观及其翻译　罗良功
24. 探析自译——问题与方法　桑仲刚
25. 转喻的图式——例示与翻译的认知路径　谭业升
26. "翻译腔"与翻译任务复杂度和译者工作记忆关系的实证研究　王福祥、徐庆利
27. 翻译研究、学术规范与文化传统　张南峰

Translation Theories

1. From Being Faithful to Source Text to Being Responsible to Source Culture: Toward a New Norm of Translation **LIU Yameng**
2. New Perspective on the Core Issues of the "Cultural Turn" **ZENG Wenxiong**
3. Yan Fu's Real Intention in Light of New Historical Materials: The Capacity and Interpretation of *xin, da, ya* in Perspective of Development **ZHOU Lingshun**
4. Dao An's "Five Losses and Three Difficulties" and Its Modern Interpretation **ZHU Chaowei**
5. Translating Is Interpreting: Redefining "Translating" from the Perspective of Philosophical Hermeneutics **ZHU Jianping**
6. A New Approach to Venuti's Foreignizing Translation Theory **JIANG Xiaohua & ZHANG Jinghua**
7. On Bell's Process Model and the Cognitive Study of Translation **LIU Shaolong**
8. On the Responsibilities of the Translator **SUN Zhili**
9. A Review, a Meta-Evaluation and an Anticipation of the Developments of Contemporary Translation Quality Assessment Models **WU Guangjun**
10. Translators' "Habitus": A New Perspective on Descriptive Translation Studies **XING Jie**
11. Opening up the Space for Translation Criticism **LIU Yunhong**
12. Cultural Translation and Glocalization **SUN Yifeng**
13. On the Components and Developments of Translation Competence **WANG Shuhuai & WANG Ruowei**
14. On Cognitive Psychology of Translation: Its Scope and Methodology **YAN Linhai**
15. Translation, Interpretation and Will-to-Power **CHEN Peiyun**

16. Contention and Reception of Deconstructionist Translation Theories: Based on "Relevant" Translation **HAN Ziman**
17. New Historicism and Translation **JIANG Xiaohua**
18. From Fidelity to Validity: A Relevance Theoretical Perspective on the Evaluation of Translation **SI Xianzhu, LIU Liqiong**
19. Legitimate Choice of SL/TL Distance in Translation **TU Guoyuan & LI Jing**
20. Poetic Rewriting in Translation **YANG Liu**
21. Text Typology and Its Implications for Translation Teaching **ZHANG Meifang**
22. Horizon Gaps as the Determinant of Interpretive Degree in Translation: A Perspective of Philosophical Hermeneutics **ZHU Jianping**
23. "Translate Poetic Ideas": On LANGUAGE Poetry and Its Translation **LUO Lianggong**
24. A Review of the Studies on Self-Translation: Problems and Method **SANG Zhonggang**
25. Schema-instance Hierarchy of Metonymy and the Mental Paths of Translation **TAN Yesheng**
26. An Empirical Study of "Translationese" in relation to Translation Task Complexity & Working Memory **WANG Fuxiang & XU Qingli**
27. Translation Studies, Academic Norms and Cultural Traditions **CHANG Nam Fung**

1

作　　者　刘亚猛

标　　题　从"忠实于源文本"到"对源语文化负责":也谈翻译规范的重构

发表刊物　《中国翻译》2006年第6期

[摘　要]　如何在放弃"忠实原则"之后重新构筑一个富有时代感的翻译规范是学界当前面临的一个重大理论问题。尽管作为该原则替代方案的"译者中心"翻译观风靡一时,但它以意义不确定为理由豁免译者正确解读原文义务的主张却忽略了在具体历史条件下和特定源语文化框架内源文本往往存在着一个局限而稳定的意义范围这一关键事实,在理论上未能自洽。在政治意识形态上,"译者中心"模式是否可取同样存疑。该模式无法排除译者的"强势"翻译造成与源文本相关各方遭受误导性表述和粗暴对待的可能性。被过分授权的译者所行使的"话语暴力"不仅在政治、法律、商业等实用翻译领域足以带来严重后果,在学术、文学等翻译领域也经常对当事方造成具有实在影响的误导及扭曲,而且其最大受害者往往不是源文本或其作者,而是他们所代表的非主流意识形态或弱势文化。鉴于此,本文主张在"忠实原则"受到质疑之后对翻译规范进行的再思考应以译者所承担的责任以及译出语的文学、智力话语传统作为必不可少的参照点,应该超越对译者责任进行理论归纳时往往只考虑到的"译者/译入语"或"译者/原文"这两大关系,转而将注意力聚焦源语文化。任何足以取代"忠实原则"的新翻译规范都应该强调译者对译出语的话语传统负有义务和责任,并要求在翻译过程中尊重源语文化作为独立的意义生成体系享有的对原文的最终解读权。这一要求的规范化将在很大程度上减小通过翻译行使话语暴力及文化霸权的可能性,有利于保护弱势源语文化。

关 键 词　忠实原则;解构;源语文化;责任;霸权主义

作者联系地址　福建省福州市仓山区金山街道公园道一号 60-1102
邮　　编　350008
电子邮箱　ymlfjfz@126.com

1

Author: LIU Yameng

Title: From Being Faithful to Source Text to Being Responsible to Source Culture: Toward a New Norm of Translation

Published in: *Chinese Translators Journal*, 2006 (6).

[Abstract]　With the principle of fidelity sufficiently discredited, how to reconstruct the norm of translation for our time is posing an increasingly formidable challenge to translation scholars. The translator-centered ideology, catapulted into popularity by radical rejection of a text- or an equivalence-centered conception of translation, is unlikely to be adopted as the centerpiece of a new paradigm, primarily for two reasons. First, it is theoretically incoherent, having based itself on a one-sided notion of the uncertainty of the ST's meaning—or on a simplistic understanding of interpretation as a "free play"—without taking into consideration at the same time the ST's relative semantic stability within the specific cultural context in which it is embedded. And secondly, despite all the claims to the contrary, the translator-centered model is suspect politically and ideologically as well: its undue empowerment of the translator often results in discursive violence against—or representational injustice for—the ST author and the source culture, causing negative material consequences to some of the parties involved. To remedy such a situation, this paper proposes that two requirements be built into any new norm of translation, to function as part of the essential constraints on the translator's behavior. These requirements are: 1) the translator should develop a sense of responsibility toward the cultural and intellectual traditions with which the ST is associated, and be guided by such a sense throughout the process of translation; and 2) the translator should show proper respect for the source culture as an independent signifying system within which the ST's meaning is ultimately determined, or for the relevant interpretive community within the source culture as the final arbiter whenever the meaning of the ST is in doubt. A source culture-oriented approach to constructing a post-fidelity new norm, which the two requirements above call into being, would go a long way toward installing a proper check on the power the translator is allowed to exercise and toward ensuring justice in the practice of translation.

Key words: fidelity; deconstruction; source culture; responsibility; hegemony

2

作　　者　曾文雄
标　　题　"文化转向"核心问题与出路
发表刊物　《外语学刊》2006年第2期
[摘　要]　翻译研究的"文化转向"这一术语源于巴斯奈特和勒菲弗尔的论文集《翻译，历史与文化论集》，指转向文化研究视角的翻译研究，将翻译视为文化和政治活动，关注翻译与文化间的相互作用、文化影响和制约翻译的方式。基于分析"文化转向"的哲学根源及其翻译学理念，本文指出，"文化转向"颠覆翻译研究的语言学派的语言转换理论，将翻译置于宏观的语境中，考察历史、社会文化因素包括意识形态、权力、赞助人、诗学、规范等对翻译操纵，其研究取向一方面拓宽了翻译研究的视角，着重考察具有普遍性的社会文化因素对翻译的制约，尤其是对文学翻译的影响，另一方面它使翻译研究带有文化研究泛化的倾向，消解了翻译研究的本体。回应"文化转向"存在的问题，我们必须明确翻译研究的任务和目标，翻译学研究应基于理性交往，回归语言，将语言转换研究与文化语境

研究相融合，并避免文化转换和翻译研究的"文化霸权主义"，实现平等的跨文化交流。

关 键 词 翻译学；文化转向；回归语言；理性交往

作者联系地址 广东省广州市海珠区仑头路 21 号

邮　　编　510320

电子邮箱　wxiongz@163.com

2

Author: ZENG Wenxiong
Title: New Perspective on the Core Issues of the "Cultural Turn"
Published in: *Foreign Language Research*, 2006 (2).

[Abstract] The term of "the cultural turn" used in translation studies taken up by Bassnett and Lefevere as a metaphor in their collection of *Translation, History and Culture*, refers to the move towards the analysis of translation from cultural studies in translation studies, focusing on the interaction between translation and culture, on the way in which culture impacts and constrains translation activity. Based on the analysis of the philosophical foundations and core theories of the cultural turn in translation studies, this paper points out that the cultural turn subverts linguistic transfer theories of the linguistic school and examines translation in its sociocultural environment and socio-cultural factors such as ideology, power, patronage, poetics, norms and conventions by which translation is manipulated. It is argued that, on the one hand, the cultural turn broadens the perspective of translation studies with emphasis on such universal constraints as social and cultural factors on translation activity especially on literary translation, on the other hand, it makes translation studies characterized with general cultural studies and dispels the ontology of translation studies.

In response to the problems of "the cultural turn", it requires our clear understanding of the tasks and objectives of translation studies, and translation studies should be based on the philosophy of rational communication, with the integration of linguistic transformation studies and cultural context in translation, avoiding the cultural hegemony in cultural transformations and translation studies in order to achieve equal cross-cultural exchanges.

Key words: translatology; the "cultural turn"; return to linguistics; rational communication

3

作　　者　周领顺

标　　题　新史料求证严复的翻译思想——从发展的角度看"信、达、雅"的包容性和解释力

发表刊物　《四川外国语学院学报》2006年第3期

[摘　要]　通过对比新的史料发现，"信、达、雅"的意义与传统上的理解稍有出入，严复的本意应该加以澄清。"信、达、雅"可以这样用英语表述：to have genuineness for the author, to have ability to help to communicate the message to the reader, and to make improvements to make the translation be better，可用 genuineness、communicability 和 improvements 代之。

　　对严复"本意"的考证虽不免会有一些臆猜的成分，但根据新的翻译事实并以发展的眼光不断增强其译论的包容性和解释力，无疑是有积极意义的。严复的翻译实践印证了他的翻译思想，其精髓确有有效指导翻译实践的作用。中国传统译论与西方译论有颇多契合之处，且往往殊途同归。

关 键 词　严复；"信、达、雅"；新史料；包容性；解释力；发展
作者联系地址　江苏省扬州市华扬西路196号，扬州大学外国语学院
邮　　编　225127
电子邮箱　zhoulingshun@163.com

3

Author: ZHOU Lingshun

Title: Yan Fu's Real Intention in Light of New Historical Materials: The Capacity and Interpretation of *xin, da, ya* in Perspective of Development

Published in: *Journal of Sichuan International Studies University*, 2006 (3).

[Abstract] In light of new historical materials, we have come to an understanding that people have somewhat distorted *xin, da, ya*, the standards of translation put forward by the well-known translator Yan Fu. *xin, da, ya* could be expressed in English as follows: 1) to have genuineness for the author, 2) to have ability to help to communicate the message to the reader, and 3) to make improvements to make the translation better. Or, in short, genuineness, communicability and improvements.

Even though the textual research of the so-called real intention may be prejudiced, it is still meaningful to enlarge the capacity of Yan Fu's standards and to strengthen their interpretations in terms of development and new practices. Yan Fu's translation practices justified his views and the essence of his views is really workable in translating. The traditional Chinese views on translations are in line with their Western counterparts, which often draw the same or similar conclusions.

Key words: Yan Fu; *xin, da, ya*; new historical materials; capacity; interpretation; development

4

作　者　祝朝伟

标　题　传事已尽，尚质而无斫凿；委本从圣，求真务令有失——道安"五失本、三不易"说源流考及现代诠释

发表刊物　《四川外语学院学报》2006 年第 6 期

[摘　要]　本文以道安"五失本、三不易"的翻译思想为中心，详细地讨论该学说提出的历史根源、哲学源起以及道安本人的宗教思想和政治抱负方面的原因，并分析道安思想中所反映出的翻译文质观、文体观和语言文化观。

　　从历史而论，道安"五失本、三不易"思想是对当时"死译"和"随意删减之自由译法"的折中与修正，其对翻译增删量的限制，有助于佛经的准确传译；就哲学而言，东晋时期道家天道观与佛家天命论相互契合，人们多采用"格义"法翻译佛经，导致译文机械生硬、质量拙劣，道安的"五失本、三不易"思想，对于纠正"削胡适秦、饰文灭质、求巧失旨"的倾向、准确传达原文意旨起到了重要作用。此外，作为一个虔诚的佛教徒，道安希望通过佛教思想的引进，为知识精英和统治阶级找到精神归宿和统治工具。因此，在佛经翻译中必须克服"格义"法的局限。道安提出"五失本、三不易"的思想，其目的是确保佛经翻译的准确性，最终实现个人的抱负。

　　"五失本、三不易"的思想反映了道安的文质观、文体观与语言文化观。从文质而言，道安认为，译者的职责是传事以尽，因而忠实是体，文质是用；就文体而论，道安的思想较早地阐述了汉语与梵文在文体上的差异，但其"胡文尚质"的思想是个人的主观论断，受当时佛经翻译重古朴的传统影响使然；在语言文化方面，"五失本、三不易"思想系统地阐述了中印在语言与文化上的差异及翻译方法，对佛教与印度文化的传播起了极大的推动作用。

　　本文一方面发掘了道安翻译思想的历史、哲学及个人根源，使当代翻

译研究者可以更好地理解其思想产生的原因,另一方面,文章结合当代语境,对道安的思想进行现代阐释,明确其译论对当代翻译研究的意义与贡献。

关 键 词 道安;五失本、三不易;文质

作者联系地址 重庆市沙坪坝区烈士墓壮志路33号,四川外国语大学

邮 编 400031

电子邮箱 zhuchaowei@sisu.edu.cn

4

Author: ZHU Chaowei

Title: Dao An's "Five Losses and Three Difficulties" and Its Modern Interpretation

Published in: *Journal of Sichuan International Studies University*, 2006 (6).

[**Abstract**] This paper focuses on the discussion of Dao An's translation theories of "Five Losses and Three Difficulties", offering the historical and philosophical background as well as his personal religious reason and political ambition. Besides, it elucidates An's ideas on "*wen* (florid linguistic form)" and "*zhi* (literary content)", styles of language in translation, and the differences between the Chinese and Indian languages and cultures.

An's idea on translation, as regards history, comes from his intention to rectify the word-for-word or too liberal translation methods, warning translators against free addition or reduction to unsure an accurate translation. In terms of philosophy, translators in the East Jin Dynasty tended to naturalize the Sanskrit concepts with traditional Chinese counterparts as a result of the conformity between the Taoist philosophy of nature and the Buddhist fatalism, leading to rigid renditions of a poor quality. Criticizing the wrong methods while providing guidance, An's idea is conducive to the correct understanding and accurate translation of the original Sanskrit texts. Moreover, An's proposition of the "Five

Losses and Three Difficulties" can be attributed to his personal goal of helping the intellectuals to be spiritually settled, and his political pursuit of supporting the ruling class through the translation of Buddhist scriptures.

An's "Five Losses and Three Difficulties" are also an expression of his ideas on *wen* and *zhi*, and his understanding of stylistic, linguistic and cultural differences between the Indian and Chinese languages. Despite the debate on the differences of *wen* and *zhi*, An holds that the translator should go beyond these differences to ensure a faithful translation of the original text. In terms of the stylistic differences of the Indian and Chinese languages, he thinks that Sanskrit is plain whereas Chinese is florid, which is a personal understanding resulting from the mainstream practice of Buddhism translation. Regarding the linguistic and cultural differences between the two languages, Dao An highlights his translation methods in accordance with these discrepancies, facilitating the spread of Indian Buddhist culture into China at that time.

The digging of the historical, philosophical and personal reasons for the proposition of An's translation theories can help translation scholars to better understand him. Meanwhile, an interpretation of his ideas in conformity with the modern translation context aids considerably in our attempts to rethink his contributions to contemporary translation studies.

Key words: Dao An; "Five Losses and Three Difficultie"; *wen* and *zhi*

5

作　　者	朱健平
标　　题	翻译即解释：对翻译的重新界定——哲学诠释学的翻译观
发表刊物	《解放军外国语学院学报》2006年第2期
［摘　要］	本文从哲学诠释学角度出发对翻译进行了重新界定，认为翻译即解释，具体地说，翻译的过程就是，在跨文化的历史语境中，具有历史

性的译者使自己的视域与源语文本的视域互相发生融合而形成新视域,并用浸润着目的语文化的语言符号将新视域重新固定下来形成新文本的过程。

该定义强调翻译的解释性特征,并运用伽达默尔哲学诠释学的视域融合概念对这一传统的西方诠释学命题注入了新的内涵。该定义中各要素的基本逻辑关系如下:

1)翻译就是解释,解释就是视域融合。

2)翻译过程中的视域融合不仅发生在理解阶段,而且发生在表达阶段。

3)理解阶段的视域融合是指译者使自己的视域与源语文本视域互相发生融合而形成新视域的过程;表达阶段的视域融合是理解阶段视域融合的继续,是指译者将刚形成的不稳定的新视域用目的语的语言符号重新固定下来形成新文本(即目的语文本)的过程。

4)由于两次视域融合的发生,目的语文本视域已不同于源语文本视域,但二者并非截然不同,而是一种同中有异、交叉互补的关系。

5)视域融合后形成的新视域之所以不同于其前的任何一个视域,是因为参与融合的各方(包括译者、源语文本和目的语语言)的视域都具有历史性。

6)翻译所在的跨文化历史语境对新视域的形成也发挥了重要作用。

7)在所有各方中,译者在视域融合中始终处于主动地位,译者是历史性和主体性的统一体。

8)该定义体现了描述性、动态性、开放性、译者因素和文化因素等特征。

关 键 词 哲学诠释学;翻译;解释;视域融合
作者联系地址 湖南省长沙市岳麓区麓山南路 2 号,湖南大学外国语学院
邮 编 410082
电子邮箱 zhujianpinghzh@126.com

5

Author: ZHU Jianping

Title: Translating Is Interpreting: Redefining "Translating" from the Perspective of Philosophical Hermeneutics

Published in: *Journal of PLA University of Foreign Languages*, 2006 (2).

[Abstract] The paper redefines translating from the perspective of philosophical hermeneutics. It holds that translating is interpreting. Specifically, translating is the process in which the translator with his history fuses his own horizon with that of the ST in a cross-cultural historical situation and forms a new horizon, and then he constructs a new text, namely, the TT, by using the newly acquired horizon in the TL, which is soaked with the TC.

That translating is interpreting is a traditional proposition in the Western hermeneutics, and this paper infuses into it something entirely new by applying H. G. Gadamer's (1900-2002) concept of "fusion of horizons". The following explains the logical relationship among all parts of the definition.

1) Translating is interpreting which is the process of fusion of horizons.

2) In translating, fusion of horizons occurs not only in understanding but also in expressing.

3) Fusion of horizons in understanding is the process in which the translator fuses his own horizon with that of the ST and forms a new horizon, and in expressing fusion of horizons occurs when the translator continues to fix the newly acquired fluid horizon in the TL to construct a new text, namely, the TT.

4) The two fusions of horizons lead to a TT which is different from its ST in some way. Specifically, the TT and its ST are two different and autonomous texts with certain degrees of similarity and certain overlapping parts.

5) The reason for the difference between the new horizon formed after each

fusion and those existing before their fusion is the historicity that the horizons of all the parties involved in fusions, i.e. the translator, the ST and the TL, have.

6) The cross-cultural historical situation in which translating occurs also plays an important role in the formation of the new horizon.

7) Among all the parties involved in translating, the translator, which is the unity of historicity and subjectivity, is always the one who plays the most decisive role in the fusions of horizons.

8) The above definition of translating is characterized with being descriptive, dynamic and open, as well as taking translator and culture into consideration.

Key words: philosophical hermeneutics, translating, interpreting, fusion of horizons

6

作　　者　蒋骁华、张景华
标　　题　重新解读韦努蒂的异化翻译理论——兼与郭建中教授商榷
发表刊物　《中国翻译》2007年第3期

[摘　要]　郭建中于1998年最早介绍了韦努蒂的异化翻译理论；2000年郭先生较系统地阐发了韦努蒂的异化翻译理论；同年稍晚，他在其专著《当代美国翻译理论》中专辟一节（第八章第二节），更系统地阐述了韦努蒂异化翻译理论的来源、内容及其影响。郭先生始终认为韦努蒂异化翻译理论是典型的解构主义翻译理论。后来持相同观点的还有不少学者，如邓红风（2003）、任淑坤（2004）、封一函（2006）等。我们查阅了不少西方有关文献，但迄今尚未找到与郭先生类似的观点。另外，韦努蒂异化翻译理论引进后，我国译界出现了一场对异化和归化的讨论。据不完全统计，仅2000年到2005年底年我国学术刊物上有关归化异化的论文多达300余篇。这些论文，概括起来，大约有以下两种情况：1）认为异化翻译基本上相

当于直译,如,谭惠娟(1998),刘重德(1999),郑海凌(2001),孙致礼(2002)等;2)认为异化翻译是直译的延伸,其内涵比后者丰富,如,朱志瑜(2001),王东风(2002),葛校琴(2002),尹衍桐(2005)等。可问题是,既然异化翻译与直译不完全相等,那异化翻译的内涵究竟有哪些方面呢?本文将探讨几个关键问题:1)韦努蒂异化翻译理论的内涵;2)韦努蒂的译者著作权思想与其异化理论的内在联系;3)韦努蒂的异化翻译理论是否属于解构主义翻译理论。

关 键 词 韦努蒂;异化翻译理论;解构主义
作者联系地址 澳门高美士街,澳门理工学院语言暨翻译高等学校
电子邮箱 xhjiang@ipm.edu.mo

6

Author: JIANG Xiaohua & ZHANG Jinghua
Title: A New Approach to Venuti's Foreignizing Translation Theory
Published in: *Chinese Translators Journal*, 2007 (3).

[Abstract] Ever since Venuti's foreignizing translation theory was introduced into China in 1998, misunderstandings and/or misinterpretations have not been rare to be found in publications. This paper attempts a new approach to Venuti's foreignizing translation theory, trying to make clear the following three questions: 1) what are the connotations of Venuti's foreignizing translation theory? 2) what is the inner link between Venuti's translator authorship thought and his foreignizing translation theory? and 3) can Venuti's foreignizing translation theory be subsumed under the deconstruction school of translation?
Key words: Venuti; foreignizing translation theory; deconstruction

7

作　　者　刘绍龙
标　　题　论双语翻译的认知心理研究——对"翻译过程模式"的反思和修正
发表刊物　《中国翻译》2007年第1期
［摘　要］　随着对西方人文科学理论流派的引进和国外翻译理论研究的深入，我国的翻译理论研究正朝着科学化、多元化的方向发展。其中，对翻译实践主体——译者的翻译心理研究已引起翻译理论界的关注。翻译理论要谋求发展就必须研究翻译（内在）过程，实现从只重译品向译品与过程并重的研究转向。本文旨在通过对"翻译过程模式"及其理论思想的七点修正和对"过程"研究的重新思考说明：1）翻译过程的实质是心理的而非物质的；2）译品是由过程来实现的，译者只有理解其内在过程才有望改进翻译技巧、提高译作质量；3）贝尔的翻译过程模式并非铁板一块的真理，对其进行科学、合理的认识和反思将有益于学术心理的健康发展和翻译认知科学的不断创新。

在反复研读"过程"模式之"分析"和"合成"两个主要环节及其相关内涵的基础上本文指出了该过程模式潜在的七点问题：1）过于圆滑的"非线性"辩解；2）过于单一的箭头线条；3）过于线性的"小句"加工；4）过于孤立、"偏远"的认知加工器；5）过于笼统、含混的"记忆系统"；6）过于独立、抽象的"语义表征"；7）过于晦涩、隐含的概念诠释。其中的"过于"意指模式设计者在分析和描述该模式的两个主要构成阶段、三个操作层面及其相关成分和功能时表现出的较为极端、粗放的分析和假设。

最后，在对贝尔模式进行反思的基础上，本文围绕"过程"提出了有待深入思考的几个问题，如：源语解码和译语编码是否享有共同的心理机制和相同的认知运作策略？译者翻译心理与其翻译行为和效果存在何种关系？如何培养健康、高效的翻译心理及加工机制？

关 键 词　双语翻译；过程模式；译者心理；加工机制

作者联系地址　浙江省杭州市下城区潮王路 18 号，浙江工业大学外国语学院

电子邮箱　lsldvd@126.com

7

Author: LIU Shaolong

Title: On Bell's Process Model and the Cognitive Study of Translation

Published in: *Chinese Translators Journal*, 2007 (1).

[Abstract] Most researchers of translation in China have been so preoccupied with describing and interpreting Bell's process theory of translation that hardly any effort has been made to subject it to a systematic cognitive examination and a critical assessment. Taking this situation into account, the author of this paper undertakes to rethink Bell's process model and comes up with three claims involving "process" research, as well as seven drawbacks to the Process Model.

The three claims made by the author are: 1) translating is by nature a complex cognitive process; 2) since target texts result from such a process, its understanding holds the key to improving translation; and 3) Bell's psychological model of translation is necessarily fallible, and a critical reexamination of the model would help to deepen our understanding of the psychology of translation.

The seven drawbacks to Bell's model can briefly be summarized as follows: 1) the over-saponaceous justification on the non-linearity of the Model; 2) the over-simplex arrow lines much used in the Model; 3) the over-linear processing of "clause" highlighted in the Model; 4) the over-isolate and-remote cognitive processor claimed in the Model; 5) the over-general and ambiguous "memory system" illustrated in the Model; 6) the over-independent and-abstract "semantic representation" stated in the Model; 7) the over-obscure or hard-to-understand concepts and interpretations as regards the whole Model.

Finally, the author thinks there is still much to be thought through regarding the translating "process" and its cognitive research, e.g., 1) Do translators or interpreters share a mental mechanism and cognitive processing strategies in terms of source-language decoding and target-language encoding? 2) What is the relationship between translator's cognitive mind and his/her translating performance and effect? 3) How could a translator's healthy, efficient cognitive mind and processing mechanism be developed?

Key words: bilingual translation; process model; translator's mind; processing mechanism

8

作　　者　孙致礼
标　　题　译者的职责
发表刊物　《中国翻译》2007年第4期
[摘　要]　翻译传统的"忠实观"打破之后，译者在认识上存在困惑，本文意图为译者提供一种思维框架来解开这种困惑。随着翻译理论的发展，人们认识到翻译这种极其复杂的社会文化交际行为受制于文本性质、翻译目的、社会文化语境、语言差异等多重因素，忠实不应该是衡量译作的唯一标准，同时也并不存在绝对忠实的翻译。于是译者负有哪些职责、应产出什么样的译文，就成为需要讨论的问题。本文借助安德鲁·切斯特曼总结的五种翻译伦理模式来探讨译者的职责问题。

译者的职责包括：1）再现原作：如无其他制约因素，译者的基本职责是准确透彻解读原文、尽可能多地传达原文在语言层面和文化层面的真实意义；2）完成委托人的要求：满足该要求，带来委托人预期的结果，就是成功的翻译；3）符合目的语社会文化规范：译者既要注意不给目的语语言文化带来不应有的侵犯，又要对源语语言文化给予足够的尊重；4）满足目的语读者需求；译者既要考虑到源语和目的语语言文化间的巨大差异，又要注意适度提高读者的阅读情趣和接受能力；5）恪守职业道德：译者应该从民族利益出发判断译介价值，选择自己能够胜任的任务，一旦接受任务就必须竭尽全力去完成；译者还要孜孜不倦提高自己的翻译水平，努力成为合格的翻译人才。上述五个方面共同规范、平衡、制约着译者的翻译活动，而译者寻求平衡与和谐的过程，就是产出合理译文的过程。

本文的意义在于：1）结合中国的翻译实际；2）借助切斯特曼的分类模式探讨译者身处的"张力网"，从而系统化译者的思考对象。

关 键 词　忠实/不忠实；伦理问题；译者的职责
作者联系地址　河南省洛阳市涧西区广文路2号院45栋东门
邮　　编　471003
电子邮箱　sunzhili_215@sina.com

8

Author: SUN Zhili

Title: On the Responsibilities of the Translator

Published in: *Chinese Translators Journal*, 2007 (4).

[Abstract]　Faithfulness, the utmost standard of translation held for a long time, was somehow overthrown with the development of translation studies, when it is gradually revealed that the extremely complex social communicative act called translation is defined by a variety of factors such as the text type, translation skopos, social and cultural contexts, and differences between source and target languages. It turned out that faithfulness should not be regarded as the only standard, and that no translation is absolutely faithful to the original. Thus, what the translator's responsibilities are becomes a question. This paper attempts to answer this question within the framework of the five translation ethics analyzed by Andrew Chesterman.

The translator's responsibilities are: 1) Representing the source text. It is the basic responsibility of the translator to approach the ST as accurately as possible and then covey it in the TT as truly as possible both in language and in culture; 2) Meeting the commissioner's requirements. The meeting of the requirements and the achieving of the expected result equate to a successful translation; 3) Abiding by the target social cultural norms. The norms in TT should not be unduly violated and norms in the ST should be respected; 4) Satisfying the target reader's need(s). The needs of learning something new and modifying those already in the TT culture should be met; 5) Abiding by professional ethics. The translator should only introduce those worthy texts and the texts s/he is capable of handling. S/he should spare no efforts in completing the translation well. The five responsibilities act together to regulate the translator's behavior, and the translator, in his/her struggle for a balance between the five, is thus able to produce a justified target text.

Key words: faithful/unfaithful translation; ethics of translation; translator's responsibilities

9

作　　者　武光军
标　　题　当代中西翻译质量评估模式的进展、元评估及发展方向
发表刊物　《外语研究》2007年第4期
[摘　要]　翻译质量评估研究一直是当代中西翻译界研究的核心问题。本文首先厘定了翻译质量评估的性质及理论定位。翻译质量评估就是译文评价，评价就是价值判断，是主体按照一定的标准对客体的价值进行判断的过程。翻译质量评估有两个基本的属性：客观性和主体性。翻译质量评估应是主观与客观、定性与定量的有机统一。

然后，全面梳理了当代中西方翻译质量评估模式的进展。本文认为西

方当代真正意义上的翻译质量评估模式主要有两大类：原则参照模式与参数参照模式。原则参照模式的翻译质量评估模式的特点是，只在翻译质量评估的宏观层面上制定纲领性的原则作为译文评价的标准，没有具体的评估指标。当代西方的翻译质量评估原则参照模式又可分为：反应原则参照模式、语篇类型原则参照模式和功能原则参照模式。参数参照模式就是评估人根据自己的判断预先设计出一组自己认为最相关的参数，赋予各个参数一定的权重，然后以参数为参照将原文与译文进行对比，最后对译文作出评价或定级。当代中国翻译理论界对翻译质量评估这一重大课题也进行了许多研究。与西方相比，中国的翻译质量评估研究有一个明显的特点，就是将其纳入翻译标准研究的名下。

其次，我们对当代中西翻译质量评估模式进行了一次元评估。在对评估研究的评估方面，我们认为研究者首先要厘定评估中的两个核心概念"对等"和"错误"。在对具体评估活动的评估方面，我们认为评估中一定要考虑模式的准确性、可行性、实效性。

最后，本文指出未来合理的翻译质量评估模式应包含两个层次上的评估：整体上的模糊评估与局部上的精确评估。

关 键 词　翻译质量评估模式；元评估；发展方向

作者联系地址　北京市朝阳区定福庄南里 1 号，北京第二外国语学院英语学院

电子邮箱　wuguangjun@bisu.edu.cn

9

Author: WU Guangjun

Title: A Review, a Meta-Evaluation and an Anticipation of the Developments of Contemporary Translation Quality Assessment Models

Published in: *Foreign Languages Research*, 2007 (4).

[Abstract]　The study of translation quality assessment (TQA) has been one of the focuses of contemporary Chinese and western translation studies. This paper firstly defines the nature and theoretical position of translation quality assessment. It was proposed that translation quality assessment is the evaluation of translation, and "evaluation" means value judgment. The theoretical position of translation quality assessment in translation studies can be seen from two perspectives. On the one hand, it belongs to applied translation studies. On the other, it can be categorized as value theory in translation studies.

Afterwards, a comprehensive review of the development of contemporary Chinese and western TQA models is made. This paper argues that the models of translation quality assessment in contemporary western countries fall under two main categories: principle- referenced models and parameter-based models. A lot of researches on the issue of TQA have also been carried out by contemporary Chinese translation theorists. Compared with the West, there is an obvious feature of the study of TQA in China, which is the inclusion of TQA in the study of translation criteria.

In addition, a meta-evaluation is made of the models of contemporary Chinese and western TQA. As to assessment of the researches on TQA, it is proposed that the two core concepts "equivalence" and "error" must be clarified. As to the second level, it is argued in the paper that the accuracy, feasibility and effectiveness of the models of TQA must be taken into consideration when evaluating the quality of the translation.

Last but not least, suggestions for future studies of TQA are offered in the paper. It is argued that a reasonable TQA model should include two levels of assessment: the globally fuzzy evaluation and the locally accurate evaluation.

Key words: translation quality assessment; meta-evaluation; development

10

作　　者　邢　杰
标　　题　译者"思维习惯"——描述翻译学研究新视角
发表刊物　《中国翻译》2007 年第 5 期
[摘　要]　翻译社会学是翻译研究历经语文学、语言学和文化研究阶段之后的又一重要理论方法。翻译与社会之间联系紧密，翻译产生于社会，也与社会整体环境密不可分。翻译作为一种跨语言、跨文化的交际活动，亦遵从一定的社会运行机制。翻译涉及人与人、人与机构、机构与机构甚至是翻译主体与机器之间的交流互动，在这个过程中，就包含了生产、传播、接受和社会交际等各个方面。然而，无论影响翻译的各种因素有多复杂，翻译社会学的框架有助于研究者把视角始终聚焦于译者作为社会人的角色上。通过考察译者的"思维习惯"（habitus）、"资本"（capital）及其身处其间的"场域"（field），打通主观与客观、内部与外部及宏观与微观之间的关联，从而构建翻译这一社会实践领域的全景。

本文尝试从诞生于文化社会学的"思维习惯"概念入手，考察其理论渊源、存在方式及其对描述翻译学的充实与完善。"思维习惯"作为"认知"和"社会"视角的二维融合，充分彰显译者本身对翻译行为的决定性作用。通过内化为译者本身的性情，"思维习惯"直接影响到译者对翻译的理解、态度乃至所采用的翻译策略。这补充了以往描述翻译学侧重"规范"影响下的解释框架，认为翻译行为的诱因可能并不仅仅在于外部因素的干预，也可能是源自主体自发的行为。透过"思维习惯"，我们能够看到译者违反"规范"，体现"多变性"、"创造性"乃至充分进行"个人发明"的可能性，从而为更全面地解释翻译这一多元、杂和系统中涵盖的各类现象提供了足够的空间。当然，在分析"思维习惯"对译者的影响时，也应力图避免庸俗决定论的倾向。

关 键 词　翻译社会学；描述翻译学；思维习惯；场域；资本；规范
作者联系地址　广东省广州市白云区白云大道北 2 号，广东外语外贸大学

高级翻译学院
电子邮箱　xingjie.xj@gmail.com

10

Author: XING Jie

Title: Translators' "Habitus": A New Perspective on Descriptive Translation Studies

Published in: *Chinese Translators Journal*, 2007 (5).

[Abstract] Following philological, linguistic and cultural paradigms in Translation Studies (TS) throughout its history, an emerging sociology of translation has come to the fore since the end of the 20th century. It is believed that as both a process and product, translation is embedded in social contexts and, consequently, governed by various social rules. Thus, methodologically informed by different branches of social theories and by employing sociological concepts such as Bourdieu's *habitus*, *capital* and *field*, researchers in TS find themselves in a better position to examine translators as social agents and their relations to other agents and various institutions, as a result of which translation as a field of social practices could be constructed and translators' behaviors could be described, interpreted and, if possible, predicted in the future. In this paper, the author argues that the cultural sociological concept *habitus* adds significantly to the interpretive framework of Descriptive Translation Studies. By drawing our attention to the integration of the cognitive and the social in a practitioner's "disposition", *habitus* balances the current "norm-oriented" model of interpretation with the revelation that what accounts for translational phenomena may not primarily be the intervention of external factors, but includes the translator's subjective pursuit as well. With the insights this concept provides, we understand better how translators violate "norms", show "variability" and "creativity", or conduct "private inventions". Employing *habitus* without succumbing to its deterministic tendency would thus enable us to come to firmer grips with so complex and heterogeneous a field as translation.

Key words: Sociology of translation; descriptive translation studies; habitus; field; capital; norm

11

作　　者　刘云虹
标　　题　论翻译批评空间的构建
发表刊物　《中国翻译》2008年第3期
［摘　要］翻译的繁荣与批评的缺席已越来越成为一对矛盾。一方面，翻译事业理性、健康的发展离不开翻译批评，另一方面，翻译批评长期处于非理性状态，甚至陷入一种尴尬境地，对翻译实践中出现的重大问题常常以缺席者的姿态出现。从总体上看，导致翻译批评无力和缺席状态的根本原因在于翻译界尚未建立起积极而有效的批评空间，从而限制和束缚了翻译批评的开展。基于这样的认识，本文立足于翻译批评的对象、主体和标准三大要素，从翻译批评话语权的重构、批评精神的树立以及价值评价体系的建立等维度对如何构建翻译批评空间加以探讨。第一，重构翻译批评失落的话语权。翻译批评话语权的失落，主要表现在对某些重大翻译问题和翻译现象的漠视以及自身理论建设不完善所导致的对翻译理论建设的缺席两方面。因此，构建积极、有效的翻译批评空间，首先应促使翻译批评摆脱目前的失语和缺席状态，在理论与实践双重意义上重构其失落的话语权。第二，树立科学的翻译批评精神。在众多评论文章所营造的表面繁荣背后，翻译批评潜藏着危机，存在着诸多亟待解决的问题。造成这一现状的重要原因之一是批评主体缺少客观、平等、宽容的批评精神。因此，构建积极、有效的翻译批评空间，必须树立科学的翻译批评精神，凸显批评的建设性，强调批评主体应明确责任意识，遵循客观公正、平等宽容的批

评原则。第三，建立科学的价值评价体系。构建积极、有效的翻译批评空间，需呼吁翻译界和出版界联合起来，共同建立科学的价值评价体系，从翻译标准的探讨和翻译出版机制的完善两方面保证翻译价值得以最大限度地体现。

关　键　词　翻译批评；空间；话语权；批评精神；评价体系
作者联系地址　江苏省南京市栖霞区仙林大道 123 号，南京大学外国语学院
电子邮箱　ningyunhan@126.com

11

Author: LIU Yunhong
Title: Opening up the Space for Translation Criticism
Published in: *Chinese Translators Journal*, 2008 (3).

[**Abstract**]　The prosperity of translation and the absence of criticism have become more and more contradictory in that the rational and sound development of translation cannot be separated from criticism and the latter has long been in an irrational and even awkward position, with its absence concerning the key issues in translation practice. The major reasons for its weakness and absence lie in its development restrictions due to the failure to open up its positive and effective space. Accordingly, this paper tries to discuss how to open up the space through the reconstruction of the discourse power, and the establishment of the spirit and the evaluation system. First, reconstruct the lost discourse power of criticism. The loss of the power means the indifference to some key issues and its absence in the construction of translation theories. Therefore, the establishment of the space needs its urged escape from the absence, and reconstruction of its lost power both in theory and practice. Second, establish the scientific spirit of translation criticism. Behind the prosperity in many papers, there has been the crisis together with many urgent problems, partially due to the lack of the objective and tolerant criticism spirit. Thus, the establishment of the space requires its scientific spirit, the focus on its constructiveness, and the necessity for its subjects to define their responsibilities and follow the objective, equal and tolerant principles. Third, set up the scientific evaluation system. The establishment of the space calls for the collaboration of translators and published ins to build up the scientific system, and ensure translation values to the fullest extent in the exploration of standards and the improvement of publishing mechanisms.

Key words: translation criticism; space; discourse power; criticism spirit; evaluation system

12

作　　者　孙艺风
标　　题　文化翻译与全球本土化
发表刊物　《中国翻译》2008年第1期

[摘　要]　这是一个日趋全球化的世界，本土化力量在跨文化交际的全球语境下，使得人们对翻译在跨文化交流中的关键性角色的看法，产生了范式性转变。翻译活动催生了全球化的商业文化，同时也支配着翻译的运作。全球化商业文化的出现又触发隐忧；文化间接触的增多可引致文化殖民，并进而形成一个威胁本土文化生存的同质化世界。因此，为应对全球化而（重新）建立本土文化地域和文化身份的极端重要性毋庸置疑。同时，经由翻译，一种业已普遍化和正处于普遍化进程中的文化语言，正唤醒并强化对本土文化的身份认知。翻译活动乃本土现实的组成部分，而本土现实与以跨族文化为标志的全球化浪潮密切相关。有鉴于此，文化翻译成功与否取决于本土知识，而后者再通过协商的办法，产生出目标语读者可接受的并具有本土色彩的文化话语。

关　键　词　全球本土化；文化改造；本土知识；翻译策略

作者联系地址　澳门氹仔大学大马路，澳门大学英文系
电子邮箱　sunyf@umac.mo

12

Author: SUN Yifeng
Title: Cultural Translation and Glocalization
Published in: *Chinese Translators Journal*, 2008 (1).
[Abstract]　In an increasingly globalized world, localization forces shape a powerful paradigmatic shift in viewing the vital role of translation in the global context of cross-cultural communication. The emergence of globalized commodity culture is attributable to translation and dictates the ways in which translation is undertaken. It also raises the troubling possibility of cultural colonization as a consequence of cross-cultural encounters, thereby creating a homogenized world that threatens to destroy local culture. It is therefore a question of primary importance to (re)establish cultural location and identity in response to globalization. Through translation, a universalized and universalizing world of transnational cultural language reawakens and reinforces cultural identification. Translation activities are part of local realities in relation to the global negotiating an acceptable cultural discourse for the target reader.
Key words: glocalization; cultural transformation; local knowledge; translation strategies

13

作　　者　王树槐、王若维
标　　题　翻译能力的构成因素和发展层次研究
发表刊物　《外语研究》2008年第5期

[摘　　要]　翻译能力的构成因素和发展层次是翻译教学理论研究的起点。本文第一部分深入述评了国内外翻译能力构成和发展阶段的研究文献。翻译能力的构成因素学说包括：1）天赋说；2）自然展开说；3）自然展开修正说（自然展开+社会—功能说）；4）建构说；5）转换说；6）策略或认知说；7）语篇协调说；8）生产—选择说；9）交际说；10）语言—语篇能力说；11）多因素均力说。翻译能力发展阶段的学说包括：1）Presas从心理语言视角出发的四阶段说；2）Chesterman从技能发展视角出发的五阶段说；3）Kiraly从建构主义视角出发的三维度、三层次的"译者能力"说；4）Toury从社会—规范视角出发的二阶段说；5）PACTE从策略发展视角出发的二阶段螺旋上升说。之后对这些学派做出了评价。

　　本文第二部分提出了"翻译能力的综合模式"，它包括六个因素：1）语言—语篇—语用能力；2）文化能力；3）策略能力；4）工具能力；5）思维能力；6）人格统协能力。之后阐述了翻译能力诸因素发展的阶段特征。1）翻译技能发展维度，发展顺序是译理→译技→译艺→译道；2）翻译策略发展维度，发展顺序是局部策略→整体策略→监控策略；3）翻译思维发展维度，发展顺序是具象思维→形象思维→抽象思维；4）翻译创造性发展维度，发展顺序是翻译普遍性→翻译个体性；5）文化能力发展维度，发展顺序是认识能力→比较能力→协调能力；6）翻译人格发展维度，发展顺序是片面性人格→全面性人格。

关 键 词　翻译能力；构成因素；发展层次
作者联系地址　湖北省武汉市洪山区珞瑜路1037号，华中科技大学外国语学院
电子邮箱　wangshh@hust.edu.cn

13

Author: WANG Shuhuai; WANG Ruowei
Title: On the Components and Developments of Translation Competence
Published in: *Foreign Language Research*, 2008 (5).
[Abstract] The study of how translation competence is constituted and developed is the basic question in translation teaching research. In the first part of this paper, the co-authors comprehensively review the eleven schools on the components of translation competence and the five perspectives on the phases of translation competence development. In the second part, a comprehensive model of translation competence is proposed. The model holds that translation competence comprises six sub-competences, i.e. linguistic-textual-pragmatic competence, cultural competence, strategic competence, tool competence, logic competence, and personality regulating competence. Of which the linguistic-textual-pragmatic component is the pivot. The co-authors also contend: 1) in the dimension of translation skills, the four phases that students will experience are: translation knowledge—translation skill—translation art—translation rationale; 2) in the dimension of translation strategy, the three phases are: local strategy—global strategy—monitoring strategy; 3) in the dimension of translation thinking, the three phases are: concrete thinking—imagic thinking—abstract thinking; 4) in the dimension of translation creativity, the two phases are: translation universality—translation individuality; 5) in the dimension of cultural competence, the three phases are: recognition competence—comparison competence—coordinating competence; 6) in the dimension of personality regulating, the two phases are: partial personality-comprehensive personality.
Key words: translation competence; components; developments

14

作　　者　颜林海
标　　题　试论翻译认知心理学的研究内容与方法
发表刊物　《四川师范大学学报（社会科学版）》2008年第2期

[摘　要]　随着翻译研究的深化，翻译研究途径和方法越来越丰富。至今，翻译研究已从最初译者的心得体会、经验杂感逐渐走向了理性化、学科化；从对单一的翻译现象研究转向对翻译的学科性质的探索；从归约式研究过渡到了描写性翻译研究；从研究途径的单一性趋向于翻译研究的多途径整合性，即翻译的跨学科研究。目前，翻译研究吸纳了语言学、文艺学、交际学、文化学、历史学、哲学、符号学等学科的理论体系，并分别形成了相应途径的翻译研究，对翻译学科建设作出了巨大贡献。这些途径都忽略了译者翻译过程中的心理活动。本文以认知心理学为理论框架对翻译过程的认知本质进行了分析，并构想了翻译认知心理学的研究目的、内容与方法。

　　认知心理学是以研究大脑信息加工为核心的心理学，所谓信息加工，就是大脑输入、变换、简化、加工、存储、恢复和使用信息的过程，即"获得"和"使用"信息的过程。而翻译作为一种认知行为，译者的整个翻译过程就是一个"获得"和"使用"（即加工）信息的过程。因此，认知心理学同样适用于翻译过程的研究，并在此基础上，本文旨在构建翻译认知心理学及其研究内容和方法。翻译认知心理学的研究内容主要是翻译认知加工系统的建构及其运用，翻译认知加工系统包括翻译认知加工机制、翻译语言加工模式和翻译图式认知加工，这三者构成了翻译认知加工的基本原理。翻译认知心理学的研究方法包括有声思维法、影像观察法、计算机日志监控记录法、鼠标屏幕录像法和追溯式观察法。

关　键　词　翻译；认知；翻译认知心理学
作者联系地址　四川省成都市锦江区静安路1号，万科城市花园45-1-302
电子邮箱　yanlinhai@sina.com

14

Author: YAN Linhai
Title: On Cognitive Psychology of Translation: Its Scope and Methodology
Published in: *Journal of Sichuan Normal University,* 2008 (2).
[Abstract] The in-depth of translation studies is always accompanied by more research approaches and methods. Translation studies has been turned from the description of translation experience or random thoughts to the theorization and disciplinization of translation, from the study of translation phenomena to the exploration of disciplinary nature of translation studies, from the prescriptive studies to the descriptive studies, from the monotony to the diversified integration in approaches. Now, lots of achievements have been made in translation studies from various approaches, such as linguistics, literature, communication, culture, history, philosophy, semiotics and so on. But all these approaches almost exclude the mental activity of the translator in translating. In view of the above facts, this paper aims to take cognitive psychology as its framework. Based upon the modern cognitive theory, this paper discusses the possibility of constructing the cognitive psychology of translation. The author supposes that the cognitive psychology deal with the cognitive information-processing model of translation, which can be applied to both comprehension and expression of the translation. He also introduces a few research methods: thinking-aloud protocols, translog, camtasia retrospective interview. At last he concludes that the cognitive psychology of translation deals with the information-processing mode of translation.
Key words: translation; cognition; cognitive psychology

15

作　　者　陈佩筠
标　　题　翻译、诠释、权力意志
发表刊物　《中外文学》2009 年第 38 卷第 2 期

[**摘　　要**]　翻译与诠释两个概念之间有一些共通之处，翻译与诠释都必须面对一个根本问题：我们在翻译什么？诠释什么？当这个问题以"什么"作为起始时，这个「什么」就不可避免地指涉某个尚未明了的东西，某种无可名状、不可辨别，却又并非不存在的东西。因此，翻译与诠释往往处于一种进退两难的处境，一方面，诠释需要参照，也就是说，它必须根据某个既已存在的文本进行阅读与解释；另一方面，也正因为诠释必须以不同方式述说，它扮演着差异的角色，每一个诠释都与其他诠释不同。每一次的诠释目的既相同也不同。翻译的概念与诠释相似，却又绝非同一，原文作为翻译的参照点理应是对于译文而言的客观来源，因此"忠于原文"向来是翻译的指导原则。然而，也正因为译文与原文不可能完全相同，翻译的任务也就在于表现差异。翻译与诠释最不同的地方，或许可以简略地说是翻译比诠释更关注译出语与译入语之间的转换。

倘若要思考翻译与诠释所处的两难处境，"意义"的问题举足轻重。我们甚至可以说，每个翻译与诠释之间上演著作者、读者、译者、诠释者等人之间的意义控制的斗争。换言之，各种不同类型的文本参与者都企图夺取意义决定的和合法与优越的地位。本文从尼采的"权力意志"的概念作为主轴，以葡萄牙籍诺贝尔文学奖得主萨拉马戈所著之《里斯本围城史》为例，试图寻找一个新方向，以重新思索翻译语诠释共同面临之两难处。

关 键 词　翻译；诠释；权力意志；里斯本围城史；忠于原文
作者联系地址　台湾新北市淡水区英专路 151 号，淡江大学英文系
电子邮箱　jill@mail.tku.edu.tw

15

Author: CHEN Peiyun

Title: Translation, Interpretation and Will-to-Power

Published in: *Chung Wai Literary Quarterly*, 2009 (Vol.38, No.2).

[Abstract] Interpretation and translation have something in common, i.e. both interpretation and translation must confront a fundamental question: what is to be interpreted/translated? Interpretation, as well as translation, is situated in a double-bind, since the reference is dispensable for interpretation, and yet, interpretation is by nature a differential element for any given text. Hence, interpretation needs a ground as its destination and yet, at the same time, its destination necessarily designates differences. Similar to yet by no means identical with interpretation, translation is involved with this double-bind, which means, an objective standard for translation cannot be discarded, but translation is never an innocent vehicle for communication between different linguistic systems—this is the source of the complexity of translation.

To think about the double-bind in which translation and interpretation are situated, the issue of "meaning" must be raised; hence the determination of meaning in any given text embodies the struggle for the control of meaning between author, reader, interpreter and translator. This paper attempts to present an understanding of this struggle for the control of meaning in terms of Nietzsche's notion of will-to-power along with the example explained in José Saramago's *The History of the Siege of Lisbon* in order to seek a new way to reconsider the principles of fidelity, which have long determined the criteria of interpretation and translation.

Key words: translation; interpretation; will-to-power; *The History of the Siege of Lisbon; the principle of fidelity*

16

作　　者　韩子满
标　　题　解构主义翻译理论的论争与接受——以"确当的"翻译为例
发表刊物　《外国语文》2009年第1期

[摘　要]　对于德里达所提出的"确当的"翻译这一概念，翻译界有三种不同的理解。第一种理解认为"确当的"翻译就是德里达在论文中定义的翻译，是与原文最等值的译文，使用的语言最正确、最贴切、最中肯、最充分、最合适、最有针对性、最单义、最地道，是德里达设定的翻译标准，代表了他的翻译理想；第二种理解对于何为"确当的"翻译与第一种理解一样，但认为德里达并不认同这种翻译，更不是要以此设立一种翻译标准，而是将其设为理想翻译的对立面，作为批评的对象；第三种理解认为，德里达在文中分析了翻译理论中通常所理解的"确当的"翻译，指出这一概念内在的基本矛盾，但对这一概念作了修改，成为自己的翻译目标。结合德里达文章本身以及他的整体理论发展脉络来看，只有第二种理解最接近德里达的原意。之所以形成这三种不同的理解，特别是错误的理解，原因在于有些学者还不适应德里达特有的解构式的书写风格，或是不适应德里达的解构主义理论，或是阅读时没有注意文中的细节，忽略了德里达的提示。这三个原因也是德里达翻译理论，乃至整个解构主义翻译理论在翻译界，特别是中国翻译界的传播中存在的问题。要真正领会解构主义翻译理论的精髓，使这种哲学化的翻译理论发挥其应有的解释力，帮助人们更好地认识各种翻译现象，我们首先应该尽量适应解构式的写作风格，特别注重文本中的细节，从细节中把握理论推演的线索；其次尽量熟悉解构主义哲学及文学理论，在解构主义的理论背景下来解读解构主义翻译理论文献；再次是要有开放的心态，不根据自己的先入之见来附会解构主义翻译理论，而是尽量站在解构主义理论的立场上，来解读这种翻译理论。

关 键 词　"确当的"翻译；解构主义；德里达

作者联系地址　河南省洛阳市 036 信箱 30 号
电子邮箱　zimanhan@sina.com

16

Author: HAN Ziman

Title: Contention and Reception of Deconstructionist Translation Theories: Based on "Relevant" Translation

Published in: *Foreign Language and Literature,* 2009 (1).

[Abstract]　There are three different understandings of the concept of "relevant" translation proposed by Jacques Derrida in "What is 'Relevant' Translation". The first is that Derrida's claim can be taken at its face value, and a "relevant translation" is taken by him to be the most equivalent version to the original, in a target language that is most appropriate and most univocal. It is standard set by Derrida for translation, standing for his ideal of translation; the second understanding agrees with the first one on the definition of "relevant" translation, but contends that such translation is not what Derrida embraces; rather it is described by Derrida as the opposite of good translation, as what translation should not be; the third understanding is that Derrida takes "relevant" translation as his aim of translation as an elaborate analysis and revision of such translation. A close reading of Derrida's article shows that the second understanding is more likely to be what is really meant by Derrida. The three different understandings, the two wrong ones in particular, may be ascribed to the fact that many translation scholars, both in the west and in China, have difficulty in comprehending Derrida's unconventional writing. These scholars are not familiar with Derrida's deconstructionist thinking as a whole, failing to pay enough attention to the details mentioned by Derrida. The failure to understand Derrida is indicative of the problems with the reception of deconstructionist translation theories and deconstruction. To solve the problem, translation scholars should read more Derrida, familiarizing themselves with deconstructionist writing and theories, and approaching deconstruction theories with as little pre-conception as possible.

Key words: "relevant" translation; deconstruction; Derrida

17

作　　者　蒋骁华
标　　题　新历史主义与翻译
发表刊物　《澳门理工学报》2009年第3期
[摘　要]　新历史主义视域中的翻译这个课题，国内外学者已有一定研究，如：2003年，美国威士廉大学（Wesleyan University）出版的《历史与理论》（*History and Theory*）杂志曾开辟"翻译与历史学"（Translation and Historiography）研究专栏，发表了与翻译和历史有关的系列学术论文；再如：Venuti (2005)、朱安博（2005）等。这些研究主要探讨了文本（包括翻译文本）的历史性、权力话语与翻译和翻译研究的关系等，对我们有诸多启发。但新历史主义与翻译究竟有怎样的理论关系？新历史主义对翻译究竟有怎样的影响？这些问题，尚需我们进一步探索。

　　新历史主义的理论特点可概括为四点：1) 多学科整合和新方法的整体挪用。新历史主义从人类学、哲学、阐释学、文化诗学、政治学、宗教学等学科和解构主义、女性主义、西方马克思主义、福柯的权力话语思想、后殖民理论等新方法中汲取了养料。2) 从历史话语含混处发掘历史权力运作的真相；3) 注重作品意义的重释；4) 强调历史和现实的互动。从与翻译和翻译研究的相关性角度，我们还可以将新历史主义的理论特点进一步概括为四点：1) 多学科性；2) 反传统；3) 强调权力话语；4) "文本的历史性"。从多学科性、反传统、强调权力话语这三个角度研究翻译的文献已经比较多，本文不赘述。本文专门从"文本的历史性"这个角度探讨文本的历史性和多重翻译之间的理论关系,并从三个方面分析了在新历史主义视域中文化、历史如何通过翻译被重写。

关 键 词 新历史主义;翻译;文本的历史性

作者联系地址 澳门高美士街,澳门理工学院语言暨翻译高等学校

电子邮箱 xhjiang@ipm.edu.mo

17

Author: JIANG Xiaohua
Title: New Historicism and Translation
Published in: *Journal of Macao Polytechnic Institute*, 2009 (3).
[Abstract] New Historicism underlines semantic indeterminacy and multiple interpretations of a text through the philosophy of "historicity of texts". This idea provides a new theoretical support for multiple interpretations and multi-faceted translations of a text. This paper explores the theoretical relationships between "the historicity of texts" and the possibility of multi-faceted translations, and analyzes from three perspectives how culture and history might be rewritten through translations in the framework of New Historicism.
Key Words: New Historicism; translation; the historicity of texts

18

作　者 司显柱、刘利琼
标　题 论译文的效度和信度
发表刊物 《中国翻译》2009 年第 3 期
[摘　要] 传统语码模式(即编码—解码模式)在解释人类言语交际行

为时存在不足，无法弥补语义表征和真正要表达思想之间存在的差距。为了避免这种不足，关联理论借鉴语用学的最新发展成果提出了明示-推理模式，从而更新了译文评价模式。"明示"和"推理"是交际过程的两个方面，分别对应说话人和听话人。"明示"指说话人明确地向听话人表示意图的一种行为，而翻译的成功在于"推理"的成功，即译文读者能明了原文作者明确向原文读者表示的意图。为了保证译文读者的推理结论与原文读者相同，必须考虑前提部分（话语信息）和共有语境两个方面。这就将译文读者的认知语境置于一个至关重要的位置。如果译文读者的认知语境与原文读者的认知语境重合，提供相同前提自然能提出相同的结论；但是如果这两者冲突或是欠缺，就只能通过修改前提的方式（即修改话语信息）来保证推理结论的相同。因此，关联翻译观不再将信度（译文语码辩证统一地向原文语码趋同的程度）至于翻译标准的首要地位，而是认为效度（译文读者通过阅读译文识别原作或原作者的交际意图的程度）才是翻译的第一要义。理想的译文自然是效度和信度的高度统一，但是，一般而言，在两者无法兼顾的情形下，翻译应首先要保证译文的效度，在此前提下，追求更高的信度。

关 键 词　效度；信度；明示—推理模式
作者联系地址　北京市朝阳区定福庄南里 1 号，北京第二外国语学院高级翻译学院
电子邮箱　20160026@bisu.edu.cn

18

Author: SI Xianzhu & LIU Liqiong
Title: From Fidelity to Validity: A Relevance Theoretical Perspective on the Evaluation of Translation
Published in: *Chinese Translators Journal*, 2009 (3).
[Abstract]　　Avoiding the deficiency of the traditional coded model and

benefiting from the latest development in pragmatics, relevance theory proposes an ostensive-inferential model to explain human communication through speech. With this new model, the success of translation is measured by how thoroughly readers of target texts can understand the intentions of the speaker expressed in the original texts. In other words, translation is judged by whether the same inferences can be made by readers of different texts. It is then proposed in this article that changes have to be made in texts when those two types of readers have different cognitive contexts. Only in this way can readers fully understand the communicative intentions of the original author or the original text through reading translations. This innovative model has led to the formulation of a new approach to explaining and evaluating translation activities whereby validity, instead of fidelity, is taken as the central criterion for evaluating translation. While ideally, translation should show a unity of high validity and high fidelity, when we cannot have both simultaneously, the translator should first aim for validity, pursuing fidelity only when the demand for achieving validity is met.

Key words: validity; fidelity; ostensive-inferential model

19

作　　者　屠国元、李　静
标　　题　距离合法性视角下译者当译之本的知情选择与情感同构
发表刊物　《中国翻译》2009年第4期
［摘　要］　翻译活动的自身命意在于语际之间的信息等值转换，然而事实上译作与原作之间却无法实现彻底的等值等效，这是译界的共识。待翻译的原作文字不光是字典上定义了的符号，其深层的文化蕴涵超乎字典之外。静止的词典释义只能设定词汇和语言单位的编码意义，而翻译要承递的是有机的词汇、语句组合在特定社会文化土壤中表征的外化价值，因此译文严格地再现原作几无可能，任何翻译天生就隐藏了距离的合法性。20

世纪西方哲学界发生的从认识论主体哲学转向语言论的解释哲学为翻译距离的合法性存在提供了充分的理论依据。翻译作为语言间的转换，转换过程中意义的增添、失落、扭曲、变形等距离标记在解释哲学那里都能够得到有力的阐释。

但是，译者作为翻译的主体，在翻译过程中会始终奉守翻译的圣命，实现等值等效。明知虽不能至，却依然心向往之，努力消除距离，争取实现语言文化信息的完美再现。为此，我们认为，译者一是要在选材上发挥主体能动性，知情选择当译之本；二是要在翻译中与原作者产生共鸣，情感同构。文学翻译是文学作品再创作过程，一部好的翻译作品并不是"客观"、"无情"的结果，而是结合了各种心理因素进行情感交流的文学磨合产物。在翻译的时候，如果译者选择与自己性情相近、阅历相似、风格相近的作品，也就是做到了知情选择当译之本来翻译的话，译者就能和原作者产生共鸣，"性情相投"，"感同身受"，也就更能够调整其主观能动性，深入理解并刻画出作者和作品的精神实质、风格气质和艺术美感，也就是实现了与原作世界的情感同构，最大限度地消融译作与原作的距离。

关　键　词　距离；合法性；选择；同构；译者

作者联系地址　浙江省宁波市江北区风华路 818 号

邮　　　编　315211

电子邮箱　tuguoyuan@126.com

19

Author: TU Guoyuan & LI Jing

Title: Legitimate Choice of SL/TL Distance in Translation

Published in: *Chinese Translators Journal*, 2009 (4).

[Abstract]　A common fact in the circle of translation studies is that the nature of translation is the equivalent transference of messages between two different languages, but full equivalence can not be achieved between TL and SL. What the translator faces is not just the linguistic symbols printed in the original work but the distinct cultures and values embodied in the linguistic symbols, thus it is not an easy task for the translator to do, which implies the legitimacy of distance between TL and SL. The translator, as the subjective in translating, knows clearly that it is impossible to produce a target language text which can be fully equivalent to the original text, but will still keep in mind her or his duty and mission to achieve full equivalence. So she or he is always in pursuit of narrowing the distance between TL and SL. Grounded on the above, this paper looks from a hermeneutical perspective into the issue of what distance should be legitimately maintained between SL and TL in translation. It suggests that the translator decide on what deserves translating first before she or he responds sympathetically to the original text, for such an approach could best keep SL and TL at an optimum distance from each other, making it more likely to come up with a properly rendered translation.

Key words: distance; legitimacy; choice; composition; translator

20

作　　者　杨　柳
标　　题　翻译的诗学变脸
发表刊物　《中国翻译》2009年第6期
[摘　要]　翻译学理论与诗学的跨学科研究成为晚近翻译研究领域的一大亮点。译者应怎样在翻译中对原文进行适当的诗学改写，以增强翻译的创造性与艺术性，成为值得深究的学术问题。本文试图从诗学视角出发来解读翻译的改写活动。通过对《伊利亚特》《狼图腾》《天演论》和《牛虻》等译本的分析，揭示不同文化语境下的诗学地位、诗学态度、经典文学形式和多种意识形态对诗学改写的操纵作用，以及典型的翻译诗学形式在文学、文化和社会的演进过程中扮演的重要角色。

翻译的诗学模式并非一成不变。诗学构建中有三种决定性的操纵因素，即诗学地位和诗学态度、经典文学形式和多种意识形态。在不同文化语境下，诗学地位和译者的诗学态度会发生变化，从而使译本发生新的诗学变形；经典文学形式对于翻译的诗学改写也有着一定的导向作用；多种意识形态也操纵着翻译诗学的构成和改变。

翻译诗学对于民族文学与文化的发展与重构具有积极的推动作用。本文以桐城翻译诗学、白话翻译诗学与杂合翻译诗学为例，分析了翻译诗学改写对于社会变革、文化启蒙与文化多样性的影响，强调了翻译诗学的改写对于拓宽民众视野、凸显译者地位、增强翻译特色的重要意义。

本文从中外文学翻译实践出发，系统总结了影响翻译诗学改写的因素，分析了翻译诗学改写的文化与社会价值，对跨学科翻译理论的进一步细化及文学翻译实践具有参照和借鉴作用。

关 键 词 改写；操纵；诗学；文学翻译
作者联系地址 江苏省南京市汉口路 22 号，南京大学海外教育学院
邮 编 201093
电子邮箱 whyareyouhappy@sina.com.cn

20

Author: YANG Liu

Title: Poetic Rewriting in Translation

Published in: *Chinese Translators Journal*, 2009 (6).

[Abstract] Interdisciplinary research in translation theory and poetics has become one of the highlights in recent translation studies. How translators should rewrite the original texts in translation so as to enhance the creativity and artistry of translation becomes an academic question worthy of further study. A poetic analysis of different versions of *Iliad*, *Wolf Totem*, *Evolution & Ethics and Other Essays*, and *The Gadfly* shows that since different cultures assign different status or have different attitudes to poetic discourse, vary in their ways of canonizing literary forms, and are informed with different ideologies, the rewriting practice in translation is always subject to manipulation by cultural factors. The translated poetic forms, in return, typically play an important role in the reformation and evolution of literature, culture and society.

The poetic form of translation is not fixed. There are three dominant manipulative factors in the construction of poetics, namely, poetic status and poetic attitude, classical literary form and a variety of ideologies. Under different cultural contexts, the status of poetics and the poetic attitude of the translator will change, leading to a poetic transformation of the translated version. The classical literary form also plays a guiding role in translation. Besides, the composition and change of translation poetics is manipulated by various ideologies.

Translation poetics plays a positive role in promoting the development and reconstruction of national literature and culture. Taking the translation poetics of Tongcheng School, vernacular translation poetics and hybrid translation poetics for example, this paper analyzes the influence of translation poetics on social reform, cultural enlightenment and cultural diversity and emphasizes the importance of rewriting of translation poetics in broadening people's horizons, highlighting translators' status and strengthening translation features.

Based on the practice of Chinese and foreign literary translation, this paper systematically summarizes the factors influencing the poetic rewriting in translation, analyzes the cultural and social values of translation poetics, and serves as reference for the further refinement of interdisciplinary translation theory and literary translation practice.

Key words: rewriting; manipulation; poetics; literary translation

21

作　　者　张美芳
标　　题　文本类型理论及其对翻译研究的启示
发表刊物　《中国翻译》2009 年第 5 期
［摘　要］　文本类型理论由德国功能主义学派的代表人物卡塔琳娜·莱思（K. Reiss 1971）首次提出。她根据功能语言学家卡尔·布勒（Karl Bühler）的语言功能三分法把文本划分为三种主要类型，即信息型（informative）、表情型（expressive）和操作型（operative），并建议根据文本功能及其相对应的语言特点和使用的交际情景采取相应的翻译策略。信息型文本主要是表现事实、信息、知识、观点等，翻译时应以简朴明了的白话文传递与原文相同的概念与信息。表情型文本用于表达信息发送者对人对物的情感和态度，翻译时应采用仿效法，以使译文忠实于原作者或原文。操作型文本旨在感染或说服读者并使其采取某种行动，译者可用编译或适应性的方法以达到感染读者的目的。

莱思的文本类型理论具有评价与规范意义。评价意义包括对所处文化情景中翻译功能的鉴定；规范意义是指对未来的专业翻译工作者进行培训，要求他们译出合适的、满足客户需要的作品，并且要求译者寻求充分的理据来保护其译作免受委托人和使用者的不合理批评，因此具有很强的实践指导意义。本文详细阐述莱思的文本类型理论、追溯其理论根源，简述其他学者提出的相关观点，并结合英汉译例讨论了文本类型理论对翻译研究，尤其是对英汉翻译研究的启示。

本文的意义在于通过示例来探讨文本类型理论，提出了可进一步研究的设想：1）文本功能理论有助于客观地分析翻译文本的功能；2）有助于译者了解不同功能的文本所具有的语言特点；3）有助于译者采取适当的翻译策略。

关　键　词　文本类型；语言功能；翻译策略
作者联系地址　澳门氹仔大学大马路，澳门大学 E21-4065 室
邮　　编　00853
电子邮箱　mfzhang@umac.mo

21

Author: ZHANG Meifang
Title: Text Typology and Its Implications for Translation Teaching
Published in: *Chinese Translators Journal*, 2009 (5).

[Abstract] Text typology in Translation Studies refers to the theory developed by Katharina Reiss in the early 1970s for translation quality assessment. Based on Bühler's three-way categorization of language functions, Reiss suggests that all texts be classified into three types: informative, expressive and operative. She also links the three functions to their corresponding language dimensions as well as to translation strategies. The informative text is mainly employed to represent facts, information, knowledge and viewpoints, and the translator should use "plain prose" to transmit the full referential content of the source text. The expressive text, with an aesthetic language dimension, expresses the sender's feelings and attitude, identifying methods should be used to transmit the aesthetic and artistic form of the expressive text. The operative text is effect-oriented, and should be translated with adaptive methods to elicit the desired response from the target receiver and to create an equivalent effect among them.

Reiss's text typology theory is both evaluative and normative. On the one hand, it can be used to evaluate the function of a translation in certain cultural situations; on the other hand, the normative nature enables the translation practitioners to be trained to produce adequate (functional) translations to satisfy the clients and to shun from unreasonable comments from the commissioners and users with convincing justifications. Therefore, the theory is very helpful in translation practice. After giving an overview of Reiss's text typology and other scholars' terminology in this area, this article explores possibilities of applying the theory to the study of Chinese-English translation by analyzing some translation cases.

Significance of this research is that its analysis has provided some assumptions for further study in the future: 1) text typology theory is helpful in objectively analyzing the function of the target text; 2) it is valuable for the translator to understand linguistic features of texts with different functions; and 3) it is useful for the translator to adopt suitable translation strategies.

Key words: text types; language functions; translation strategies

22

作　　者　朱健平

标　　题　视域差与翻译解释的度——从哲学诠释学视角看翻译的理想与现实

发表刊物　《中国翻译》2009年第4期

[摘　要]　本文从哲学诠释学视角探讨了视域差与翻译的解释度之间的关系。翻译的解释度有"理想的解释度"和"实际的解释度"之分，一方面翻译标准要求译者在翻译过程中应该把握一个理想的解释度，而翻译现实却表明，翻译中实际的解释度常会偏离理想的解释度。

无论是理想的解释度还是实际的解释度都与视域差有关。视域差是指与翻译过程密切相关的各个因素的视域之间所存在着的差异。直接影响翻译解释度的视域差主要有三种：目的语文化与源语文本的视域差影响理想的解释度，译者与源语文本的视域差影响实际的解释度，而导致实际的解释度偏离理想的解释度的除了译者与源语文本的视域差外，还有译者与目的语文化的视域差。

一般而言，理想的解释度与目的语文化和源语文本的视域差成正比。该视域差越大，目的语文化所允许的理想解释度就会越大；反之，目的语文化所期待的理想解释度就应该越小。目的语文化与源语文本的视域差并非固定不变的，而是一种动态的存在。因而理想的解释度同样也是一种动态的存在。由于译者无论是与目的语文化还是与源语文本都存在着视域差，因此，在翻译实践中，即使是这种动态的理想解释度实际上也是不可能达到的，译者在翻译中的实际解释度常会或多或少偏离理想的解释度。一方面，译者视域中拥有目的语文化视域所没有的独特视域，另一方面，译者无法将所有的目的语文化视域全部纳入自己的视域中。译者与目的语文化的这种视域差正是导致实际解释度偏离理想解释度的主要原因之一。

关 键 词 视域差；理想的解释度；实际的解释度；翻译标准；哲学诠释学
作者联系地址 湖南省长沙市岳麓区麓山南路1号，湖南大学外国语学院
邮 编 410082
电子邮箱 zhujianpinghzh@126.com

22

Author: ZHU Jianping

Title: Horizon Gaps as the Determinant of Interpretive Degree in Translation: A Perspective of Philosophical Hermeneutics

Published in: *Chinese Translators Journal*, 2009 (4)

[Abstract] The paper explores the relationship between the horizon gaps and interpretive degrees in translating from the perspective of philosophical hermeneutics. There are two types of interpretive degrees in translating, the ideal degrees and the actual degrees. On the one hand, various translation criteria expect or require that the translator ensure an ideal interpretive degree in translating while numerous translation realities indicate that the actual interpretive degrees often deviate from the ideal ones. Both ideal and actual interpretive degrees are closely associated with the horizon gaps, or the differences between the horizons of various factors related to translating/ translations. Usually the interpretive degrees in translating are directly influenced by three kinds of horizon gaps: the ideal interpretive degrees are influenced by the gaps between the target culture (TC)'s horizon and the source text (ST)'s horizon; the actual interpretive degrees are influenced by the gaps between the translator's horizon and the ST's horizon; while the gaps between the translator's horizon and the TC's horizon, together with those between the translator's horizon and the ST's horizon, lead to a deviation of the actual interpretive degrees from the ideal ones.

Generally, the ideal interpretive degrees are in direct proportion to the gaps between the TC's horizon and the ST's horizon. The greater the gaps, the greater the ideal degrees that the TC would allow or expect, and vice versa. However, the ideal interpretive degrees are not unchangeable. On the contrary, they are constantly changing, from time to time, from place to place, from culture to culture, and from text to text, since the gaps between the TC's horizon and the ST's horizon do not remain unchanged at all times and in all places. This indicates that the ideal interpretive degrees should be regarded as a dynamic, rather than static, concept. However, as the ideal interpretive degrees are in reality unreachable due to the gaps between the translator's horizon and the source culture (SC)'s horizon and those between the translator's horizon and the TC's horizon, the actual interpretive degrees always deviate more or less from the ideal ones. On the one hand, the translator's horizon includes part of his unique horizon that the TC does not have, and on the other hand, the translator cannot possibly incorporate the whole horizon of the TC into his own. The gaps between the translator's horizon and the TC's horizon are one of the major causes of the deviation of the actual interpretive degrees from the ideal ones.

Key words: horizon gap; ideal interpretive degree; actual interpretive degree; translation criteria; philosophical hermeneutics

23

作　　者　罗良功
标　　题　"翻译诗学观念":论美国语言诗的诗学观及其翻译
发表刊物　《外国文学研究》2010年第6期
[摘　要]　本文提出"翻译诗学观念"的诗歌翻译原则,并以美国语言诗为个案,通过探讨语言诗的诗学观与诗学实践,论述了这一翻译原则对于语言诗翻译的必要性和意义。作为诗歌翻译原则,"翻译诗学观念",就是以认同原作者的诗学观作为诗歌在跨语言传播中的核心价值为前提,在诗歌的译文文本中再现原诗文本所体现的原作者的诗学观;也就是说,在充分把握原诗作者的诗学观及其在具体诗歌中体现方式的基础上,在译语中用相应的策略将原诗作者的诗学观及其在诗歌中的表现方式再现出来。本文认为,语言诗的语言观、美学观、政治观等诗学观赋予诗歌的语言和其他文本形式以空前的责任,使之成为诗歌意义的一部分和意义生成机制,对语言诗的翻译必须按照语言诗的诗学观在译语系统中复现原诗的语言策略和文本形式,唯其如此,才能复现原诗意义及其意义生成机制。
关 键 词　"翻译诗学观念";诗学观念;语言诗;诗歌翻译
作者联系地址　湖北省武汉市洪山区珞喻路152号,华中师范大学外国语学院
邮　　编　430079
电子邮箱　luolianggong@163.com

23

Author: LUO Lianggong

Title: "Translate Poetic Ideas": On LANGUAGE Poetry and Its Translation

Published in: *Foreign Literature Studies*, 2010 (6).

[Abstract] This paper proposes "Translate Poetic Ideas" as a principle of poetry translation. Taking LANGUAGE Poetry for example, this paper examines this principle based on analysis of the poetics and poetical practice of LANGUAGE Poetry. In this paper, "Translate Poetic Ideas" means the meaning and meaning-generating mechanism of the poetic form in the source language shall be reconstructed in the target language. This paper argues that the linguistic, aesthetic and political ideas of LANGUAGE Poetry endows language and other types of textual form with such great responsibility as part of the meaning or part of the meaning-generating mechanism of a poem, and thus in translating LANGUAGE Poetry it is necessary to restore the language strategies and textual form of the original poem by following the LANGUAGE Poetics so as to restore the meaning and the meaning-generating mechanism.

Key words: "Translate Poetic Ideas"; poetic idea; LANGUAGE Poetry; translation

24

作　　者　桑仲刚
标　　题　探析自译——问题与方法
发表刊物　《外语研究》2010 年第 4 期

[摘　要]　自译指"翻译"自己作品的行为或该行为的结果即自译文本。早在文艺复兴时期，尼可·奥雷斯莫（Nicole Oresme）、查尔斯·奥尔良（Charles d'Orleans）等就在拉丁文、法文、英文之间"翻译"自己的作品。二十世纪以来，涌现出了包括罗宾德拉纳特·泰戈尔（Rabindranath Tagore）、约瑟夫·布罗茨基（Joseph Brodsky）、塞缪尔·贝克特（Samuel Beckett）、弗拉基米尔·纳博科夫（Vladimir Nabokov）在内的许多著名文学自译者。在中国当代作家中，林语堂、张爱玲、萧乾、余光中、白先勇等也都曾"翻译"过自己的作品。虽然自译研究有助于进一步认识写作过程

的认知机制、翻译的本质及其过程，同时自译也可作为一种教学手段应用于翻译教学，但直到最近三十年它才引起语言、文学研究领域的关注。进入二十一世纪，越来越多的翻译研究者也开始关注该话题。

　　鉴于此，本文通过梳理国内外的相关学术成果，试图探究该领域的研究现状及存在的问题。文章发现，早期自译研究主要是文学、哲学和语言学视域的个案分析，当前的成果则多是基于女性主义、后殖民主义等文化视角的批评—解释性研究；该领域有待探究的主要问题为：自译是否为译？自译在文本、过程和功能等方面如何区别于普通翻译行为？本文指出，通过观察多样本双语文本收集实证数据，在归纳双语转换策略的基础上"重构"自译"规范"和自译"法则"，进而逐渐"构建自译理论"的描写研究，是解决上述问题的重要途径。

关 键 词　自译；研究现状；问题和方法
作者联系地址　甘肃省天水市秦州区藉河南路，天水师范学院南校区
邮　　编　741000
电子邮箱　sangzhonggang2007@163.com

24

Author: SANG Zhonggang
Title: A Review of the Studies on Self-Translation: Problems and Method
Published in: *Foreign Language Research*, 2010 (4).
[Abstract] Self-translation refers to an author's linguistic behavior of "translating" her own texts as well as the product of the process. Although the studies on self-translation may also lead to a better understanding of translation and self-translation as a method is applicable in translation teaching, it is not until the recent thirty years that self-translation has begun to attract the attention of the researchers in the fields of linguistic, cultural, literary and translation studies. Based on an investigation of the self-translation studies both in and

outside China, this paper proposes that descriptive method be adopted to probe into the essence of self-translation and to construct a theory of self-translation.

Key words: self-translation; state of arts; problems and method

25

作　　者　谭业升
标　　题　转喻的图式——例示与翻译的认知路径
发表刊物　《外语教学与研究》2010年第6期

[摘　要]　在传统对等理论框架下,转喻被看作一种偏离性的语言使用,其所得到的有关翻译的认识非常有限,无法反映转喻翻译中体现的人类认知的复杂性和动态性。本文在认知语言学框架下探讨了在翻译过程中以语境为基础并受规约限制的转喻图式的例示,阐释了基于多样性邻接关系的转喻图式—例示级阶与翻译转换、翻译变体的关联,以及它为译者提供的认知创造空间。在翻译中,基于转喻的图式—例示层级的语言分化既可表现为系统性的宏观分化,也可表现为在具体案例涉及的转喻链中不同层级上的分化,两种分化均为概念框架中多层次邻接关系选取的偏好性差异。翻译中的各类具体转喻转换,是应对语言文化规约差异而进行的创造性调整,或是出于个体操控的目的。在前者的情况下,正是语言文化差异催化了译者的认知创造。得以实现为语言表达的具体转喻用法受到了通用转喻图式的允准,转喻图式—例示级阶为译者的创造性翻译提供了认知路径。译文产出过程,则体现了一种基于概念框架中多层次的邻接关系网络在不同的层级上寻求转喻例示的认知运作。最后,文章提出对今后开展转喻与翻译关系研究的建议。

关 键 词　认知语言学;转喻;认知创造空间;翻译转换/变体
作者联系地址　上海市虹口区大连西路550号,上海外国语大学《外国语》编辑部
邮　　编　200083
电子邮箱　tanyesheng1974@126.com; tanyesheng@yahoo.com

25

Author: TAN Yesheng

Title: Schema-instance Hierarchy of Metonymy and the Mental Paths of Translation

Published in: *Foreign Language Teaching and Research*, 2010 (6).

[Abstract] Within the framework of equivalence theory, research on metonymy as a deviant use can lead to rather limited understanding of the complexity and dynamics of human cognition in translation. In the cognitive linguistic framework, this paper discusses how the context-based and convention-constrained instantiations of metonymic schemas are related to the shifts and variations in translation. It reveals how the metonymic schema-instance hierarchy based on a diversity of contiguous relations within conceptual frameworks provides the translator with a cognitive creative space. With regard to metonymic translation, cross-linguistic differences can be characterized in terms of systematic differentiation at various levels of a metonymic schema-instance hierarchy or at different stages of a metonymic chain involved in a particular case. Various metonymic shifts or variations in translation are embodiments of creative adjustment to deal with the langua-cultural preferences or for individual manipulation. In the former case, these differences are essentially preferential choices with regard to multi-level contagious relations within a certain conceptual framework and it is these differences that catalyze the translator's cognitive creation. An actual usage of metonymy which is realized in the linguistic expression of a translation event may be sanctioned by a universal metonymic schema, which provides a mental path for the translator's creative rendering. The translation production process concerned, on the other hand, can be characterized in term of searching the appropriate metonymic instantiation in the multi-level network of contiguous relations. Finally, the paper gives some suggestions on how to further explore into the issues related to metonymy in translation.

Key words: cognitive lingusitics; metonomy; creative space of cognition; shifts/variations in translation

26

作　　者	王福祥、徐庆利
标　　题	"翻译腔"与翻译任务复杂度和译者工作记忆关系的实证研究
发表刊物	《外语教学》2010年第6期

[摘　要] 传统上学界普遍将"翻译腔"形成归因于原文语言表达方式的影响和束缚导致译文不符合目的语表达习惯。翻译过程不仅是语言转换过程，本质上是译者的认知过程，翻译受到译者认知能力和翻译任务复杂度的影响。"翻译腔"的生成也是译者认知活动的结果，应在认知心理学理论框架内得到更好的解释。本研究以中国大学英语专业四年级学生为受试开展翻译实验，从认知心理视角探讨"翻译腔"与翻译任务复杂度和译者工作记忆能力之间的关系。研究发现如下：1）对于初学翻译的英语专业大学生译者而言，"翻译腔"的出现频率与翻译任务复杂度正相关，与译者工作记忆能力负相关；2）"翻译腔"与翻译任务复杂度和翻译任务复述能力间的相关关系有着深厚的认知心理动因。随着翻译任务复杂度的增加，译者认知加工负荷增加，可供工作记忆存储的容量变小，译者不得不愈来愈多地采用"边读边译"的阅读/翻译方式来不断扩容工作记忆。3）"翻译腔"的产生或许与译者的理解结果有关。理想的翻译理解始于源语视觉信号的接收终止于语义表征的生成。随着翻译任务复杂度增加，生成认知的、非语言的、具有图示性质的语义表征的难度也随之增加，译者在建立概念和命题集合时就愈来愈难完全脱离原文语言形式，译文编码时存留某些源文形式在所难免，可能导致了"翻译腔"的产生。

总之，本研究初步表明："翻译腔"的出现与翻译任务复杂度、译者工作记忆关系密切，其产生的一个重要原因是翻译任务对认知资源的需求超出了译者认知心理能力特别是工作记忆能力，译者对原文的理解无法生成非语言的、具有图示性质的语义表征。

关 键 词 翻译腔；工作记忆；翻译任务复杂度

作者联系地址 山东省曲阜市静轩西路 57 号，曲阜师范大学外国语学院

电子邮箱 wfxroger@163.commailto；xuql2011@163.com

26

Author: WANG Fuxiang & XU Qingli

Title: An Empirical Study of "Translationese" in relation to Translation Task Complexity & Working Memory

Published in: *Foreign Language Education*, 2010 (6).

[Abstract] This research, based on an empirical study in which 10 senior students of English in a Chinese university were first tasked with translating English sentences with different levels of complexity into Chinese, followed by a paraphrasing task and a semi-structured interview, probes "translationese" in relation to translation task complexity and working memory. The major findings are as follows: 1) The frequency of "translationese" occurrences is in positive correlation with translation task complexity, and it is in negative correlation with working memory capacity. 2) The relationship between "translationese" and translation task complexity as well as the translator's translation task paraphrase performance are deeply cognitively motivated. As the translation task complexity increases, the burden for the translator's cognitive processing rises, and this decreases the working memory capacity available for sustaining normal translation processing. Therefore, the translator is forced to resort to the mode of translation of "translating while reading" in order to fresh up and expand working memory capacity. And 3) as the translation task complexity increases, it becomes increasingly difficult for the translator based upon the source text to generate the semantic representation, which is supposed to be of non-linguistic and schematic nature. Therefore, it is more difficult for the translator to free himself from the confinement of the source text structures to generate the conceptions and propositions, upon which translation is expected to be produced. At this moment, when the translator tries to produce the target text, some formal features of the source text segment are expected to be transferred into the target text segment, thus resulting in "translationese".

Key words: "translationese"; working memory; translation task complexity

27

作　　者　张南峰
标　　题　翻译研究、学术规范与文化传统
发表刊物　《中国翻译》2010年第2期
[摘　要]　中国当代的翻译研究，借助于西方的理论和模式，得以蓬勃发展，已经成为一门独立的学科，但并未广泛认同和践行西方的主流学术思想和学术规范，尤其是较高层次的规范，因此与西方的翻译研究有很大差异。首先，在对学术研究的基本认识方面，仍有论者混淆研究和研究对象，忽视纯学术研究的存在或价值，把指导翻译实践视为翻译研究的唯一目标；其次，在研究的立场和态度方面，仍有不少研究者忽视论证，对研究对象和其他事物作出价值判断，让民族意识影响学术研究。这些差异之所以存在，根本原因在于，学术系统既然是西方的文化产物，它必然带着西方的文化基因；这个系统表面上是移植到了中国，但中国的文化土壤与西方不同，令西方学术系统产生了变异。文化土壤的不同，包括求知的目的、求知的途径、知识分子的社会角色、学术的自主性、社会的维系方式和权力结构等方面。西方的知识分子，可以为学术而学

术，着重理性和科学方法，崇尚自由与自主，常以独立的身份推行另类形式库。中国的传统知识分子，则强调学以致用，经世济民，崇尚权威，依附权力，推行另类形式库的常见方式是首先寻求当权者的支持。西方的学术系统，相对独立于政治与权力；中国的人文学术系统，则仍与政治和权力系统关系密切。

中国的主流文化，一直有"中学为体，西学为用"的心态，就是想引进西方的工具，同时保存中国的文化价值系统。引进工具，其实可能导致目标文化的价值观发生改变，但文化价值观的改变速度通常远远慢于引进工具的速度。"中体"与"西用"出现了不协调，这就是中国的翻译研究乃至于人文学术系统目前存在的问题。

关 键 词 翻译研究；学术；规范；文化传统；价值观
作者联系地址 香港屯门青山公路八号，岭南大学翻译系
电子邮箱 changnf@ln.edu.hk

27

Author: CHANG Nam Fung

Title: Translation Studies, Academic Norms and Cultural Traditions

Published in: *Chinese Translators Journal*, 2010 (2).

[Abstract] Translation studies in China has developed into an academic discipline in its own right with the help of Western theories and models, but it has not accepted certain academic concepts and norms dominant in the West, especially higher-level norms, such as distinction between the meta-level and the object-level and that between pure research and application, academic autonomy, and neutrality. Consequently, the application orientation, value judgements, unsubstantiated assertions and nationalistic sentiments still exist, and Western theories are sometimes misunderstood. The crux of the matter is that the academic system, carrying Western cultural genes, has been transplanted in a cultural soil that is different in terms of the purpose of seeking knowledge, the approaches to knowledge, the social role of intellectuals, academic independence, and the power structure of society. In the West there have been free intellectuals who either pursue knowledge for its own sake or promote alternative repertoires in an independent capacity, whereas traditional Chinese intellectuals pursue knowledge for the sake of application, and tend to attach themselves to power. The academic system in the West is relatively autonomous, but that in China is subordinate to the political system.

For over a century, mainstream Chinese culture has intended to import tools from the West while keeping its traditional value system intact. The importation of tools may in the long run induce changes in the value system of the target culture. However, it usually takes much longer to change value systems than tools. The incompatibility between values and tools is a problem that translation studies and the humanities in China are facing at the moment.

Key words: translation studies; academic; norms; cultural traditions; values

翻译史

1. 文化史就是翻译史——陈寅恪的历史发现与其翻译观初探　蔡新乐
2. 翻译家鲁迅的"中间物"意识——以鲁迅早期翻译方式的变换为例　崔　峰
3. 史学观念与翻译文学史写作——兼评谢天振、查明建主编的《中国现代翻译文学史（1898—1949）》　耿　强
4. 19世纪中国人关于基督教God/Spirit汉译问题的讨论　刘林海
5. 试论中国晚清翻译小说中的"译意"现象　陆国飞
6. 关于译场职司的考辨　孙海琳、杨自俭
7. 圣典与传译——六朝道教经典中的"翻译"　谢世维
8. 近代翻译之始——蠡勺居士及其《昕夕闲谈》　张政、张卫晴
9. 从林纾看文学翻译规范由晚清中国到五四的转变：西化、现代化和以原著为中心的观念　关诗珮
10. 《孔夫子》：最初西文翻译的儒家经典　梅谦立
11. 圣经汉译与佛经翻译比较研究　任东升
12. "罪过"：在明清之际耶儒对话中谈"Sin"的翻译与诠释　韩思艺
13. 中国歌曲翻译之百年回眸　何高大、陈水平
14. 天朝话语与乔治三世致乾隆皇帝书的清宫译文　王　辉
15. 非常时期的非常翻译——关于中国大陆文革时期的文学翻译　谢天振
16. 《仁王经》的西夏译本　聂鸿音
17. 早期中文法律词语的英译研究——以马礼逊《五车韵府》为考察对象　屈文生

18. 新时期英美文学在中国大陆的翻译（1976—2008） 孙会军、郑庆珠
19. 《梦溪笔谈》译本翻译策略研究 王　宏

Translation History

1. The History of Human Culture is History of Translation—An Initial Study of the Historical Findings of Chen Yinke and His View of Translation **CAI Xinle**
2. Lu Xun's "Intermediate" Consciousness and the Methodological Changes in His Early Career as a Translator **CUI Feng**
3. Underlining Historiographic Vision in Compilation of History of Translated Literature—with *History of Translated Literature in Modern China (1898-1949)* co-edited by Xie Tianzhen and Zha Mingjian as an illustrative case **GENG Qiang**
4. Nineteenth Century's Chinese Views on Rendering God (Elohim/Theos) and Spirit (Ruach/Pneuma) of Christianity into Chinese **LIU Linhai**
5. On the "Adaptation" of Translated Novels in China's Late Qing Dynasty **LU Guofei**
6. Querying the Sources of a Claim about Tang Dynasty Translation Workshop **SUN Hailin & YANG Zijian**
7. Sacred Scriptures and Transmissions—The Notion of "Translation" in Six Dynasties Daoist Scriptures **SHU-wei Hsieh**
8. The Beginning of Literature Translation in Modern China: A Case Study of Lishaojushi and *Xinxixiantan* **ZHANG Zheng & ZHANG Weiqing**
9. Westernization, Modernization, and the Concept of Basing on the Source Text: A Study of the Transformation of Norm in Literary Translation from Late Qing to May Fourth with Lin Shu as a Case Study

    Uganda Sze Pui KWAN
10. Early Translation in Western Language of Confucian Classics   **Thierry Meynard**
11. A Contrastive Study of Bible Translation and Buddhist Sutra Translation   **REN Dongsheng**
12. "Zuiguo": On the Translation and Interpretation of "Sin" in the Dialogues between Catholicism and Confucianism in the Ming and Qing Dynasties in China   **HAN Siyi**
13. 100-Year Translation of Songs in China   **HE Gaoda & CHEN Shuiping**
14. Celestial Empire Discourse and the Translation of King George III's Letter to Emperor Qianlong   **WANG Hui**
15. Particular Translation in Particular Time: A Study on the Literary Translation During the "Culture Revolution" in Mainland China   **XIE Tianzhen**
16. Tangut versions of *Kārunkarāja-sūtra*   **NIE Hongyin**
17. Early English Translations of Chinese Legal Terms: A Study Based on Robert   **QU Wensheng**
18. The Chinese Translation of Anglo-American Literature in the New Era (1976—2008)   **SUN Huijun & ZHENG Qingzhu**
19. A Research on the Translation Strategy of *Brush Talks from Dream Brook*   **WANG Hong**

1

作　　者　蔡新乐
标　　题　文化史就是翻译史——陈寅恪的历史发现与其翻译观初探
发表刊物　《外语与外语教学》2006年10期
[摘　　要]　本文试图对历史学家陈寅恪（1890—1969）在翻译研究领域的贡献进行历史综述。陈寅恪虽被视为一位历史学家，但翻译问题一直是他所关注的。他认为，高水准的译者具有与伟大学者一样的能力，因为二者都能够对传统重新加以创造和改造，不断激活文化并使之持续发展，进而一代代传下去。而他们也都将翻译视为一种促动性的力量，一种强有力的资源。如果没有翻译，文化本身就不可能存在下去。因此，人类的文化历史首先就是翻译史。本文同时也讨论了他对法成（?-?865）这位里程碑式的藏族翻译家及《几何原本》的再发现。
关 键 词　陈寅恪；翻译；历史；法成；佛教
作者联系地址　河南省开封市顺河区明伦街85号
邮　　编　475001
电子邮箱　xinlecai@163.com

1

Author: CAI Xinle

Title: The History of Human Culture is History of Translation—An Initial Study of the Historical Findings of Chen Yinke and His View of Translation

Published in: *Foreign Languages and Their Teaching*, 2006 (10).

[Abstract]　This paper is intended to present a historical survey of Chen Yin-ke (陈寅恪, 1890-1969)'s achievements in translation studies. Chen is seen as a historian, yet problems in translation remained his concern throughout his career. In his view, highly qualified translators have the same ability as great scholars, for both of them can re-create and transform cultural traditions, thus continuing and reviving human culture and passing it on to later generations, with translation always being a driving force and a powerful resource. Without translation, human culture could exist in the first place. Therefore the history of human culture is first of all the history of translation, which always rewrites the former as a multi-cultural and post-national continuity by means of a single national language. This paper also discusses his reconfirmation of Chos-grub (法成,?-?865) as a monumental Tibetan translator, and his rediscovery of an anonymous Manchu version of the *Elements of Geometry*.

Key words: Chen Yinque; translation; history; Chos-grub; Buddhism

2

作　　者　崔　峰

标　　题　翻译家鲁迅的"中间物"意识——以鲁迅早期翻译方式的变换为例

发表刊物　《中国翻译》2007年第6期

[摘　要]　诸多研究者忽略了这样一个非常有意义的现象：鲁迅翻译生涯的开山之作《哀尘》（1903）直接采用了直译的手法；而其后的几篇小说又放弃了直译法，改为编译的形式，主要包括《地底旅行》（1903）、《斯巴达之魂》（1903）、《北极探险记》（1904）、《造人术》（1905），而到了1909年，鲁迅又在其《域外小说集》中的三篇译文中重新采取了直译的手法。本文试以鲁迅早期（1903—1909）翻译方式的变换为例，从鲁迅这一阶段"中间物"意识的角度，结合当时的社会文化背景，对鲁迅的翻译思想、翻译实践等方面进行阐发。从而认识鲁迅以翻译为途径，在

中国文学、文化现代性追求中所扮演的角色；理解作为开拓者、探索者的翻译家鲁迅在思想发展、实践过程中出现的摇摆变化、矛盾错误或意气用事之处；从历时的角度去观察鲁迅与历史和未来的关系，重新评估鲁迅在中国文学史和中国翻译史上的地位。本文认为，鲁迅通过他的创作和翻译实践着他作为中国现代化进程中文学、思想的启蒙家、探索者的人生定位。对当时的中国文化、思想、国民性改造、语言文字改革，鲁迅选择的方法是一种因力图彻底而略显偏激的"破"。但鲁迅把重心始终放在以"破"为"立"这一层面上，对"立"的结果没有细加考虑，对未来希望的寄托可以说是鲁迅对"立"的结果的一种模糊意识。此外，鲁迅的这种"中间物"意识与其在中国文化转型期所做的文学文化现代性探索紧密相联。把翻译作为他追求中国文化现代性的手段之一，通过翻译来改造国民性、批判中国传统文化、改造汉语语法等。

关 键 词　鲁迅；"中间物"意识；翻译方式；现代性

作者联系地址　新加坡南洋理工大学，南洋道 14 号 HSS-03-10

电子邮箱　cuifeng@ntu.edu.sg

2

Author: CUI Feng

Title: LU Xun's "Intermediate" Consciousness and the Methodological Changes in His Early Career as a Translator

Published in: *Chinese Translators Journal,* 2007 (6).

[Abstract]　A change is observed in LU Xun's translation methods during the early years of his translation career (1903-1909). He adopted literal translation for his first work, *Les Misérables* (1903), but shifted to using adaptation for later works such as *The Soul of Sparta* (1903), *Journey to the Center of the Earth* (1903), *An Expedition to the North Pole* (1904), and *Art of Making Men* (1905), before returning to his original method of literal translation for three articles in *Collections of Stories from Abroad* (1909). This paper discusses LU Xun's "intermediate" consciousness by correlating it with changes in his methods of translation. It argues that in exploring issues in LU Xun's translational thoughts and practices, simultaneously taking into consideration the socio-cultural conditions of his time and his "intermediate" consciousness brings three advantages: it would enable us to better appreciate the key role LU Xun played in China's pursuit of literary and cultural modernity; it would open our eyes to the oscillations and conflicts he experienced as a pioneer and an explorer in the emerging field of translation; and it would provide a historical perspective from which to determine how LU Xun was situated vis-à-vis the past and the future. Such an approach allows us to re-evaluate LU Xun's position in China's literary and translation history, established through literary creation and translation. In pursuing thoroughness in revolution, LU Xun resorted to extreme means such as relentlessly condemning the traditional Chinese culture and national character. This "intermediate" consciousness is closely related to China's exploration of modernity in this period.

Key words: LU Xun; the "intermediate" consciousness; translation methods; modernity

3

作　　者　耿　强
标　　题　史学观念与翻译文学史写作——兼评谢天振、查明建主编的《中国现代翻译文学史（1898—1949）》
发表刊物　《中国比较文学》2007年第2期
［摘　要］史学观念最终决定史撰的表现形态。中国翻译文学史的撰写长期以来得不到学科理论的支撑，虽有局部史料汇编的精彩，但总体缺乏有深度的理论提升。中国翻译文学的实践自佛经翻译便已经开始，但从史

学的角度对这一活动进行梳理并以史著的形式出现则是晚近的事情。1949年建国之前，胡适（1928）、陈子展（1929）、王哲甫（1933）均在中国文学史中论述中国翻译文学的成绩。1949年之后的30多年的时间里，中国翻译文学逐渐淡出中国文学史的视野，直至彻底消失。1985年，黄子平、陈平原、钱理群共同提出"二十世纪中国文学"这一概念，目的在于打通当时"近代文学""现代文学"和"当代文学"的研究格局，在整体上把握近代百年中国文学。此概念一出，可谓吹响了"重写中国文学史"之号角。到了80年代末，在"重写文学史"口号的刺激和鼓舞下，翻译文学史的理论思考与实践才算真正起步。谢天振率先从理论上思考翻译文学在中国文学体系中的地位，进而提出完整的中国文学史应该包括翻译文学，随后对翻译文学史的理论与实践问题作了系统而深刻的探索。这在谢天振、查明建主编的《中国现代翻译文学史（1898—1949)》（2004）这本书中有着集中而明确的解答。这本书视翻译文学史为文学交流史、文学关系史、文学影响史，从而在以下三个方面创新独树：史撰内容上，涵盖作家、作品与事件三要素；体例编排上，承认并突出"披上中国外衣的外国作家"作为翻译文学史另一主体的地位；史学叙述上，彰显交流史、关系史与影响史脉络，史学分期重证据实。因此，这次史学实践定会给中国翻译文学史的理论深入和实践开拓带来新的刺激和推动，给后续研究提供可资借鉴的认识和经验。

关 键 词 史学观；中国现代翻译文学史；谢天振、查明建；历史分期
作者联系地址 上海市浦东新区沈家弄路877弄17号403室
电子邮箱 qianggeng@shmtu.edu.cn

3

Author: GENG Qiang

Title: Underlining Historiographic Vision in Compilation of History of Translated Literature—with *History of Translated Literature in Modern*

China (1898-1949) co-edited by Xie Tianzhen and Zha Mingjian as an illustrative case

Published in: *Comparative Literature in China*, 2007 (2).

[Abstract] The historiographic vision determines how history is compiled. For lack of theoretical support, the historical compilation of Chinese translated literature has produced good isolated case studies, but no deep theoretical construction. The practice of Chinese translated literature started from translation of Buddhist scriptures into Chinese more than a thousand years ago, however, to conduct a research on it from historical perspective was a recent activity. Prior to the foundation of New China in 1949, Hu Shi (1928), Chen Zizhan (1929) and Wang Zhefu (1933) all made personal accounts of Chinese translated literature in their compilation of Chinese literature history. However, during the thirty years after 1949, Chinese translated literature has been out of the vision of Chinese literature history and finally withdrew into oblivion. In 1985, Huang Ziping, Chen Pingyuan and Qian Liqun, by advocating for a concept of "twentieth-century Chinese literature", aimed to put the research of "near-modern literature" "modern literature" and "contemporary literature" under an umbrella concept. The concept promoted a trend of rewriting Chinese literature history. Under this current, in the last few years of 1980s, compilation of translated literature history was put into practice and corresponding theoretical exploration was initiated too. Xie Tianzhen took a lead in researching how translated literature can be understood in the polysystem of Chinese literature, further advocating to explore the relation between translated literature and Chinese literature from a theoretical point of view. In the book *History of Translated Literature in Modern China (1898-1949)* co-edited by Xie Tianzhen and Zha Mingjian (2004), few important questions are discussed for us to have a better understanding of the nature of history of translated literature. The book deserves recommendation for the following reasons: in terms of content, it includes original authors, texts and literary events; in terms of compilation, it highlights "foreign authors in Chinese costume" as another subject in history of translated literature; in terms of historical narration, it constructs a tradition characteristic of a communicative history, relational history and influential history, besides the periodization is based on solid evidence from raw data. In a word, the book would give a push to the development of theory and practice in writing history of Chinese translated literature.

Key words: historiographic vision; translated literature history in modern China; Xie Tianzhen & Zha Mingjian; historical periodization

4

作　　者　刘林海
标　　题　19世纪中国人关于基督教God/Spirit汉译问题的讨论
发表刊物　《北京师范大学学报》2007年第6期

[**摘　要**]　本文在梳理已有重要研究成果的基础上，以相关文献为主要材料，探讨19世纪中国学者对圣经汉译中一些关键术语的理解和认识。全文分为四部分：问题的提出、19世纪四五十年代的翻译和讨论、19世纪70年代末的激烈争论以及简短的评论。

如何用汉语词翻译圣经中的God (Elohim/Theos) 和Spirit (Ruach/Pneuma)？近代以来，就成为讨论的问题，被称为"术语问题"。不过，学界一般认为这只是外籍传教士内部的争论，中国学者并未参与。其实，查阅当时的资料就会发现，中国人对这个问题也一直进行着认真的讨论。19世纪四五十年代，何进善、徐继畲、洪秀全等就使用了"上帝"、"神天"、"天父"、"真神"等译名。19世纪70年代末，更多学者参与其中，福州征文活动和《万国公报》起了推波助澜的作用，使讨论达到高潮，这个时期出现了"造化主""真宰"等译名。中国学者的主张具有深厚的民族文化底蕴，表现了鲜明的民族特色，对中西文化交流产生重要的推动意义。

关　键　词　基督教；God/Spirit；术语问题；汉译；中国学者
作者联系地址　北京市海淀区新街口外大街19号，北京师范大学历史学

院 (100875)
电子邮箱　linhailiu@163.com

4

Author: LIU Linhai

Title: Nineteenth Century's Chinese Views on Rendering God (Elohim/Theos) and Spirit (Ruach/Pneuma) of Christianity into Chinese

Published in: *Journal of Beijing Normal University (Social Science Edition)*, 2007 (6).

[Abstract] The aim of this paper is to discuss the participation and discourses of the Chinese scholars during the course of the Bible translation into Chinese in the 19th century. It is divided into four parts: analysis of the publications in the field, the controversy in the early 19th century, the controversy in the late 19th century and a short conclusion.

The Term Question, or how to render the Biblical words God (Elohim/Theos) and Spirit (Ruach/Pneuma) into Chinese, has long been a controversy ever since the modern times. Nevertheless, it is generally considered by scholars to be an internal controversy among the Protestant missionaries to China without Chinese participations. Such assumption falls to the ground when related resources at that time come to the front. In fact, it has been discussed seriously by Chinese scholars all the time. Words such as *Shangdi*, *Shentian*, *Tianfu* and *Zhenshen*, had been used or proposed for the translation into Chinese in the late 1840s and 1850s, among others, He Jinshan, Xu Jiyu and Hong Xiuquan. More and more Chinese scholars joined the discussion in the late 1870s, highlighted by the essay competition in Fuzhou and the controversy in *Wanguo Gongbao*. It was during this period that words such as *Zaohuazhu* and *Zhenzai* were added to the list for candidacy. Deeply rooted in national Chinese culture and characterized by Chinese nationality, the solutions proposed by Chinese scholars promoted the cultural exchanges between China and the West greatly.

Key words: Christianity; God/Spirit; term question; Chinese translation; Chinese scholars

5

作　　者　陆国飞
标　　题　试论中国晚清翻译小说中的"译意"现象
发表刊物　《浙江社会科学》2007年第2期
[摘　要]　本文以翻译的"目的论"为理论观照，阐释"译意"法在晚清翻译小说中的地位，从文化传播史、文化接受史的维度加以考察晚清翻译小说中的"译意"现象。我们研究它并不是故意拔高"译意"的作用，在当前的翻译实践中推而广之，而是强调其文化功能。因为它当时的确在开启民智、促进和丰富中国近现代文学中发挥过不可小觑的作用。晚清时期，中国翻译小说空前繁荣。但是我们发现这一时段的翻译方式与传统所谓的"直译"、"意译"不尽相同，期间普遍采用一种"译意"的翻译方法。在刊物上发表译作，基本以署"某某人译述"为主。"译述"属于一种翻译变体，在翻译操作上比较自由、比较灵活，它包括译中有改、译中有评、译中有增、译中有删等操作，当然它也不是一种无序，而是强调对原作的高度的自由把握。本文将其统称为"译意"。所谓"译意"，就是"译意不译词"，译者在保持原文主要内容不变或主要故事情节完整的情况下，可以根据目的语读者的需要或阅读习惯、审美情趣进行删改、增补或发挥。其操作比"意译"还要宽松，涵盖了"直译"和"意译"的翻译方式；而且在语篇层面上进行，不以句子为基本单位。长期以来，学术界往往把"译意"和"意译"混为一谈，对其特征和意义未有足够的重视。因此，有必要界别"译意"和"意译"这两个概念，分析"译意"现象产生的社会背景及其文化意义。

关 键 词 晚清；翻译小说；"译意"；"目的论"；翻译方法
作者联系地址 浙江省舟山市定海临城新区长峙岛海大南路 1 号
电子邮箱 luguofei2005@163.com

5

Author: LU Guofei
Title: On the "Adaptation" of Translated Novels in China's Late Qing Dynasty
Published in: *Zhejiang Social Science*, 2007 (2).
[Abstract] China's translated novels enjoyed a great popularity in the late Qing Dynasty, during which the then translators universally adopted a translating method of "adaptation". "Adaptation" means to translate meaning of the original rather than words themselves. Thus, the translator might do some deletions and additions or use other manipulations so long as he kept either the main content unchanged or the completion of the main story plot according to the requirements, the reading habit and the aesthetic taste of the target readers in the process of translating the Western literary works. Its translating manipulations is much freer than "liberal translation", including the translation methods of both "literal translation" and "liberal translation". It does not take a sentence as a basic unit but is manipulated on the level of a text. However, the academic circles often confuse the "adaptation" with the "liberal translation" without attaching much importance to the characteristics and meaning of the "adaptation". Therefore, it's necessary for us to distinguish the two concepts of "adaptation" and "liberal translation" so that we can analyse the social background and cultural meaning caused by the translation method "adaptation".
Key words: The late Qing Dynasty; translated novels; "adaptation"; "Scopos theory"; translation method

6

作　　者　孙海琳、杨自俭
标　　题　关于译场职司的考辨
发表刊物　《中国翻译》2007 年第 3 期

[摘　要]　佛经翻译在中国翻译史上是很重要的一个阶段，其中的译场特别是译场中的职司问题又是研究佛经翻译的一个重要课题。有关译场职司的记载，我们最先看到的是马祖毅的文章（1980）、《中国翻译简史》（1984、1998）与（中国翻译史）（上）（1999）和陈福康的《中国译学理论史稿》（1992）。之后看了曹仕邦（1963、1982、1990）、王文颜（1984）、杨廷福（1986）、苏晋仁（1998）、李德山（2002）等的著作。再之后又查阅了任继愈（1951）、吕澂（1979）、汤用彤（1982）的著作。最后主要查阅了《大正新修大藏经》中道宣的《续高僧传》和智磐的《佛祖统纪》中天息灾的记述，还有赞宁的《宋高僧传》（1987）。上述从曹仕邦到汤用彤这些作者的文章和书中关于译场职司的资料基本上都来源于道宣、赞宁和天息灾的记述。马书和陈书明确交代译场职司的资料分别出自《宋高僧传》和《续高僧传》，我们从四个方面就马书和陈书的引文和来源文献进行了考证和探询，发现引文和来源文献二者差别很大，但和天息灾的记载以及任继愈和杨廷福文章的记述非常相似，所以本文认为马书与陈书的引文出处难以令人信服。

关 键 词　译场；职司；考辨
作者联系地址　山东省青岛市城阳区长城路 700 号，青岛农业大学外语学院
电子邮箱　sunhailin2012@163.com

6

Author: SUN Hailin & YANG Zijian

Title: Querying the Sources of a Claim about Tang Dynasty Translation Workshop

Published in: *Chinese Translators Journal*, 2007 (3).

[Abstract] Sutra translation was one important phase in the history of Chinese translation and the functionaries in sutra translation workshop were paid much attention to by researchers. As for the record of translation workshop, we firstly read Ma Zuyi's article (1980), *A Short History of Translation in China* (1984,1998) and *A Series of Translation Studies in China* (1999), and Chen Fukang's *A Short History of Translation Theory in China* (1992). Secondly, some articles and books written by Cao Shibang (1963;1982;1990), Wang Wenyan (1984), Yang Tingfu (1986), Su Jinren (1998), Li Deshan (2002), etc. are checked. Thirdly, the records of translation workshop are looked up in the books written by Ren Jiyu (1951), Lv Cheng (1979) and Tang Yongtong (1982). Lastly, we consult *Taisho Tripitaka* for Daoxuan's and Tianxizai's record, and Zanning's *The Biography of Eminent Monks in Song Dynasty*. Ma and Chen clearly said that they referred to Zanning's *The Biography of Eminent Monks in Song Dynasty* and Daoxuan's *A Sequel to the Biography of Eminent Monks*. But there are some differences. Further textual research shows that the true sources lie elsewhere, most likely in Tianxizai's record of the Song Dynasty and in publications by such contemporary scholars as Ren Jiyu and Yang Tingfu.

Key words: translation workshop; duty; textual research

7

作　者　谢世维
标　题　圣典与传译——六朝道教经典中的"翻译"
发表刊物　《中央研究院中国文哲研究所集刊》2007年第31期

[**摘　要**]　道教的天书观与圣典传译概念实际上是一个复杂的观念，其中复合了许多不同的传统，包含汉代以来借由符瑞与天授文书的天命观以及佛教译经传统。在谶纬传统中，"天"被塑造成一个有主体性、能主动传递"符命"、"天命"予受命圣王的最高权威。这类天命文书常被描述为古老字体或是无法解析的图像纹路，似乎都是无法被一般人所解读，因而需要透过圣者经过一定程序的解释或翻译，然后天的意志才可以被世俗之人所理解。这种经典传译观念又与佛教的译经传统有很深的关联性，当佛典传入汉地后，记录佛典的梵书及佉楼书被视为是天界语言。因此，佛典翻译不是单纯的异国文字转译，而是牵涉到神圣语言传译为世俗语言的传译转化问题。当道教面临这种强势而具宗教权威的神圣文字与经典大批翻译传入中国时，开始意识到道教经典的神圣性，并宣称其经典文字并非世俗文字，而是源自于天界的文字，这种神秘的天书起源于宇宙生成之时，是先天之气与道的化现，经过漫长的时间，才由诸神仙真转写，层层转译传授，最后翻译成世俗文字而成为经书。在建构天界文字系谱时，甚至将梵文给纳入这神圣的天界文字系谱中，将之视为天书之一；或者将印度梵的观念转为道教宇宙生成时先天之气的概念，而称之为梵气，而其凝成的天文称为"大梵隐语"。这些神秘的隐语并采用了佛教翻译中所使用的音译文字，使得大梵隐语看起来具有如佛教咒语般的神秘力量。其中印度文化里将梵文作为神圣语言的观念与道教的天书观被巧妙地糅合，而形成一种带有神秘符码性质的天界文字系谱。在道教天书神学的系统之下，道教的经典拥有一个根源性的神圣基础，一切的经典都是由这个神圣根源辗转翻译而来的。

关 键 词　道教；灵宝；翻译；天书

作者联系地址　台湾台北市指南路二段 64 号，宗教研究所
电子邮箱　hsiehben@hotmail.com

7

Author: SHU-wei Hsieh

Title: Sacred Scriptures and Transmissions—The Notion of "Translation" in Six Dynasties Daoist Scriptures

Published in: *Bulletin of the Institute of Chinese Literature and Philosophy*, 2007 (31).

[Abstract]　The notion of Daoist Celestial Writing was a synthesis of a variety of practices, including the Mandate of Heaven, as well as Buddhist practices and scriptural traditions. Expanding on the mythology of the auspicious celestial writs, and other portents whose mysterious appearance was proof of the ruler's authority, the Weft texts were described as ancient scripts or patterns, which needed translation in order to understand the will of Heaven. In addition, Buddhism had some impacts on the notion of "translation" in Daoist scriptural tradition, especially the idea of taking Sanskrit as a type of Celestial language. In the *Shangqing* tradition, the theory of writing not only relates to cosmology, but also already includes Sanskrit. The inspiration for celestial script lies not only in traditional Chinese notions of writing; the idea that celestial script needed transcription and translation into a human language was strongly reinforced by the introduction of Buddhism. In certain *Lingbao* scriptures, the characters of the Celestial Script are based on transliterations of Sanskrit syllables. Furthermore, they are grouped into strings of pseudo-Sanskrit words. The Celestial Script is also called "the hidden language of the Great Brahman". When this Celestial Script was translated into human script, it is written with standard Buddhist transcription characters. According to the *Lingbao* tradition,

"Brahman" refers to the "primal pneuma" which swirled in undifferentiation before the separation of *Yin* and *Yang*. This article investigates the idea of Daoist revelation as a chain of transmissions and translation that stretches across vast distances from Celestial Script to mundane language.

Key words: *Lingbao*; Celestial Writing; translation; Daoism

8

作　　者　　张　政、张卫晴
标　　题　　近代翻译之始——蠡勺居士及其《昕夕闲谈》
发表刊物　　《外语与外语教学》2007年第6期

[摘　要]　国内大多数学者认为近代文学翻译以1899年长篇小说《巴黎茶花女遗事》的问世为滥觞，林纾开创中国人翻译西方小说的先河。事实上，1873年，"蠡勺居士"翻译了英国作家利顿的小说《夜与晨》，并连续刊载于《申报》的文艺副刊《瀛寰琐纪》。从译品出版时间看，蠡勺居士早于林纾，理应视作我国文学翻译之始。然而到目前为止，学界鲜有提及"蠡勺居士"，原因是多方面的。首先是译者蠡勺居士的身份难以确定；再者译文与原文差异较大，多有编译、译写、译创的成分，无法回译，读者很难将译文与原文联系在一起，这给深入研究其作品造成一定难度；此外，蠡勺居士是否独立翻译全文还是与西方人合作以"口述——笔录"形式成书尚未可知，也需进一步探究。

本文就上述问题进行较为深入的研究，通过文本对比、史料考证、文献梳理分析，作者认为，虽然蠡勺居士的翻译小说不如林译小说社会影响大，也不如林译小说数量多，但蠡勺居士在翻译史上的地位不容撼动，不仅因为他的译品出现年代更早，更重要的是，其翻译形式远远超越晚他一代的林纾——蠡勺居士独立翻译西方小说。他的翻译形式超越了明清延续下来、传教士与华士结合形成的"口述－笔录"模式，从而使翻译活动趋于独立和成熟。蠡勺居士独立翻译标志着国人独立翻译文学作品时代的到来，更标志着中国人从此摆脱依赖传教士或西人之笔了解世界的被动局面，转而成为系统了解西方文学、社会学、政治制度等的主动行为。

关 键 词　蠡勺居士；《昕夕闲谈》；独立翻译；翻译史

作者联系地址　北京市海淀区新街口外大街19号，北京师范大学外国语言文学学院

电子邮箱　zhangzheng@bnu.edu.cn

8

Author: ZHANG Zheng & ZHANG Weiqing

Title: The Beginning of Literature Translation in Modern China: A Case Study of Lishaojushi and *Xinxixiantan*

Published in: *Foreign Language Teaching and Research,* 2007 (6).

[Abstract]　Lin Shu translated *La Dameaux Camelia* by Dumas, Ill, in 1989, which is considered the the beginning and milestone of Chinese literature translation; howerver, in 1973, Lishaojushi translated *the Night and Morning* by John Lytton, Britich novelist and had its series published in the Supplement of *Shun Pao*. Judging from the time, Lishaojushi should be the first Chinese who brought the western novel into China. But up to now, this has been ignored by the Chinese translation circles and the reasons may be as follows: 1) it is difficult to ascertain the identity of Lishaojushi; 2) there is a big difference between the translation and the original, and there are compiling, rewriting and creation; besides, whether Lishaojushi translated it independently or took the traditional translation form of "oral interpretation by westerners and word for word record by Chinese", which needs further exploration.

　　This paper studies the above-mentioned questions and by comparing the original and the translation, textual research of historical data and literature analysis, the authors come to the following findings: compared with Lin Shu,

Lishaojushi translated much less; as a result, his influence is liminted, but his contribution and his historical status should be well recoginzed because his translation appeared far earlier, and because more importantly, his translation form "oral interpretation by Westerners and word for word record by Chinese" also outran Lin Shu's. All those showed that Chinese translation was moving toward maturity, that the Chinese translator began doing his translation, independent of Western missionaries, and that some Chinese intellectuals were able to take an active step to learn western literature, sociology and political systems and so on.

Key words: Lishaojushi; *Xinxixiantan*; independent translation; translation history

9

作　　者　关诗珮

标　　题　从林纾看文学翻译规范由晚清中国到五四的转变：西化、现代化和以原著为中心的观念

发表刊物　《中国文化研究所学报》2008年第48期

［摘　要］　林纾（1852—1924）是中国翻译史上的奇葩。于19世纪末，他翻译了众多知名的世界文学到中国来，仅于20年间，出自他的译笔就有213篇外国文学。五四以来，即使是不同文学观念的作家、评论家和文学研究者，都必承认或多或少曾受林纾的影响。不过，在晚清声名远播的林纾，到了1919年的五四时代，不觉转眼二十年，却落得"桐城妖孽"、"遗老"、"亡国贱俘"、"罪人"的恶评，因而饮恨退隐历史现场。而五四时期大力批判林纾的知识人，却正是晚清时期——于青年时代——曾经沉迷林译小说的同一批人。历史上的林纾，在个人形象方面还是社会评价方面，都被分成两半。

本文认为，林纾现象在中国翻译史上虽长期被看成是"真是绝可怪诧

的事", 事实却侧写了近代中国翻译史上文学翻译规范从晚清到五四的嬗变。学者图里 (Gideon Toury) 在翻译研究的经典论文《翻译规则的本质和功用 (1995)》中, 提出了翻译规范 (norms) 的概念, 详细分析翻译活动如何受译入语社会及文化制约, 这些规范并直接影响译者的翻译策略。本文借着林纾"前誉后毁"的现象, 利用图里翻译规范理论分析文学翻译规范在中国短短数十年间, 出现了一次急遽并彻底的转变。在西力的冲击下, 晚清中国所处的时代是一个与西方话语权角力竞争的特殊历史境遇。本文论述晚清中国与西方的权力关系时, 采用"去现代化话语干扰"的方法亦接近于还原历史的角度, 分析不同历史时期的译作以及文化接受翻译过程中所产生的规范, 如何宰制社会成规的权力因素, 让晚清时译文在进入译入语社会时, 会产生偏离原著、不通文义及语句上不对等这些规范却又成为林译小说成功之本。

关　键　词　文学翻译；晚清；五四；林纾；以原著为中心；翻译规范
作者联系地址　新加坡南洋理工大学, 南洋道 14 号 HSS-03-13
电子邮箱　ugandakwan@ntu.edu.sg

9

Author: Uganda Sze Pui KWAN

Title: Westernization, Modernization, and the Concept of Basing on the Source Text: A Study of the Transformation of Norm in Literary Translation from Late Qing to May Fourth with Lin Shu as a Case Study

Published in: *Journal of Chinese Studies*, 2008 (48).

[Abstract]　Lin Shu (1852-1924) was one of the most prolific, significant and well-known translators of literature in translation history. His prolificity is phenomenal and the total number of 213 pieces of Western literary work he translated into the Chinese soil has earned him an unquestionable place in the cultural history of modern China. There were plenty of translators in the late imperial China, and many of them were more competent in foreign languages, but none could captivate the readers' mind the way Lin did. He was an expert in the archaic Tongcheng style of writing, which, once fused with Lin's new and vivid lexicons, proved irresistible to the generation of the May Fourth era, and eventually came to shape the literary taste of an era. But the wind turned quickly in those revolutionary days, when China was stumbling into the modern world. Within two decades of time, the sacred aura surrounding Lin's translation was gone, and his translation style was regarded as strange, bizarre, and unpalatable. For a long time, in the study of the history of Chinese translation, the view of the latter age has been taken for granted, and a great number of representative works on Lin's translation are focused on finding out its discrepancies from the source texts. The SL (Source text)-oriented approach certainly has its own merits, but this paper will try and take an alternate path. Drawing on the myriad discourses about Lin's translations from the late imperial to the May Fourth era and Gideon Toury's theory of norms from his seminal essay "The Nature and Role of Norms in Translation (1995)", this paper will lay down and analyze two sets of translation norms that underpin the cultural critique of Lin's translation in that period. And taking Lin as an example, it will also try to reappraise the current view about translation in late Qing from the perspective of post-colonial studies and discuss several key issues about it, such as the role of the text and the power of the translator.

Key words: literary translation; late Qing; May Fourth; Lin Shu; source-text oriented; translation norm

10

作　者　梅谦立

标　题　《孔夫子》：最初西文翻译的儒家经典

发表刊物 《中山大学学报》2008年第2期

[摘　要] 本文介绍了在中国经典西传的开端时期,西方人如何第一次阅读、理解、翻译和在欧洲传播《四书》。1579年来华的耶稣会士罗明坚很快意识到儒家经典的重要地位,在1588年返回欧洲之前,他已开始翻译四书,然而他在欧洲只能出版《大学》前面部分。随后,在华的耶稣会士使用《四书》作为语言教材学习中文。1666年,郭纳爵在江西出版了《大学》及《论语》前半部分的中文、拉丁文对照本。1667—1669年,殷铎泽在广州及果阿刻印了《中庸》的中拉对照本。1666—1670年,传教士们聚集在广州,他们之间的"礼仪之争"再次爆发,这迫使耶稣会士为了证明中国礼仪的合法性必须展示儒家经典的"祭天"和"祭祀"并不是迷信,而是符合理性。在殷铎泽的指导之下,柏应理等耶稣会士更系统地阅读宋明理学家对《四书》的评论,把大量评论翻译成拉丁文来解释《四书》原文。1687年,在法国国王路易十四世的支持下,柏应理最终出版了《中国哲学家孔夫子》。这是首次在欧洲同时出版《大学》、《中庸》、《论语》三部经典。文章指出耶稣会士在宋明理学家的评论中做了怎样的选择:以朱熹《四书章句》中的理学证明古儒思想完全符合人的自然理性;用张居正《四书直解》中的政治思想证明中国伦理生活及政治制度充满理性;也以邱俊《大学衍义补》中的考证学证明儒家经典所包含的历史记载是真实的。耶稣会士把儒家经典理解为哲学,也理解为历史,开启了中西之间的哲学与文明对话。

关　键　词 四书;宋明理学;耶稣会;诠释学

作者联系地址 广东省广州市海珠区新港西路135号哲学系锡昌堂710

电子邮箱 meiqianl@mail.sysu.edu.cn

10

Author: Thierry Meynard
Title: Early Translation in Western Language of Confucian Classics
Published in: *Journal of Sun Yat-sen University,* 2008 (2).

[Abstract] This paper presents the first dissemination of the Chinese Classics into the West. Ruggieri arrived China in 1579 and soon realized the importance of the Confucian Classics. Before his return to Europe in 1588, he had already started his translation, but he only published in Europe the preface of the *Daxue*. Later, the missionaries in China used the *Four Books* to teach Chinese. In 1666, da Costa published in Jiangxi a Chinese-Latin edition of the *Daxue* and of the first half of the *Lunyu*. In 1667-1669, Intorcetta engraved in Guangdong and Goa his translation of the *Zhongyong*. In 1666-1670, the Rite Controversy erupted again among missionaries in Guangzhou. To prove the legitimacy of the Chinese rites, the Jesuits needed to show that the sacrifices to heaven and to ancestors in the Confucian Classics are rational and not superstitious. They systematically read the commentaries on the Four Books, and translated some of them. In 1687, under the auspices of Louis XIV, Couplet finally published the *Confucius Sinarum Philosophus*. This paper shows the choices made by the Jesuits: using Zhu Xi's *Sishu zhangju* to prove that ancient texts are conform to natural reason; using the political thought of Zhang Juzheng in his *Sishu zhijie* to prove the high moral and political thought of the *Four Books*; using the method of Qiu Jun's in his *Daxue yanyibu* to prove the antiquity of Chinese history. Jesuits presented the *Four Books* as being both philosophy and history, starting the philosophical and cultural dialogue between China and the West.

Key words: *Four Books*; Song-Ming lixue; Jesuit; hermeneutics

11

作　　者　任东升
标　　题　圣经汉译与佛经翻译比较研究
发表刊物　《上海翻译》2008 年第 3 期
［摘　要］文章从宗教经典翻译发生论入手，探讨圣经汉译与佛经翻译在

翻译实践上的相似性以及两者产生差别的历史文化原因。圣经翻译有一语多译的传统，因而带有世界性特征；佛经翻译的中心在中国，地区性特征明显。其次，西方圣经翻译历来与民族集团和宗教政治的需要密切相关。第三，西方圣经翻译以输出为主导策略，策动者和赞助人在源语文化一方，带有"征服文化"色彩，符合基督教拯救灵魂、皈依基督的普世目的；佛经翻译以输入为主导策略，策动者在目的语文化一方，带有"使节文化"意味，符合佛教对主体悟性的倚重。最后，西方圣经翻译张扬基督教文化，在基督教国家，宗教性始终被尊崇为圣经文本的主导性价值或首要价值；佛经翻译从一开始就与中国传统哲学及美学结合，哲理性和文学性被尊崇为汉译佛典的主导性价值或首要价值。

圣经汉译与佛经翻译都以汉语为依归，以传播本教教义、塑造本教教徒身份为主要目的，均受到中国统治阶级意识形态的影响，反过来对中国社会各个层面产生深刻影响，对中国语言和文学的发展起到积极作用。圣经和佛经在中国语境下均得到诗意的诠释，这说明中国的诗学传统和文人读经传统对宗教文本发挥了重塑作用。两者的差异则反映出佛教来源地印度文化圈和圣经来源地欧洲文化圈之间的巨大差别，折射出佛教文化的"使节文化"内涵和基督教文化的"征服文化"特点。在外来文化面前，中国文化并不是被动的，而是与外来文化积极互动。这正是民族文化自主和自卫的体现，也是不同文化之间得以平等交流的保证。

关　键　词　圣经汉译；佛经翻译；比较研究；使节文化；征服文化
作者联系地址　山东省青岛市松岭路 238 号，中国海洋大学外国语学院
邮　　编　266100
电子邮箱　dongsheng_ren@ouc.edu.cn

11

Author: REN Dongsheng

Title: A Contrastive Study of Bible Translation and Buddhist Sutra Translation

Published in: *Shanghai Journal of Translation*, 2008 (3)

[Abstract]   This paper, starting with the translation and circulation of religious cannons from the genetic perspective, discusses the similarities in translation practice between Chinese Bible translation and Buddhist Sutra translation, followed by a tentative exploration of the historical and cultural reasons for their differences. Firstly, having been translated to multilingual versions and currently in the ascendant, Bible translation boasts a worldwide event, while Buddhist Sutra translation is a regional event since it took place in China. Secondly, Bible translations in the West has all the way been closely related to the interests of Christian sects or traditions or religious politics. Thirdly, to output the Christian values and cultures dominates the translation strategies adopted by initiators and sponsors of Bible translation, aiming at cultural conquest over the others', which is in accordance to the universal Christian idea of converting every soul to Christ by saving every soul. In contrast, with the target-language culture as translation initiator, Buddhist Sutra translation employs input as primary strategy, and consequently, it is characterized by diplomatic culture, which is in accordance with the Buddhist's emphasis on individuals' insights. Finally, since Bible translations in the West publicizes Christian values and culture, the religious nature has been constantly favored as Bible's leading or first value in Christian countries, in contrast with philosophy and aesthetics Buddhist Sutra translation prefers, since the two are highlighted from the very beginning.

Both translation traditions in China, aim at spreading their own teachings by Chinese language and establishing the identity of their believers in China. Both are influenced by Chinese ruling ideology and in turn exert profound impacts on all levels of Chinese society, playing a role in enriching Chinese language and literature. The fact that both have been interpreted poetically in Chinese context suggests that the two are reshaped by Chinese traditional poetics and Chinese scholars' inclination of interpreting classics. The discrepancy between the two translation traditions reflects not only the great differences between the "Indian cultural circle" — the source of Buddhism, and the "European cultural circle"— the origin of the Bible, but also the characteristics of the Buddhist's diplomatic culture and the Bible's conquering culture. In face to foreign cultures, Chinese culture has not been in a passive position, but actively interacted with them, indicating the importance of being the master of its own culture and defending national culture, which is the guarantee for equal exchanges between different cultures.

Key words: Chinese Bible translation; Buddhist Sutra translation; contrastive study; diplomatic culture; conquering culture

12

作　者　韩思艺
标　题　"罪过"：在明清之际耶儒对话中谈"Sin"的翻译与诠释
发表刊物　《神学关键词：基督教文化学刊》2009 年第 1 期

[摘　要]　自明清以来，基督宗教在中国的传播已有四百年的历史，但是基督宗教中"罪"的观念始终为中国人所不解甚至拒斥。这不仅是因为基督宗教传统与中国文化传统之间存在着诸多的差异，将"sin"翻译为"罪"也是导致中国人对这个观念误解的一个重要原因。本文首先探讨了明清之际传教士将"sin"翻译为"罪"的由来，以及反教儒者对"罪"的批评，以便从反教儒者的角度理解中国人对基督宗教的"罪"的认识。其次，通过阐述明清之际天主教关于"罪"的神学思想，并分析研究宋明理学传统中对于"罪过"的相关论述，从中寻找耶儒双方可以相互理解和会通之处。由此得出将"sin"翻译为"罪过"，将有助于中国人更好地理解并接受基督宗教"sin"的观念。在儒家传统中，"罪过"一词既有"获罪于天"，接受上帝审判的宗教性的含义；也有违背儒家的礼制和法度等伦理性的含义；还有过分的欲望、情感等道德质量方面的含义。"罪过"一词虽然笼统模糊却比较全面，反倒不容易被儒家学者所误解，并能广泛为儒家学者所接受，因此比"罪"的翻译更为妥帖全面。在日常生活中，人们常常会

说道:"罪过,罪过"。分析其语义,"罪过,罪过"是对自己的过错的承认和道歉;分析其源头,"罪过"一词本来就与佛教和道教中的忏法有关,带有一定的宗教性。当人们使用这个词时,不是对某一事物的评价或论断,而是对自己的过错所怀的悔改之心。在基督宗教的传播中,固然不可缺少"天国近了,你们当悔改"的宣告;但"罪过,罪过"的"口头禅",也有助于提醒基督宗教的宣讲者们需要有颗谦卑的心。

关 键 词 罪;过;宗教对话

作者联系地址 北京市海淀区中关村南大街27号,中央民族大学宗教研究院

电子邮箱 hsiyi@hotmail.com

12

Author: HAN Siyi

Title: "Zuiguo": On the Translation and Interpretation of "Sin" in the Dialogues between Catholicism and Confucianism in the Ming and Qing Dynasties in China

Published in: *Critical Terms in Theology: Journal for the Study of Christian Culture*, 2009 (1).

[Abstract] Ever since the Ming and Qing Dynasties, the Christian religion has been in China for four hundred years, however, as one of the basic conception in Christianity, "sin" always could not be understood or even rejected by Chinese people. It is not only because of the big difference between the Christianity tradition and the Chinese culture, but also because of the misunderstanding from the translation of "sin". This paper points out that firstly it is the missionaries in the Ming and Qing Dynasties that translated "sin" into "crime", and secondly it is the anti-Christian Confucian scholars who severely criticized the Christian concept "sin". The author offers analysis on the Chinese understanding of "sin" from the perspective of anti-Christian Confucian scholars. Besides, through clarifying the Catholic theological thought on "sin" in the Ming and Qing Dynasties, and by illustrating the related statements of "sin" in Neo-Confucianism tradition, the paper tries to find out the basis on which Christianity and Confucianism could understand each other or even have a dialogue. The paper suggests that translating "sin" to "zuiguo (transgression)" would better enable the Chinese people to understand and accept the Christian concept "sin".

Key words: sin; "zuiguo (transgression)"; religious dialogue

13

作　　者　何高大、陈水平
标　　题　中国歌曲翻译之百年回眸
发表刊物　《名作欣赏》2009 年第 10 期
[摘　要]　音乐是全人类共同的语言，一个民族的歌曲往往能跨越国界被其他民族广为传唱，像《雪绒花》《友谊地久天长》《莫斯科郊外的晚上》《红河谷》等等这样翻译过来的外国歌曲可以说足足影响了好几代中国人，而中国的《茉莉花》也远渡重洋，为世界各国人民所喜爱，是翻译让这些歌曲成为全人类共同的精神财富。因此，本文在历时性地回顾了我国歌曲翻译的百年历程的基础上，从共时的角度综述了其研究现状，再进一步反思造成我国歌曲翻译从鼎盛到衰退的主要原因，并据此对歌曲翻译的未来做出展望，希望有更多的人关注这一边缘领域。我国的歌曲翻译始于清朝末年，五四运动以后，西风东渐，许多外国歌曲和音乐开始大量译入，至五六十年代臻于繁荣，出现了大量脍炙人口的好歌。"十年文革"曾导致歌曲翻译工作一度中止，但拨乱反正后的八十年代又迎来另一个辉煌时期。然而，今日的歌曲翻译已如昨日黄花，昔日辉煌不再，整体出现了"六多六少"的状况：外文的原版歌曲多，译成中文的少；学唱外语歌曲的多，

从事歌曲翻译（配译）的少；外译中多，中译外少；欧美流行歌曲译品多，多元化多民族歌曲译品少；歌词翻译的多，歌曲配译的少；译配的作品多，真正能入唱的少。导致这一现状的原因之一在于歌曲文本本身独特的文体特征，既有文学性又有音乐性，翻译难，导致好译本越来越少——不仅要做到"美诵"、"美奏"、"美韵"、"美意"，还得做到"美唱"和"美感"，其审美效应还得指向唱者和听者，既要"切唱"还要"切听"。原因之二在于学界很少有人对歌曲翻译理论进行研究探讨，甚至在歌曲翻译标准上都没有任何共识。

关 键 词 歌曲翻译；百年回顾

作者联系地址 广东省广州市天河区五山路483号，华南农业大学外国语学院

电子邮箱 tall168@126.com; helen.csp@163.com

13

Author: HE Gaoda & CHEN Shuiping

Title: 100-Year Translation of Songs in China

Published in: *Masterpieces Review*, 2009 (10).

[Abstract] Music is the universal language of mankind, and songs of a nation can often travel across the national boundaries and be widely sung by other peoples. The translated songs such as "Edelweiss", "Auld Lang Syne", "The night on Moscow's Outskirts", etc. have influenced several generations of Chinese people, and "Jasmine Flower" of China is also loved by the people all over the world. It is the translation that makes these songs the common spiritual wealth of all mankind. The paper, based on a diachronic summarization of 100-year's history of song translation in China and a synchronic analysis of its current situation, explores the main causes for the song translation's decline, with an attempt to encourage more and more people to pay attention to the field. In China, song translation began earlier in the late period of Qing Dynasty and flourishes in 1950s and 1960s when a large number of best songs were translated. There was an interruption during the Cultural Revolution and the 1980s witnessed another glorious period of song translation. Now, song translation has inevitably declined and never resumed to the original state of prosperity. There are two main reasons for it. Firstly, the unique stylistic features of song texts are overlooked by most translators, which in turn resulted in the defective nature of most target texts. For a song text, since its reception is indispensably carried out by two participants – the singer and the listener, its function involves both the singer and the listener: for the singer, the translation should be singable; for the listener, the translation should be enjoyable. Secondly, the researches into song translation are very scanty and there is even no consensus on the standard of song translation.

Key words: song translation; 100 year's history

14

作　　者　王　辉
标　　题　天朝话语与乔治三世致乾隆皇帝书的清宫译文
发表刊物　《中国翻译》2009 年第 1 期
[摘　要]　乔治三世致乾隆皇帝的国书是马戛尔尼访华事件（1792—1794）中的重要文献。国书以英文写就，配有拉丁语和汉语副本，由马戛尔尼在觐见仪式上面呈乾隆。保存在清宫档案中的汉语副本显示，英方以对等的姿态表达友好交往意愿的国书，经由翻译，变成了向中方输诚纳贡的"英吉利国表文"。

从国书到表文的奇特变化，论者往往衡之以忠实观做出批评，但如果从话语的角度加以考察，则不难看出这种翻译现象的必然性。国书看似平等、友好，但其实是大英帝国话语体系的产物，它所构建的中英双方关系，提出的平等交往、派驻使节、通商护侨等要求，体现的均是英方认知、想象、改造世界的方式，与大清帝国的话语体系尤其是朝贡话语建构的宗藩关系是格格不入的，必然被视为对清廷话语秩序的挑衅，也必然受到天朝话语机制的审查与改写。

　　本文的研究发现，清宫档案中的汉语副本，并非马戛尔尼使团进呈的译本，而是清廷按照朝贡话语生产的译本，目的是将英国纳入朝贡体系，维护清廷的话语秩序。

关 键 词　乔治三世；乾隆；国书；翻译；话语
作者联系地址　广东省深圳市南山区南海大道3688号，深圳大学外国语学院
邮　　　编　518060
电子邮箱　wanghui@szu.edu.cn

14

Author: WANG Hui

Title: Celestial Empire Discourse and the Translation of King George III's Letter to Emperor Qianlong

Published in: *Chinese Translators Journal*, 2009 (1).

[Abstract] King George III's letter to Emperor Qianlong is an important document in the first British Embassy to China headed by Lord Macartney. It is a deft blending of arrogant assertions and persuasive conciliation, and proposes trade and communication between Britain and China on equal terms. The Chinese version which reached Emperor Qianlong, however, presents the British King as the prince of a vassal state entreating for commercial favors in most humble terms.

　　This article traces the production of this remarkable version, and attributes its metamorphosis to the workings of the Celestial Empire discourse. King

George's apparently friendly letter is actually a product of Britain's imperial discourse and embodies its colonial desire, the identities of Britain and China and their relationship constructed therein goes every bit against those mapped out by the Qing China's Celestial Empire discourse and could only be perceived as a challenge to the latter, and as such it had to be radically rewritten to be acceptable to the Qing court.

Research indicates that the Chinese version of King George's letter kept in the Qing archives is not the one presented by the embassy, but a new version translated by the Qing court and a product of China's tributary system discourse, which explains why British discursive claims are invariably defeated, disciplined or tamed.

Key words: King George III; Emperor Qianlong; letter; translation; discourse

15

作　　者　谢天振
标　　题　非常时期的非常翻译——关于中国大陆文革时期的文学翻译
发表刊物　《中国比较文学》2009 年第 2 期
[摘　要]　在中国翻译史上，1966 至 1976 年中国大陆"文革"时期的文学翻译属于非常时期的非常翻译。在这一人类历史上罕见的非常时期，政治、意识形态、国家政权、政党对翻译的干预和控制，都达到了极点：从翻译对象的选定，翻译过程的组织，到最后翻译文本的审定、署名形式，等等，都进行了操控。与此同时，翻译家的自主性和对翻译对象的选择权利完全被抹杀，翻译家完全沦为一具任人摆布的翻译机器。"文革"期间，翻译出版的主要是苏联、美国、日本三国的当代文学作品，以及少数的其他国家的作品。这些译作没有公开出版发行，而是以一种特有的"内部发行"的形式在一个特定的、比较有限的圈子内发行、流传和被阅读。"文革"期间的文学翻译，首先是被用来充当这一时期执政党党内不同政治集团之

间的斗争工具。当时主管国家意识形态的是"四人帮"集团,他们有意选择反映苏联领导干部贪污腐化、享受特权生活的文学作品进行翻译,借这些作品影射他们的政治对手,即"文革"中所说的"走资派"。其次,它还要充当当时中国与国际上不同政党之间的斗争工具。"文革"期间中共与苏共反目,还认定美苏两个超级大国在争夺世界霸权,于是能够揭露所谓"苏修与美帝争霸世界"的小说和电影剧本等,就被翻译了出来。最后,其实是"文革"中文学翻译的最主要的目的,就是为当时中国大陆占主导地位的意识形态服务。当时中国的主流意识形态是"无产阶级在夺取政权以后必须要继续革命,否则党就会变'修(正主义)',资本主义就会复辟,劳动人民就会吃'二遍苦'"。于是"文革"期间就翻译出版了特别多的反映所谓"苏联劳动人民悲惨生活""苏共干部专横跋扈、腐化堕落"的作品,以此证明进行"文化大革命"是完全正确的。

关　键　词　文学翻译;文化大革命;翻译的操控
作者联系地址　上海市虹口区大连西路550号,上海外国语大学高级翻译学院
电子邮箱　swgfxtz@163.com

15

Author: XIE Tianzhen

Title: Particular Translation in Particular Time: A Study on the Literary Translation During the "Culture Revolution" in Mainland China

Published in: *Comparative Literature in China*, 2009 (2)

[Abstract] In the translation history of China, the literary translation during the "Culture Revolution" (1966-1976) in Mainland China is unique. In this very rare period of human history, the intervention and control of translation from politics, ideology, state power and political parties went to the extreme, ranging from the selection of translation materials, the organization of translation processes, to the inspection of the final translated texts and forms of signature, etc. In the meantime, the translator's autonomy and their rights of choosing the translation materials were completely deprived of, which reduced the translator to a manipulated translation machine. During the "Cultural Revolution", the published translations were mainly contemporary literary works from the Soviet Union, the United States and Japan, plus a few works of other countries. These translations were not publicly available, but were distributed, circulated and read in a specific and relatively limited circle in a unique form of "internal issue". Literary translation during the "Cultural Revolution" was used in the first place as a tool of strife between political groups within the ruling party. The "Gang of Four", then in charge of state ideology, deliberately selected for translation of literary works that reflected the corrupt and privileged life of leading cadres in the Soviet Union, and used these translated works to hint at their political opponents who were called "capitalist roaders" during the "Cultural Revolution". Secondly, literary translation also served as a tool of struggle between political parties in China and in the world. During the "Cultural Revolution", the Chinese Communist Party quarreled with the Soviet Communist Party and held that the two superpowers of the United States and the Soviet Union were struggling for world hegemony, which led to the translation of novels and screenplays, etc. that could bring to light the so-called "Soviet revisionism and American imperialism contending for the world". Finally, the most important purpose of literary translation during the "Cultural Revolution" was to serve the dominant ideology in Mainland China, which was that "the proletariat must continue its revolution after seizing power, otherwise the party will become the 'revisionist', and capitalism will be restored and the working people will 'suffer the second round'". Consequently, during the "Cultural Revolution", many translations were published of the works reflecting the so-called "miserable life of the working people of the Soviet Union" and "despotic, corrupt officials of the Soviet Communist Party", in order to justify the "Cultural Revolution".

Key words: literary translation; the "Culture Revolution"; the manipulation of translation

16

作　　者　聂鸿音
标　　题　《仁王经》的西夏译本
发表刊物　《民族研究》2010 年第 3 期
［摘　要］《仁王护国般若波罗蜜多经》是中国佛教史上著名的"疑经"之一。其西夏译本 1909 年出土于内蒙古额济纳旗的黑水城遗址，今藏俄罗斯科学院东方文献研究所。西夏文《仁王经》实际上分属两个不同的译本，即 11 世纪的初译本和 12 世纪的校译本，前者保留着西夏惠宗秉常的译经题记，后者在 1194 年由智能法师奉罗太后敕命校订并在纪念仁宗的法会上散施。校译本对初译本的改动表现在三个方面：第一，改动个别用字，这些改动有的会与原字形成语音通转关系，其形成原因尚不清楚；第二，调整语序以适应党项语法习惯，例如把初译本里"现成佛身"改作符合党项语法的"现身成佛"；第三，重新翻译了经文中的咒语。在仁宗时代之前，西夏人翻译咒语时习惯据汉字读音硬译，《仁王经》的校译本则完全抛开了不空金刚原来的汉译，而改以梵文为据，并采用了特殊的格式来表现梵文的复辅音，力求使读出的西夏语音最大限度地接近梵文原本。

此前中国学术界仅仅是从夏译佛经的题款中概略地了解到当时曾经发生过大规模的佛经校译，但对具体的校译细节还几乎一无所知，原因是除了西田龙雄之外还很少有人利用同一佛经的新旧两种译本从事过细致的对勘研究。将来如果有条件取得各种佛经的各种译本进行综合对勘，那么我们必然能够从中总结出西夏校译佛经的具体原则和规范，从而为中国佛教史补充新的、不可或缺的一页。

本文首次公布了校译本的一则发愿文和一则题记并加上了汉译和注释。
关 键 词　佛教；西夏；仁王护国般若波罗蜜多经；翻译

作者联系地址　北京市海淀区新街口外大街19号，北京师范大学励耘6
　　　　　　　楼5门303
邮　　编　100088
电子邮箱　nhy54116@sina.com

16

Author: NIE Hongyin

Title: Tangut versions of *Kāru☐karāja-sūtra*

Published in: *Ethno-National Studies*, 2010 (3).

[Abstract]　The Tangut versions of *Kāru☐karāja-rā☐☐rapāla-prajñāpāramitā- sūtra* were unearthed from the Khara-khoto ruins in 1909 and now housed at the Institute of Oriental Manuscripts, Russian Academy of Sciences. The said sūtras may be regarded as two different translations, i.e., an original one at the beginning of the 11th century and a collated one in the 12th century. The former preserved a translator's affix of the Xixia Emperor Huizong and the latter was a present in a Buddhist ceremony to commemorate the Emperor Renzong. The modifications of the collative version on the original one are shown in three aspects: 1) a few characters were changed under the phonemic interchangeability; 2) some word orders were changed to accord with Tangut grammar; and 3) mantras in the sūtra were re-transcribed. Before the era of Renzong, Tanguts used to transcribe the mantras only according to the sound of Chinese characters, but the collated version of the *Kāru☐karāja-sūtra* ignored the classical Chinese version by Amogavajra and gave the new transcription directly according to Sanskrit original in order to be close to its Sanskrit pronunciation.

　　Up to the present, Chinese academic realm has realized some roughly information of collating Buddhist works than its working details at that time, because there are few scholars, except Nishida Tatsuo, work on the collation research between the two versions of one and the same sūtra. If in the future we are able to get various versions of various sūtras, the detailed principles and standards will be summarized through collation research and the new light will be thrown on the history of Chinese Buddhism.

A Tangut vowing article and a postscript are published in the present paper with Chinese transition and commentaries.

Key words: Buddhism; Xixia; *Kāru☐karāja-sūtra*; translation

17

作　　者	屈文生
标　　题	早期中文法律词语的英译研究——以马礼逊《五车韵府》为考察对象
发表刊物	《历史研究》2010年第5期

[摘　要] 本文将法学研究、译学研究、史学研究的方法与策略融合在一起，典型列举了马礼逊译《五车韵府》（1819年）中十则中国古有法律词语（如"犯流罪""囚笼""合同""状师""衙门""八议"等）的英译情况，分析了马礼逊的翻译得失及马氏译本反映出的早期西方人的中国法律观。

选择《五车韵府》为研究脚本的原因有以下几点。第一、马礼逊《华英字典》是世界上第一套汉英双语字典，也是早期汉外字典的集大成之作，《五车韵府》作为《华英字典》的一部分，极具代表性。第二、马礼逊本人对中国法律有较为深入的研究，因此其《五车韵府》对中文法律词语的英译能代表当时的翻译水平。第三、研究中国"前法学移植时期"或法学近代化开始以前中文法律词语的英译概况，1819年无疑是一个合适的年份。

文章认为《五车韵府》的中文法律词语英译仅是中文法律概念进入英语世界的一次尝试，在中西初识的过程之中，法律翻译在"西法东渐"（即西方近代法律原则与制度在中国的移植与传播）中扮演的角色远大于其在"中法西传"（即中国传统法律文化在西方的传播）中所发挥的作用。马礼逊《五车韵府》无论从翻译策略、效果及影响等方面均未达到稍后的英文法律词语汉译同样的效果。文章认为，后世汉英双语词典的编纂受到了马礼逊翻译策略和翻译范式的影响。《五车韵府》树立了晚清时期双语词典几乎由外国传教士编写、阅读对象主要是外国人的传统。

关 键 词 《五车韵府》；马礼逊；法律翻译史；词典；法律翻译

作者联系地址 上海市松江区龙源路 555 号，华东政法大学集英楼 C202

电子邮箱 qu_kevin@qq.com

17

Author: QU Wensheng

Title: Early English Translations of Chinese Legal Terms: A Study Based on Robert Morrison's *Wuche yunfu*

Published in: *Historical Research*, 2010 (5)

[Abstract] *Wuche yunfu* is a bilingual dictionary of Chinese and English compiled by Robert Morrison and named after an early Qing exemplar. The Chinese legal terms contained in the dictionary are from a pre-modern discourse system familiar to the Chinese of the time. From his translation of legal terms in the major branches of Chinese law including criminal law, civil law, procedural law, basic law and feudal law, we can see that Morrison's translation was the first attempt to convey Chinese legal concepts to the English-speaking world. As such, it played quite an important role in communication between Chinese and Western legal cultures. Morrison's translation strategies and paradigms had an influence on the later compilation of bilingual dictionaries of Chinese and English.

The effects and impact of Morrison's translation of Chinese legal words cannot be compared with the later Chinese translation of English legal terms. The communications between the two systems are somehow unidirectional, not interactive. China is more like a recipient than a donor. Nonetheless, Morrison's translation took a solid step towards Chinese and Western legal culture communication. The later compilations of Chinese-English bilingual dictionaries are all influenced by Morrison's translation strategies and paradigms. It also established the tradition that the bilingual dictionaries in the late Qing Dynasty be compiled mostly by the foreign missionaries and for the purpose of meeting mainly the reading demand of Westerners in China or those who want to learn Chinese in the West.

Key words: *Wuche yunfu*; Robert Morrison; legal translation history; dictionary; legal translation

18

作　　者　孙会军、郑庆珠
标　　题　新时期英美文学在中国大陆的翻译（1976—2008）
发表刊物　《解放军外国语学院学报》2010年第2期
［摘　要］　1976年10月，中国结束"文革"，进入了改革开放的新时期。中国文学逐渐兴盛起来，这在很大程度上得益于新时期外国文学在中国的大量译介。新时期的外国文学翻译，特别是英美文学翻译，在经过了"文革"十年的禁绝之后，逐渐焕发了生机，并在二十世纪八十年代出现井喷之势在中国翻译史上书写了新的篇章。本文尝试对新时期英美文学在中国大陆的翻译情况进行总体描述和阶段考察，对新时期的英美文学翻译史进行总结。这一工作是在数据统计的基础上进行的。笔者对1976年10月到2008年出版的英美文学作品单行本进行认真统计，考察新时期英美文学翻译总体发展情况和变化趋势，并尝试对其背后的原因进行分析和解释。我们注意到新时期英美文学翻译的发展情况并不是一成不变的，大致可以

分成三个发展阶段——解冻阶段、复兴阶段和繁荣发展阶段。1976年10月到1978年11月,是英美文学翻译的解冻阶段。在这一时期,出版社开始突破文化大革命时期的严格限制,经过精心挑选,出版了少量外国文学翻译作品,其特点是以重印"文革"之前出版过的外国古典文学译著为主。1978年11月到八十年代末,是外国文学界拨乱反正以及英美文学翻译复兴的阶段,许多曾经遭到禁绝的英美文学作品,包括现代派作品以及后现代作品等逐步获得了翻译的合法性,开始被陆续译介给中国读者,并成为新时期外国文学翻译的主流。这一时期见证了英美文学作品译介的井喷时期。进入二十世纪九十年代以后,我们的社会逐步走进了一个相对稳定、多元、开放、民主的时代,政治气氛宽松之程度是前所未有的,为英美文学翻译创造了很好的条件,使我国的英美文学翻译在2006年又进入了新的高峰。

关 键 词 新时期;英美文学翻译;翻译史

作者联系地址 上海市虹口区大连西路550号,上海外国语大学1号楼324室
电子邮箱 sunhuijun@163.com

18

Author: SUN Huijun & ZHENG Qingzhu

Title: The Chinese Translation of Anglo-American Literature in the New Era (1976—2008)

Published in: *Journal of PLA University of Foreign Languages*, 2010 (2)

[Abstract] China's New Era began after the end of Cultural Revolution in October 1976 with the adoption of "Reform and Opening-up" policy in 1978 by the Chinese government. It followed that foreign literature, especially Anglo-American literature, which had been regarded as taboo during the Cultural Revolution, once again began to be translated into the Chinese language in large numbers, giving rise to the development of Chinese literature in Chinese mainland. This paper intends to give an overall description of the history of Anglo-American literature translation, grasping the general tendency of the historical development, and making some explorations into the different phases of this new Era the basis of statistics of published Chinese versions of Anglo-American literature. The history of Anglo-American literature translation are classified into three phases in this paper: the phase of revival (1976 to 1978), the phase of prosperity (1978-1989), and the phase of stable development (1990-2008). The features of each phase are identified and accounted for in detail in the paper.

Key words: New Era; Anglo-American Literature translation; translation history

19

作　　者　王　宏
标　　题　《梦溪笔谈》译本翻译策略研究
发表刊物　《上海翻译》2010 年第 1 期
［摘　要］《梦溪笔谈》是知名度最高、影响最大、传播最广的中国古代笔记体裁作品，已被先后译成多种国外文字。然而，该书至今尚无英文全译本。本文作者以胡道静的《梦溪笔谈校证》为蓝本，历时四年半，将《梦溪笔谈》全书译为英文。我们在翻译《梦溪笔谈》时制定的总原则是，译文要做到"明白、通畅、简洁"，同时我们借鉴德国功能主义学派代表人物 Katharina Reuss 的翻译类型学和文本内容决定文本形式的理论，根据《梦溪笔谈》特殊的文本类型和所包含的不同条目内容制定具体的翻译策略。笔者指出，在翻译类似《梦溪笔谈》这样的鸿篇巨作时，根据该文本类型以及不同条目内容制定不同的翻译策略不仅十分必要，而且完全可行。笔者还强调指出，译者解决具体问题时采取的具体翻译措施也是影响翻译质量的重要因素。

关 键 词 《梦溪笔谈》；文本类型；条目内容；翻译策略
作者联系地址 江苏省苏州市姑苏区十梓街 1 号，苏州大学外国语学院翻译研究所
邮　　编 215006
电子邮箱 hughwang116@163.com

19

Author: WANG Hong

Title: A Research on the Translation Strategy of *Brush Talks from Dream Brook*

Published in: *Shanghai Journal of Translators*, 2010 (1).

[Abstract]　Being the most popular, most influential and most widely-read ancient Chinese sketch-book, *Brush Talks from Dream Brook* (Meng Xi Bi Tan) has been translated into different languages in the world; however, a complete English translation is yet to be made. After four and a half years' drudgery, the author of this paper has finished translating the whole book of *Brush Talks from Dream Brook* into English. Our translation is based on Hu Daojing's *Brush Talks from Dream Brook, a Variorum Edition* and the basic translation principle we stick to is "clarity, smoothness and conciseness". In the meantime, drawing references from translation typology put forward by Katharina Reiss and from the linguistic theory that the form is decided by its content, we lay down specific rules for translating different jottings of the book. The author of this paper argues that in translating the encyclopedic work such as this, laying down different translation strategies for different contents is not only necessary, but also highly applicable. He also points out that the specific measures the translator takes when solving specific problems in translation are also important factors influencing the quality of translation.

Key words: *Brush Talks from Dream Brook*; text types; contents; translation strategy

翻译文学与文化

1. 言意之辨与象意之合——试论汉诗英译中的言象意关系　刘华文
2. 意识形态与文学翻译——论梁启超的翻译实践　罗选民
3. 文化自主意识观照下的汉典籍外译哲学思辨——论汉古典籍的哲学伦理思想跨文化哲学对话　包通法
4. 叙述学和文体学在小说翻译研究中的应用　方开瑞
5. 翻译的本意——《枫桥夜泊》的五种汉学家译文研究　胡安江
6. 绝妙寒山道——寒山诗在法国的传布与接受　胡安江
7. 《汉书》在西方：译介与研究　李秀英、温柔新
8. "直译文体"的汉语要素与书写的自觉——论横光利一的新感觉文体　王志松
9. 从糅杂看杜甫《秋兴》诗的互文性翻译　罗选民
10. 莎士比亚翻译与"跨文化剧场"交流——以台南人剧团"莎士比亚工作坊《奥赛罗》"呈现为例　陈淑芬
11. 翻译与性禁忌——以 *The Color Purple* 的汉译本为例　韩子满
12. 译者的性别意识与翻译实践——谈性别视角下的《紫色》四译本　李红玉
13. 论比较文学的翻译转向　谢天振
14. 追寻老子的踪迹——《道德经》英语译本的历时描述　辛红娟、高圣兵
15. 文学及文体翻译的重要性——以约瑟夫·康拉德的小说《黑暗的心》的中文译本为例　余文章
16. 艾米·罗厄尔汉诗英译艺术探析　张保红

17. 翻译间性与徐志摩陌生化诗歌翻译　陈　琳
18. 翻译黑倪的后现代救赎　高家萱
19. 张爱玲笔下的自我译述以及华人全球化　江宝钗、罗　林、王璟
20. 古诗歌"意境"翻译的可证性研究　包通法、杨　莉
21. 亲近中国？去中国化？从晚清香港"总督"的翻译到解殖民"特首"的使用　关诗珮
22. 典籍英译中的"东方情调化翻译倾向"研究——以英美翻译家的汉籍英译为例　蒋骁华
23. 晚清翻译小说的误读、误译与创造性误译考辨　裘禾敏
24. 鲁迅小说英译历程综述　汪宝荣
25. 《论语》英译与西方汉学的当代发展　王　琰
26. 民族志视野中的《格萨尔》史诗英译研究　王治国
27. 伯顿·沃森英译《楚辞》的描写研究　魏家海
28. 论古汉诗词英译批评本体论意义阐释框架——兼论社会文化语境关联下的主题与主题倾向性融合　曾利沙

Translated Literature and Culture

1. The Relationship of *Yan* (Language), *Xiang* (Image) and *Yi* (Meaning) and Its Implications for C-E Translation of Poems   **LIU Huawen**
2. Ideology and Literary Translation: A Brief Discussion on LIANG Qichao's Translation Practice   **LUO Xuanmin**
3. On Trans-cultural Philosophy-based Equal Dialogue in Translation of Ancient Classics of Han Culture   **BAO Tongfa**
4. Narratological and Stylistic Perspectives on Fiction Translation   **FANG Kairui**
5. The Intention of Translation: A Study on the Five English Versions of the Poem "Feng-Qiao-Ye-Bo"   **HU Anjiang**
6. On the Dissemination and Reception of Hanshan's Poetry in France   **HU Anjiang**
7. A Review of the Translations and Studies of *The History of the Former Han Dynasty* (*Han Shu*) in the West   **LI Xiuying & WEN Rouxin**
8. Chinese Elements and Writing Consiousness of "Tyokuyakubuntai"—On Riyiti Yokomitu's Shinkankakubuntai   **WANG Zhisong**
9. Hybridity, Intertextuality and the Translation of Du Fu's *Qiuxing* Poem   **LUO Xuanmin**
10. Shakespearean Translation and Theatrical Interculturalism—Take Tainan Zen Theatre Troupe's "Shakespeare Workshop—Othello" as an Example   **CHEN Shu-fen**
11. Translation and Sex Taboo—A Case Study of the two Chinese Translations

of *The Color Purple*   **HAN Ziman**
12. Translators' Gender Consciousness and Their Translation Practice — On the Four Translations of *The Color Purple* from a Gender Perspective   **LI Hongyu**
13. On the Translation Turn in Comparative Literature Studies   **XIE Tianzhen**
14. Diachronic Description of *Tao Te Ching* in the English World   **XIN Hongjuan & GAO Shengbing**
15. Literature and the Importance of Stylistic Translation: A Study of the Chinese Translation of Joseph Conrad's *Heart of Darkness*   **Isaac YU**
16. A Study on Amy Lowell's Art of Translating Classical Chinese Poems into English   **ZHANG Baohong**
17. Translational Interness in Xu Zhimo's Alienizing Verse Translation   **CHEN Lin**
18. Translating Seamus Heaney's Postmodern Redemption   **KAO Chia-hsuan**
19. Cultural Self-Translation and Chinese Globalization: Eileen Chang's *The Rouge of the North* (Yuan Nü)   **CHIANG Baochai, Rollins, J.B. & WANG Jing**
20. A Verifying Outlook on Translation of Ideo-imagery in Classical Chinese Poetry   **BAO Tongfa & YANG Li**
21. To Embrace Chinese? To De-sinicize? The Translation of the Term "Governor" in Late Qing Period and the Use of the Term "Chief Executive" in Post-colonial Hong Kong   **Uganda Sze Pui KWAN**
22. "Orientalization" as Seen from Western Translators' Translations of Chinese Classics   **JIANG Xiaohua**
23. A Textual Study of Misreading, Mistranslation and Creative Mistranslation in Translated Novels in Late Qing Dynasty   **QIU Hemin**
24. Lu Xun's Short Stories in English Translation: A Descriptive Study   **WANG Baorong**
25. Recent Renditions of *The Analects* and Their Impacts on Contemporary

Development of Sinology in the West   **WANG Yan**
26. On English Translation of Epic *Gesar* from the Perspective of Ethnopoetics   **WANG Zhiguo**
27. A Discriptive Study of Burton Watson's English Translation of *Chu Ci*   **WEI Jiahai**
28. On Constructing an Ontology-based Interpreting Framework for Criticism of Diversified English Versions of Ancient Chinese Poetry   **ZENG Lisha**

1

作　者　刘华文
标　题　言意之辨与象意之合——试论汉诗英译中的言象意关系
发表刊物　《中国翻译》2006 年第 3 期

[摘　要]　言、象、意作为中国古代哲学和诗学的核心范畴其关系定位代表了中国古代的语言哲学和诗学理念，从最初"言"和"象"这两种分别代表着概念思维和象思维的符号体系彼此独立，到逐渐携手共同服务于"意"的表达，在这个发展脉络的背后"言不尽意"这一语言哲学观念充当着促使象表述加入言表述的主要理据。"言"被看作是获得"意"的权宜性和临时性的工具，"意"一经获得，"言"就被弃置一边，即使借助"言"获得了所谓的"意"，这个"意"也不是圣人之意或含有"道"的天意。既然"言"在达意能力上有所欠缺，而"言"又毕竟是达意的重要手段，于是，"象"就担负起加强"言"的达意能力的责任。"象"之所以比"言"有着更强的表意能力，原因在于它与"道"在有无关系层面上是同构的，都是集有无于一身的。"言"和"象"融合之后，改变了"言"在表述"意"中的单打独斗局面。虽然象表述并没有取代言表述，但是"象表述"的加强很大程度上消除了概念性的名言思维，凸显了语言意象性的诗意旨趣。意象作为象表述的重要元素其实就是言表述中和了象表述后的结果。诗歌中的语言是意象性的语言，而诗歌中的意象则是语言中的意象。语言表述因为有了意象而更加趋向于以象表意，也就是趋向一种诗意性的言说。既然在诗歌创作中，"象"或"意象"承载了中国诗人们的诗学主张，相应地，中国古典诗歌语言就呈现出强烈的象表述特征，而言表述则处于次要地位。于是，当以象表述作为诗性表述特征的中国古典诗歌在翻译成具有强言表述特征的英语时，翻译者面临着两种表述方式的取舍，同时也就会影响到言象意之间的关系。

关　键　词　言；象；意；概念（名）思维／言表述；象思维／象表述；意象；汉诗英译

作者联系地址　上海市闵行区东川路 800 号，上海交通大学外国语学院 508 室
邮　　编　200240
电子邮箱　shl0068@sina.com

1

Author: LIU Huawen

Title: The Relationship of *Yan* (Language), *Xiang* (Image) and *Yi* (Meaning) and Its Implications for C-E Translation of Poems

Published in: *Chinese Translators Journal*, 2006 (3).

[Abstract]　*Yan* (language), *xiang* (image) and *yi* (meaning) are three key categories in classical Chinese philosophy and poetics. Initially, *yan* and *xiang* were deemed to be independent of each other and to embody respectively two distinctive modes of thinking, i.e., the conceptual and the imagistic thinking. However, they have been mutually merged to serve the expression of *yi* (meaning). What has motivated the participation of *xiang* in the expression of *yi* is the philosophical notion that meaning (*yi*) is always in excess of verbalization (*yan*). According to this notion, *yan* was only deemed expedient in getting access to *yi* and would be disposed of once *yi* was acquired, and even the so-called *yi* thus obtained falls short of the authentic *yi* of sage or *Tao*. Since *yan* is insufficient in capturing *yi*, *xiang* is relied on to complement *yan* in the expression of meaning. *Xiang* is isomorphic with *Tao* in terms of the relationship between being and non-being, for both incorporates being and non-being within themselves. Imagistic expression counteracted the conceptual thinking to a great extent, and gives full play to the imagistic poetic orientation. The fusion of verbal expression and imagistic expression gives birth to image (*yixiang*). The poetic language is an imagistic one, and the image in poetry is embedded in language. In classical Chinese poetry, image is laden with ancient Chinese poets' poetic appeal. Therefore, classical Chinese poetry assumes a distinct characteristic of imagistic expression, with verbal expression being secondary. When mapped onto the verbalization-dominated English in C-E translation of ancient Chinese poems, the relationship of the three elements is liable to undergo a re-alignment.

Key words: *yan* (language), *xiang* (image), *yi* (meaning), conceptual thinking, verbal expression, imagistic thinking, imagistic expression, image, C-E translation of poems

2

作　　者　罗选民
标　　题　意识形态与文学翻译——论梁启超的翻译实践
发表刊物　《清华大学学报(哲学社会科学版)》2006年第1期
[摘　要]　有关梁启超的研究甚多,但其翻译实践和翻译思想仍未受到足够的重视。对于梁启超而言,翻译是社会启蒙和政治变革的利器。经历了维新变法的失败后,梁启超开始转向文学,以翻译西方小说为手段来引进西方的启蒙思想,抨击朝政,改造社会。他的翻译实践主要有四个方面的特色:首先,在选材上,他主要取西方政治小说翻译,试图借用西方的社会政治思想,实现国民素质的改造,最终达到其政治改革的目的。其次,在翻译策略上,他选择从日文转译西学,使得很多西方的概念和语词在中国被很好地接受并固定下来,至今为人所用。再次,在翻译手段上,他大量进行操控和改写,以思想家和政治家的眼光看待外国文学,最为重视的是文学的价值观,然后才是文学的艺术性,希望通过置换和改写促进一种新的意识形态,新的国民性的形成。最后,在传播渠道上,他选择通过新闻报报刊作为翻译发表的阵地,他的翻译多以连载形式刊发在自己和他人创办的报刊上,如《清议报》、《新民丛报》、《新小说》等,形式活泼多样,

既译且评，相得益彰，深为当时民众欢迎，这也是其小说翻译产生重大影响的一个重要条件。梁启超的翻译理论有深厚的佛学基础，对今天的译学研究仍有指导意义和借鉴价值，但他的翻译实践具有明显的意识形态特征，是在政治学的背景下进行的，打上了鲜明的时代烙印，有明显的功利观。我们应该从文化社会等诸多非艺术因素去审视它，从而充分肯定其翻译在历史上所起到的积极作用。从一个侧面反映了二十世纪前后中国知识分子学习西方、追求民主的心路历程。

关 键 词 翻译；意识形态；新学语；操纵；重写；传播

作者联系地址 广东省广州市白云区白云大道北 2 号，广东外语外贸大学外语研究与语言服务协同创新中心

邮　　编 510420

电子邮箱 luoxm@tsinghua.edu.cn

2

Author: LUO Xuanmin

Title: Ideology and Literary Translation: A Brief Discussion on LIANG Qichao's Translation Practice

Published in: *Journal of Tsinghua University (Philosophy and Social Sciences)*, 2006 (1).

[Abstract] Studies on Liang Qichao are abundant, yet examinations into his translation practice are few. For him, translation is a great tool for social enlightenment and political reform. After the failure of the Reformation Movement in the 1890s, Liang turned to literature and had made prodigious efforts in translating Western novels, which were considered a way of debunking the dark society and the bankrupted Qing government, and a way of introducing Western civilization to his fellow people. His translation practice may be summarized as follows: (1) As for source text selection, he was mainly interested in political novels, which would be most helpful in transforming people's mindset and thereby facilitate sociopolitical reform. (2) As for translation strategy, he chose to retranslate the Western works and introducing new terminologies through Japanese renditions, which proved to be very successful. (3) In terms of translation method, he often resorted to manipulation and rewriting. He approached literature from the perspective of a political thinker and attempted to translate first and foremost for advancing new values, and then arts and other things. (4) In terms of publication, he used the newspapers and periodicals, such as *Qingyibao*, *Xinmincongbao*, and *Xinxiaoshuo* as the front for communicating translation. This greatly increased the circulation and influences of his translations. Rooted in Buddhist studies, Liang made his translation theory still illuminative for translation studies today. His translation practice around the turn of the 20th century was, however, ideological in nature, reflecting partially on modern Chinese pioneers commitments for democracy and freedom in their hard-won procession of learning from the West.

Key words: translation; ideology; new terms; manipulation; rewriting; communication

3

作　者　包通法
标　题　文化自主意识观照下的汉典籍外译哲学思辨——论汉古典籍的哲学伦理思想跨文化哲学对话
发表刊物　《外语与外语教学》2007年第5期
[摘　要]　语言表征样态是人经验世界的外化表征，人的本质在于其语言性，人凭自己的感官给予心理经验体认外在事物，凭自己的心智能力"造出"外在事物。因此，语言体现的是一种特定的民族群体将感知的精神体

验分类和范畴化。本文认为,1) 以文言文写就的中国古代典籍是先贤们按照客观的表象,抽象整体思辨体悟和阐述的两个世界(主观与客观)以及生命价值观的固化物质符号形式,其话语阐述形态,如哲学和伦理术语尤以其汉语"语义过载"特质而体现和承载我典籍中东方式的抽象,整体深邃的哲学思辨观和方法论;2) 因而对其进行跨文化翻译研究必然超出一般语言学和文化学研究的范畴;3) 传统汉译英典籍翻译实践大都基于"结构主义"语言学思辨观和方法论,以"语言自主实体"的翻译认知范式有意无意将我先哲哲学精神构式和样态纳入"西方中心"的理念内而实践之;4) 而后殖民主义理论"文化平等对话"的文化自觉意识和阻抗式翻译方法论等则提供了一种新的视角和方法论,关注我元典籍的话语表征样态就是关注我华夏民族世界观和价值观,可以使我们摆脱"语言自主实体"的翻译认知范式;5) 故本文提出为我中华哲学精神立言,以创与化的方法论翻译我元典的术语体系,实现东西方文化平等对话,为张扬我古典籍中有别于西方思想哲学形态提供一种可资途径。

关 键 词 典籍;道;仁;思辨范式;术语
作者联系地址 江苏省无锡市滨湖区蠡湖大道1800号,江南大学外国语学院
邮 编 214036
电子邮箱 baotongfa@163.com

3

Author: BAO Tongfa

Title: On Trans-cultural Philosophy-based Equal Dialogue in Translation of Ancient Classics of Han Culture

Published in: *Foreign Languages and Their Teaching,* 2007 (5).

[Abstract] Language is not only a self-identity subject, but also an outward expression of a national philosophy that grasps the world and human. Therefore, the ancient Chinese classics (linguistic expressions and academic terms) of philosophy and ethics bear rich historical accumulation of how our ancients categorized the universe, the society and their life, and personality aesthetics development over the past 2,000 years. And it is of every reason that their translations and their translation studies must go beyond the boundary that linguistics can cover. However, the past practice of translating our classics always followed the Occidental thinking mode and methodology consciously or unconsciously. As is known to all, language expressions reflect the thinking mode and the outlook of a nation, and the foreignization in the Post-colonialism in translation lays a solid argument "to have an equal dialogue" and offers a fresh perspective and methodology in translation of Chinese classics of philosophy and ethics. So in the end the paper proposes the views and approaches on foreignized translation of ancient Chinese classics in linguistic expression especially on foreignized translation of the academic terms born with Chinese culture category and connotation.

Key words: classics; Daoism; Ren-ism (philosophy of Goodness); thinking paradigm; academic term

4

作　　者　方开瑞
标　　题　叙述学和文体学在小说翻译研究中的应用
发表刊物　《中国翻译》2007年第4期
［摘　要］叙述学和文体学的某些方法和视角，可以用于叙述话语的分析。近二三十年来，这两个学科均有了值得注意的新的发展，在关注文本形式特征的同时，也将文本外因素纳入考察范围。这为小说翻译研究将文本的形式分析与文本外因素的分析联系起来，提供了更多的可行性。本文就此进行了探索，并提出了相关的分析模式。首先，可参照热奈特提出的叙事范畴分析模式，根据文本的具体情况，在时间、语体、语式

等三个方面，对源本和译本作对比研究。其次，可从如下角度对译本和源本作叙述和文体分析：1）故事和情节是否与源本一致；2）是否存在文体变换以及变换的形式与效果；3）译本是否存在人物形象变形问题，以及导致人物形象变形的原因；4）源本和译本中的性别政治，其构建方式和语境的关联；5）源本和译本分别存在哪些互文性因素；6）不同时期出现的译本在以上方面各自反映出何种翻译策略，这些策略与相关历史、社会、文化语境有着何种联系。将叙述学和文体学用于小说翻译研究，要把对结构的分析和语言表达的分析结合起来，把文本形式的分析与文本主题的分析结合起来，把对文本内语境因素的分析和文本外语境因素的分析结合起来。这一研究模式的意义在于以下两个方面：首先是与叙事文本的性质吻合。叙事文本有其文学特性，当代叙述学和文体学为该特性的研究提供了方法论。其次是理论框架和方法论方面的创新。这种研究弥补了宏观研究未给予文本描写足够关注之不足，从而在微观分析和宏观考察之间建立对接，克服单纯的文本形式分析和宏观研究存在的局限性。

关　键　词　叙述学；文体学；小说翻译研究
作者联系地址　广东省广州市白云区白云大道北 2 号，广东外语外贸大学英文学院
电子邮箱　fangkr2005@163.com

4

Author: FANG Kairui

Title: Narratological and Stylistic Perspectives on Fiction Translation

Published in: *Chinese Translators Journal*, 2007 (4).

[Abstract]　Some narratological and stylistic methods and perspectives can be applied to an analysis of narrative discourse. And new developments worthy of note in the two principles over the past couple of decades have made it more feasible to take into account extra-textual factors while discourse features continue to engage critics' attention. This paper is an attempt to investigate the above applicability, and suggests the following analytical models. On the one hand, a comparative or contrastive study can be made of the problems of narrative in the three categories (tense, aspect and mood) proposed by Gerard Genette, and of textual properties of particular importance. On the other hand, efforts can be made to probe into the following questions: 1) whether the story and the plotting remain unchanged in the target text; 2) whether there are stylistic shifts, how the shifts are formed, and what effects are produced; 3) whether character deformation exists, and how it is engendered; 4) what gender politics exist in the source and the target texts, and how they are textually and contextually constructed; 5) what intertextual elements exist in the source and the target texts; and 6) what strategies are applied to the translation of a text in different historical periods, and how the strategies are related to historical, social and cultural contexts. In applying narratology and stylistics to fiction translation studies, one needs to integrate structuralist research with stylistic analysis, formalist description with thematic evaluation, and textual criticism with extra-textual exploration. The above analytical models are significant in the following ways. First, they are fit for the nature of narrative. Second, they help remedy the approaches reproved for their neglect of textual description. Macro- and micro-examinations can be thereby connected so as to overcome the limitations in formalist research and macro-examinations.

Key words: narratology; stylistics; fiction translation studies

5

作　者　胡安江

标　题　翻译的本意——《枫桥夜泊》的五种汉学家译文研究

发表刊物 《天津外国语学院学报》2007年第6期

[摘 要] 《枫桥夜泊》是唐代诗人张继的一首传世七绝。对于这首脍炙人口同时又通俗浅白的诗作，汉学家们一向青睐有加。本文从韦特·宾纳、伯顿·华生、黄运特、王红公和加里·斯奈德五位汉学家的译诗入手，探讨翻译的本质以及由此而涉及的汉诗英译过程中的诸多问题。就《枫桥夜泊》的五个汉学家译本而言，宾纳的译文出现时间最早，然而该译文无论在形式上还是内容上都不能令人满意；相较于宾纳，华生的译文在用韵和意象的处理上，均略胜一筹；黄运特的译文以注释见长，作为学术翻译的典型代表，践行着其"粉碎不同语言资本间'光滑无痕'交易的目标"；王红公的译诗感性自由，作为诗人译者，他的译文与其说是翻译，毋宁说是仿作；而斯奈德的译诗，从用词的凝练到意象并置手法的运用，从简略的句式到自由的节奏，无不流露出意象派诗歌的痕迹。可以说，在中国古典诗歌的翻译过程中，宾纳最早发现了王维和道家诗学并受其影响创作了大量的仿中国诗，华生集儒释道传统于一身，自由游弋于中国的千年诗歌长河，黄运特在翻译过程中体验到了学术注释与文化传递的乐趣，王红公与杜甫超越时空"相遇"后借用杜诗作为自我表达与诗歌创作的方式，而斯奈德则成为众人瞩目的"美国寒山"，其言行和诗歌无不渗出一阵阵的"寒（山）"意。简言之，唐诗《枫桥夜泊》在汉学家们的译笔之下获得了本雅明所说的"来世"。对于这首已经被"陌生化"的诗作的重新阅读与谈论，无疑可以让中国读者从另一个视角品味本土语言和文化的独特魅力。而对于目标语文化背景中的译者们而言，译诗的过程同时也是他们认识和了解源语文化，以及获取创作灵感的一种绝佳手段。由是观之，目标文化与源语文化之间的有序互动，正是翻译的本意。

关 键 词 翻译的本意；《枫桥夜泊》；汉学家；目标文化；源语文化

作者联系地址 重庆市沙坪坝区壮志路33号，四川外国语大学翻译学院

邮 编 400031

电子邮箱 haj1410@163.com

5

Author: HU Anjiang

Title: The Intention of Translation: A Study on the Five English Versions of the Poem "Feng-Qiao-Ye-Bo"

Published in: *Journal of Tianjin Foreign Studies University*, 2007 (6).

[Abstract] Feng-Qiao-Ye-Bo is an often-anthologized quatrain poem by the Tang poet Zhang Ji. Based on its five versions by Witter Bynner, Burton Watson, Huang Yunte, Kenneth Rexroth and Gary Snyder, this paper explores the intention of translation and other problems involved in poetry translation. Bynner's version is the earliest one; however, it is acceptable neither in form nor in content. Watson's version, compared with Bynner's, is much better both in its rhyme usage and image interpretation. Huang Yunte, a typical scholar-type translator, advocates the usage of explanations to achieve his academic goal. Rexroth, on the other hand, is a poet-type translator. His version is not so much a kind of translation as imitation. Besides, Snyder's version belongs to the family of imagist poetry, using brief words, juxtaposed images, simple patterns and free rhythms. In general, Bynner composes imitations of Chinese poems under the influence of Wang Wei and the Taoist poetics, Watson shows his skillfulness at Chinese poetry with the internalization of Confucianism, Buddhism and Taoism, Huang emphasizes the importance of academic explanations, Rexroth expresses himself through Du Fu's poetry, and Snyder is indeed the American Hanshan. In short, Feng-Qiao-Ye-Bo has won Walter Benjamin's "afterlife" while translated by Sinologist. The re-reading of this defamiliarized poem undoubtedly will deepen our understanding of the source culture, and the process of translating provides a good way for translators to get to know the source culture better in the meantime. This sort of orderly interaction between the source culture and target culture is surely the real intention of translation.

Key words: the intention of translation; Feng-Qiao-Ye-Bo; Sinologist; target culture; source culture

6

作　　者　胡安江
标　　题　绝妙寒山道——寒山诗在法国的传布与接受
发表刊物　《中国比较文学》2007年第4期
[摘　要]　由于主体文化规范的制约，寒山诗在中国文学史千百年的语内之旅中受尽冷遇。然而，相较于上述的寥落景象，寒山诗的语际之旅却妙趣横生，所到之处获得了几乎所有中国"主流诗人"们也许永远都无法与之比肩的成就。可以说，从故国文学史的"被边缘化"到译入语文化语境中的"被经典化"，寒山诗在文学史书写中谱写了光辉绚烂的篇章，在翻译文学经典中更是塑造了一个不朽的传奇。在法国，寒山诗的翻译与研究肇始于敦煌学专家吴其昱1957年发表于《通报》的《寒山研究》专论。之后，寒山诗在法国经历了短暂的沉寂期。1975年，由法国汉学家雅克·班巴诺翻译的《达摩流浪者：寒山诗25首》问世，标志着首个寒山诗法译本的完成。1985年，由郑荣凡（音）和哈维·科勒合译的《寒山：绝妙寒山道》，以及由卡雷·帕特里克翻译的《云深不知处：流浪汉诗人寒山作品集》相继问世，将法国的寒山诗译介引向新的高潮。2000年，日本学者柴田真澄夫妇的法文译著《碧岩录：语录与禅诗》出版，在新世纪的法国延传并续写了寒山诗的辉煌。概括而论，寒山诗在法国的翻译与研究已然成了欧洲寒山学研究的风向标。而寒山诗在法国的流布与经典化，原因大致如下：首先，战后欧洲所勃兴的"中国文化热"，推动了以中国古典诗歌为翻译与研究核心的法国汉学的发展。其次，敦煌学研究的发展，促使法国汉学家们不可避免地将寒山纳入其关注视野。再次，自由诗在法国的发端，使文学研究者们对于通俗而自由的寒山诗风趋之若鹜。同时，美国"垮掉派运动"的影响，以及青年人对于存在主义哲学"反抗"特质的追捧，无疑使寒山成了欧洲年轻

一代心目中的隔世知音。最后，世界性的禅学研究热潮，也催生了禅味十足的寒山及其诗歌在汉学研究重镇法国的广泛传布与接受。

关 键 词 寒山诗在法国；传布与接受
作者联系地址 重庆市沙坪坝区壮志路 33 号，四川外国语大学翻译学院
邮 编 400031
电子邮箱 haj1410@163.com

6

Author: HU Anjiang
Title: On the Dissemination and Reception of Hanshan's Poetry in France
Published in: *Comparative Literature in China*, 2007 (4).

[Abstract] Due to the constraints of the main cultural norms, Hanshan's poetry suffers a cold reception within the history of Chinese literature. Compared with the above-mentioned situation, however, the cross-cultural reception of Hanshan's poetry has been proved to be a great success. In France, the translation and studies of Hanshan's poetry could be traced back to Wu Chi-yu's "A Study of Han Shan" published in *T'oung Pao* in 1957. In 1975, the first French version of Hanshan's poetry, the French sinologist Jacques Pimpaneau's *Le Clodo du Dharma: 25 poèmes de Han-shan*, had been published. In 1985, *Han Shan: Merveilleux le Chemin de Han Shan* by Cheng Wingfan and Hervé Collet, and *Le Mangeur de Brumes: L'oeuvre de Han-shan, Poète et Vagabond* by Carré Patrick, had come out in succession. In 2000, Maryse et Masumi Shibata's *Le Recueil de la Falaise Verte: Kōans et Poesies du Zen* had been published, in which included 27 poems by Hanshan. In general, the translation and studies of Hanshan's Poetry in France has become the weathervane for European Hanshan Studies. The reasons for its dissemination and canonization can be concluded as follows: Firstly, the Chinese culture boom has promoted the development of sinology in France. Secondly, the flourish of Dunhuang studies has made the French sinologists put their eyes on Hanshan's poetry. Thirdly, the emergence of free verse in France has popularized Hanshan's poetry within the literary circle. Besides, the influence of the beat movement in America and the pursuit of existentialism have undoubtedly made Hanshan an intimate friend for the younger generation in Europe. Finally, the global Zen boom has also contributed to the dissemination and reception of Hanshan's poetry in France.

Key words: Hanshan's poetry in France; dissemination and reception

7

作　　者　李秀英、温柔新
标　　题　《汉书》在西方：译介与研究
发表刊物　《外语教学与研究》2007年第6期，第456—462页
［摘　要］　随着中国国力的不断提升，中国迫切需要加强中国文化的国际亲和力，以便为中国未来的发展营造一个有利的国际环境。一个国家的国际亲和力是一种软实力，是扩大其国际影响力的重要基础。它依赖于这个国家的文化在国际的认同程度，而文化的国际认同度来源于这个文化的对外传播路径和方法。过去几个世纪以来，西方汉学对中国文化的对外传播发挥了重要作用，影响了西方过去和现在的中国观。不同的西方汉学家从不同视角研究了中国典籍，也采用了不同的翻译模式来译介中国的典籍。研究西方汉学对于中国典籍的译介与研究，对于中国了解西方过去和现在的中国观、西方人对待中国文化的思维方式及其形成路径、当前中国文化翻译的方法定位等具有重要意义。作为中国第一部纪传体通史，《汉书》是继《史记》之后中国史学的又一部鸿篇巨著。《汉书》在西方的译介与研究已经有百余年的历史。国内外的一些学者已就此做了一些梳理。随着更多资料被发现，重新整理和分析这些译介与研究成果对于当前中国文化对外传播具有重要的理论和实践意义。西方对《汉书》的译介主要有英国

汉学家伟列亚力的节译、美国汉学家德效骞的节译、美国著名翻译家华兹生的节译等。西方对《汉书》的研究主要包括对《汉书》作者班固的撰史态度及中国史学方法、《汉书》版本考证、班昭的历史学与文学成就、《汉书》反映的中国古代社会、经济制度及其对外关系、汉代哲学、宇宙观、法律、《汉书》中的历史人物等。这些译介与研究反映了西方特定的历史、社会、文化语境，西方汉学的研究传统和不同的翻译模式以及对中国典籍中的文化底蕴的接受状况。

关 键 词 《汉书》；翻译；西方

作者联系地址 辽宁省大连市甘井子区凌工路 2 号，大连理工大学外国语学院

邮　　编 116023

电子邮箱 xiuyingli@dlut.edu.cn

7

Author: LI Xiuying & WEN Rouxin

Title: A Review of the Translations and Studies of *The History of the Former Han Dynasty* (*Han Shu*) in the West

Published in: *Foreign Language Teaching and Research*, 2007 (6), pp. 456-462.

[Abstract] As China rises in the world, it is essential that China make itself better understood in the world, which has significantly positive implications for the world order China needs for its future development. International affinity is a soft power, a base on which a nation can build its international influence. It comes from the international recognition that a national culture receives, which in most cases result from the way that the national culture travels in the world. In the past few centuries, Western Sinology has played an important role in introducing Chinese culture to the West, which has had a strong impact on the China image in the West. Western Sinologists have investigated Chinese classics and translated them differently. To understand the past and current China Image in the West and the appropriate approach for translating Chinese culture in the present context, it is necessary to do a survey about previous translations and studies. As the first dynastic historical text in the Annals-Biography format, *Han Shu* is a monumental work known after *Shi Ji*. It has been translated and examined in the West for more than a century. Some surveys have been done by scholars worldwide. As more research data become available, it is theoretically and practically important that previous research and translations regarding *Han Shu* be revisited and reviewed. The major Western translations of *Han Shu* include partial English translations by British Sinologist Alexander Wylie, American Sinologist H. H. Dubs and American translator Burton Watson, etc. The major research themes cover Ban Gu's attitude towards history and China's historiography, the textual criticism, Ban Zhao's historiographical and literary achievements, the Chinese social, economic systems and foreign affairs, the philosophical and cosmological outlook and the laws of the Han Dynasty, and the historical figures in *Han Shu*, etc. These translations and researches were produced within the Western Sinological tradition under specific historical, social, cultural contexts, and demonstrate how the culturally loaded Chinese classics have been received in the West.

Key words: *Han Shu;* Translation; The West

8

作　　者　王志松
标　　题　"直译文体"的汉语要素与书写的自觉——论横光利一的新感觉文体
发表刊物　《外国文学评论》2007年第3期
[摘　要]　日本新感觉派文学，无疑是在同时代西欧的未来主义、表现主义等各种现代主义文艺思潮的刺激下诞生的。但就横光利一（Riyiti

Yokomitu)的新感觉文体的形成而言,不可忽视的是福楼拜著、生田长江(Tyoukou Yikuda)译《萨朗波》的"直译文体"对其产生的重要影响。横光的新感觉文体最初受到日本文坛广泛关注的是,1924年发表于《文艺时代》(*Bungeijidai*)创刊号上的小说《头与腹》(*Atama narabini hara*),但其文体的新感觉特色早在1923年发表的小说《日轮》(*Nitirin*)中便已经显现出来。有关《日轮》与《萨朗波》之间的影响关系,日本学者已经作了较多的实证性研究,认为生田所采用的浓厚的"翻译腔调"——即"直译文体"是造成《萨朗波》的文体奇异性、并最终影响《日轮》新感觉文体的主要原因。然而,研究者们在提及"直译文体"时,仅仅是置于与日本传统文体断裂的欧化层面上来论述的,并未注意到"直译文体"本身特定的形态和内涵。所谓"直译",就是把两种语言语序与词义的对应关系放在首位的一种翻译方式。但英语的语法结构与日语相距很大,相对而言汉语的语法顺序则与英语较为接近。因此,日本明治时期的"直译"一般采用汉文体。明治大正时期的"直译文体"不仅是对欧美文体的模仿,同时也是对近代以前的公共文体——"汉文体"——的改造利用,并再造了大量新的"汉语"。本文从考察"直译文体"的内涵入手,重新梳理《萨朗波》与《日轮》的影响关系,探讨横光的新感觉文体的性质和书写意识,以及日本现代主义文学与民族主义关系的问题。

关　键　词　新感觉;直译文体;汉语要素;书写
作者联系地址　北京市海淀区新街口外大街19号,北京师范大学外国语言文学学院
邮　　　编　100875
电子邮箱　wangzs@bnu.edu.cn

8

Author: WANG Zhisong

Title: Chinese Elements and Writing Consiousness of "Tyokuyakubuntai"—On

Riyiti Yokomitu's Shinkankakubuntai

Published in: *Foreign Literature Review,* 2007 (3).

[Abstract] Shinkankaku School of Japan, no doubt, was stimulated by Modernism schools. However, when talking about Shinkankakubuntai of Riyiti Yokomitu, one work cannot be overlooked is *Salammbô,* which is written by Gustave Flaubert and translated by Tyoukou Yikuda. The "Tyokuyakubuntai" in this book influenced Riyiti Yokomitu a lot. The first work of Yokomitu's Shinkankakubuntai that received considerable attention was the novel *Atama narabini hara* published on *Bungeijidai* in 1924, but before that, his *Nitirin* published in 1923 already earned him some public's attention. Japanese researchers have made empirical studies on the connection between *Nitirin* and *Salammbô,* suggesting the "translating accent" adopted by Yikida, i.e. "tyokuyakubunntai" was the main factor that contributed to *Salammbô's* characteristics, and influenced the Shinkankukabuntai in *Nitirin.* While analyzing "tyokuyakubuntai", researchers tended to put it into the big picture of European literature, which cut off its connection with Japanese traditional culture, and thus, neglected the features and connotations of it. The "tyokuyaku" in Japanese Meiji Period used Chinese writing a lot. "Tyokuyakubuntai" in Meiji Taisho Period was not only the imitation of European style, but also the reconstruction of "kannbuntai" used before modern era. This paper started from the connotation of "tyokuyakubuntai", re-combed the relations between *Salammbô* and *Nitirin, explored Shinkankakubuntai's feature and* the author's writing consousness, and explained the relations between Japanese Modernism and Nationalism.

Key words: Shinkankaku; tyokuyakubuntai; Chinese elements; writing

9

作　者	罗选民
标　题	从糅杂看杜甫《秋兴》诗的互文性翻译
发表刊物	《翻译学报》2008 年第 2 期

[摘　要] 互文性是文学批评、语言学和翻译研究的新课题，主要包含显性互文性和成构互文性两大类。糅杂是显性互文性的一种形式，出现在词汇层面，是过去的和现在的语汇的交织融汇，给人以似曾相识的印象。但糅杂与显性互文性的其他形式如引用、镶嵌不一样，其用据通常无法考证，而后者则可以根据读者/译者的阅读经验而追本溯源。由于糅杂的语汇内涵更加丰富，更加耐人寻味，所以需要更多的创造性阅读。本文以杜甫《秋兴》诗八首之一为蓝本，先对原作炉火纯青的糅杂运用进行互文性分析，解读其与前代相关诗文的互涉及其产生的情感效果，然后取 W. J. B. Fletcher，吴钧陶，A. C. Graham 三位译者对该诗的英文翻译，对比分析其中糅杂的跨文化处理及其互文表现效果。文章认为，在显性互文性中，糅杂是最难翻译的。就此首《秋兴》诗的翻译而言，Graham 在这方面的表现最值得称道。他的译文虽然在忠实性、诗歌韵律等方面有些不足，但明显更好地保留了原诗的多义性，对原诗的意蕴与互文空间也有更为理想的跨文化处理和传达，从而更有效地激发了译诗读者的情感共鸣和文化想象。文章最后指出，为了在译文中体现糅杂所包蕴的丰富意象，译者需要细心品味原文，进行创作性的阅读，在目的语中找出同质的语汇，得体地表现在译文之中。唯有如此，诗歌翻译才能做到"达"和"美"。

关 键 词　糅杂；互文性；翻译；杜甫《秋兴》诗
作者联系地址　广东省广州市白云区白云大道北 2 号，广东外语外贸大学外语研究与语言服务协同创新中心
邮　编　510420
电子邮箱　luoxm@tsinghua.edu.cn

9

Author: LUO Xuanmin

Title: Hybridity, Intertextuality and the Translation of Du Fu's *Qiuxing* Poem

Published in: *Journal of Translation Studies,* 2008 (2).

[Abstract] Intertextuality is a new research agenda in literary criticism, linguistics and translation studies. It can be divided into manifest intertextuality and constitutive intertextuality. Hybridity is a form of manifest intertextuality in the lexical level. As a fusion of words in the past and the present, it often gives us an impression of familiarity. Different from other forms of manifest intertextuality, for example, quotation and embedding, it is hard to decide the source a hybridity refers to. It demands more engaging reading to understand the rich connotations of the word utilized. This paper presents a case study of one of the eight *Qiuxing* poems by the Tang Chinese poet Du Fu. It first conducts an intertextual analysis of Du's masterful use of hybridity, explaining how his words relate to those of the early dynasties and what emotional effects they might engender. Then it examines three translations of this poem by, respectively, W. J. B. Fletcher, Wu Jun-tao, and A. C. Graham, comparing their cross-cultural renderings of hybridity and the intertextual space they have. It is pointed out that hybridity is the most difficult in translating manifest intertextuality. Graham did the best jobs in the translation of this poem of Du Fu. He better preserves the multiple meaning potentials of the original poem and skillfully renders the rich connotations and intertextual projections of the poetic words in the original. This helps stimulate sympathy and cultural imagination from the target text readership. Finally, it concludes that to translate the abundant meanings and images behind the use of hybridity, the translator needs to read the original carefully, engagingly and creatively and then search for words with similar intertextual potentiality to be placed properly in the target text. Only so may poetry translation achieve expressiveness and beauty.

Key words: hybridity, intertextuality; translation; Du Fu's *Qiuxing* poem

10

作　　者　陈淑芬

标　　题　莎士比亚翻译与"跨文化剧场"交流——以台南人剧团"莎士比亚工作坊《奥赛罗》"呈现为例

发表刊物　《文山评论：文学与文化》2008年12月

[摘　要]　"跨文化剧场"像是彼得·布鲁克（Peter Brook）将印度史诗《摩可婆罗多》*Mahabbarata*改编为戏剧，因其运用西方表演技巧；或者巴芭（Barba）重新为日本人或印度舞者排演的《浮士德》；再者，日本导演铃木（Suzuki）以传统戏剧表演程序中的姿势与声音，诠释莎士比亚或希腊悲剧。"跨文化"的范畴像是剧场实践的交换、互惠部分则包括表演方法、舞台景观（mise en scene）、和改编外国素材如莎士比亚剧本。

台南人剧团的"莎士比亚工作坊"课程，尝试各类跨文化"演出"的可能性，此课程的多文化（multiculture），从英国文艺复兴时期的剧作家——莎士比亚的悲剧《奥赛罗》（Othello），在台湾重新出版印行大陆方平所翻译的中文译本，导演是英国请来的印裔英籍非洲肯尼亚出生的贾丁得·韦玛（Jatinder Verma）。学员有国光豫剧队的队员、台南的演员——其中有台湾人、外省人、含原住民血统的学员；乐师部分有一台湾民谣弹唱的月琴师及一鼓手等多元跨领域"演出"。

"工作坊"第一部分是《奥赛罗》的剧本翻译探讨与练习，导演依据的是英文版本，指导说中文的演员工作，如此的工作模式，导演必须更深层进入文本翻译细节：像是字句、行间隐意、莎士比亚透过字里行间的舞台指示等等。第二部分"跨文化戏剧交流"聚焦于三个最有转换性与实验性的：1) 演员与表演；2) 有关"他文化"戏剧的训练；以及 3) 对身体的实验。最后"跨文化剧场"交流需要经过正式演出的过程，层层筛选与弥合不同剧种间的悍格，只有少数来源文化（source culture）的元素，可以进入目标文化（target culture）。

关 键 词 跨文化剧场；贾丁得·韦玛；奥赛罗；来源文化；目标文化
作者联系地址 台湾台东市大学路二段 369 号 95092
电子邮箱 epker1012@nttu.edu.tw

10

Author: CHEN Shu-fen

Title: Shakespearean Translation and Theatrical Interculturalism—Take Tainan Zen Theatre Troupe's "Shakespeare Workshop—Othello" as an Example

Published in: *The Wenshan Review of Literature and Culture*, December 2008 (Vol.2 No.1).

[Abstract] Theatrical intercultural directors include Peter Brook, adapting the Indian epic *The Mahabbarata* into theatrical performance, by the borrowing of Western performing techniques, and Eugenio Barba, rehearsing Ego Faust for Japanese and Indian dancers. Moreover, the Japanese director Tadashi Suzuki adopted gesture and voice from the traditional theatrical conventions to perform Shakespeare or Greek tragedy. The scope of interculturalism ranges from exchange of theatrical practices, reciprocal benefiting performing methods, mise en scene and adapting foreign materials like Shakespearean plays.

"Shakespeare Workshop", held by Tainan Zen Theatre Troupe, aimed at possibilities of intercultural performances — its multiculture including from British Renaissance playwright Shakespearean Othello, rendered by Fang Ping, a Mainland Chinese, the director Jatinder Verma, a Binglish (an Indian-African English), to acting participants like *yiju* (Henan Opera) and Tainan Zen troupe members, who varied from Taiwanese, mainlanders to aboriginal descents.

Musical parts invited a stringed musician, expert at Taiwanese folk songs, and a drummer, joining in this cross-cultural performance.

The first part of workshop started with discussion of script translation and practice. The director used an English script, guiding the Mandarin-speaking actors. This mode of team work brought the director further into the details of translated script such as words, between lines, and stage directions hidden in the text. The second part of theatrical intercultural exchange focused on the three most transferable and experimental areas: actor and performance, 'other' cultural training and body experiment. Lastly theatrical intercultural exchange needed the formal production, through the process of consciously selective transcoding among divergent cultures, only few of source cultural elements can emerge in the target culture.

Key words: cross-cultural theatre; Jatinder Verma; Othello; source culture; target culture

11

作　者　韩子满
标　题　翻译与性禁忌——以 *The Color Purple* 的汉译本为例
发表刊物　《解放军外国语学院学报》2008年第3期
［摘　要］　对于西方文学作品中的性描写，大陆的译者在翻译时历来比较谨慎，往往会做特殊处理，比如删除或淡化，理由是中西方伦理要求不同，汉语译文中不能保留露骨的性描写，但实际上他们特殊处理并不仅仅是露骨的性描写，原因也不是中西伦理差异，而是中国文学翻译中的性禁忌，这一点从 *The Color Purple* 的两个汉译本中可以清楚地看出来。该英语小说中的性描写主要有继父及丈夫对主人公 Celie 的强暴、Celie 与其女性好友 Shug 之间的性冲动、有关 Celie 身体尤其是性器官的描写，以及有关性行为的脏话。四类描写都比较节制，更说不上露骨，生动地表现了小说中

女主人公所遭受的伤害，增强了小说故事的真实性和感染力，体现了小说作者提倡的"妇女主义"思想，顺应了小说情节发展的要求，暗示了小说中人物之间的权力关系。直接提及性器官和性行为的语句在两种译文中都被删去了，对含蓄一些的性描写，两种译文程度不同地进行了删除，或淡化处理，有时还采用汉语文学作品中常见的淡化手法，对于暗示性行为的脏话，两种译文都作了淡化处理。这些翻译方法淡化了原文中女主人公所遭受的伤害，破坏了故事的真实性，使其艺术感染力大打折扣，遮蔽了作者的"妇女主义"思想，破坏了小说情节发展的连贯性，整体上降低了小说的思想和艺术深度，给读者理解小说造成了一定的障碍，甚至会误导读者和研究者。实际上，类似于原文中的性描写，在同时期汉语原创小说中屡见不鲜，因此，所谓中西伦理差异的解释根本站不住脚。最根本的原因还是在于两位译者或者是出版者对于外国文学汉译，有强烈的性禁忌。翻译者们对于性描写的态度，完全符合禁忌的特征。中国译者翻译性描写，至少体现了罗宾逊所说的三种禁忌。

关 键 词 《紫色》；性描写；性禁忌；翻译禁忌
作者联系地址 河南省洛阳市 036 信箱 30 号
电子邮箱 zimanhan@sina.com

11

Author: HAN Ziman

Title: Translation and Sex Taboo—A Case Study of the two Chinese Translations of *The Color Purple*

Published in: *Journal of PLA University of Foreign Languages*, 2008 (3).

[**Abstract**] Chinese translators are as a rule very cautious when dealing with descriptions of sexuality in Western literary works. They tend to delete such descriptions or "neutralize" them and translate them into much "cleaner" Chinese, on the conviction that moral requirements are different in China and in the West, and that the Chinese culture has little tolerance of "flagrant" erotic passages or words. But what they delete or neutralize is not limited to "flagrant" erotic descriptions, and the underlying reason is not moral difference either. The root cause for their deletions or neutralization is rather the sex taboo among Chinese translators. This finds clear evidence in the two Chinese versions of Alice Walker's *The Color Purple*. Sexuality descriptions in the novel are fourfold: the rape of the heroine by her stepfather and husband, the sexual impulse between the heroine and her female friend, the body of the heroine, her sex organs in particular, and curses implying sexual intercourses. None of such descriptions are "flagrant" and they play an important role in the novel, making the story more credible, depicting the harm inflicted upon the heroine, meeting the needs of the plot development, and thus showcasing the "womanism" advocated by the original author. The deletion and neutralization of them undermine all the functions they serve in the novel, greatly compromising the artistic value of the original novel. Judging from the comments made by the two translators and similar and even more "flagrant" erotic descriptions in Chinese novels also published in the 1990s, it can be safe to conclude that the deletions and neutralization are made not because of the moral difference between China and the West, but because the sex taboo is at work in the translation of the novel.

Key words: *The Color Purple*; description of sexuality; sex taboo; translation taboo

12

作　　者　李红玉
标　　题　译者的性别意识与翻译实践——谈性别视角下的《紫色》四译本
发表刊物　《中国比较文学》2008年第2期
[摘　要]　近年来我国译学界对女性主义翻译研究的关注不断升温，而一些研究在运用女性主义视角、探究性别因素对我国译者的影响时，将女译

者的翻译都扣上女性主义的大帽子，而将男译者的译文视作为父权主义的文本。为深化性别视角的本土化运用，考察我国语境中译者性别意识与翻译实践之间的关系，本研究以艾丽斯·沃克的妇女主义小说《紫色》中译本为研究对象，对比考察了陶洁（1998）、鲁书江（1986）、杨仁敬（1986、1987）的四个汉译本；采用定性与描写的方法，在性别视角下从译者个人背景、译者序、译文等方面，探讨了以下问题：译者的性别意识是否会给翻译带来影响？女译者一定表现出女性主义倾向，而男译者一定对性别不敏感吗？译者的性别意识在翻译中是否受其他因素的制约？研究发现，在该案例中，女译者陶洁和鲁书江的性别研究背景对她们的翻译实践的确产生了不可忽视的影响，使她们总体而言能够更贴切地把握这部女性主义名作，甚至从细微之处凸显其女性主义思想。但受性别意识还刚刚觉醒的影响，她们的翻译中偶尔也体现出父权文化的特征。而男译者杨仁敬由于缺乏对性别问题的关注，总体而言在理解和再现原文的女性主义意图上暴露出了不足。但通过纵向对比其1986年与1987年译本，研究发现男译者在翻译时也能不断向性别视角靠近，偶尔还在译文中体现出较为明显的性别意识。这可能主要与我国自上而下的妇女解放运动的影响有关。最后，研究还发现，译者的性别意识能否在翻译中彰显受赞助人和语境的限制。因此，译者的性别意识并不一定能在翻译中显露出来，有时可能被遮蔽。

关 键 词 性别意识；翻译；女译者；男译者；中国语境
作者联系地址 上海市虹口区大连西路550号，上海外国语大学高级翻译学院
电子邮箱 hyli7581@163.com

12

Author: LI Hongyu
Title: Translators' Gender Consciousness and Their Translation Practice—On the Four Translations of *The Color Purple* from a Gender Perspective
Published in: *Comparative Literature in China*, 2008 (2).

[Abstract] In order to better understand the role of translators' gender consciousness in their practice, this paper examines four Chinese translations of Alice Walkers' *The Color Purple* by TAO Jie (1998), LU Shujiang (1986) and YANG Renjing (1986, 1987). By using a qualitative and descriptive method, the paper mainly focuses on the following questions: firstly, does the translators' gender-consciousness influence their translation? Secondly, are women translators always gender-conscious, while men translators gender-unconscious? Thirdly, are translators restricted in revealing their gender-consciousness in translation in any circumstances? It finds that, concerning the women translators TAO Jie and LU Shujiang, their interest in gender related issues has a significant impact on their translations, enabling them to appreciate and reproduce the feminist theme of the novel. However, occasionally they still exhibit patriarchal ideology, which might be the result from their unthorough gender-consciousness in the early 1980s. Yang Renjing the male translator, on the other hand, who lacks gender consciousness, has generally revealed inadequacies in transferring the feminist motive of the original text. However, his 1987 version is more gender conscious than his 1986 version. It also finds that patronage and the social context affects how much the translator's gender consciousness can be revealed.

Key words: gender consciousness; translation; woman translator; man translator; Chinese context

13

作　　者　谢天振
标　　题　论比较文学的翻译转向
发表刊物　《北京大学学报》2008年第3期
［摘　要］从二十世纪五十年代起到二十世纪末，国际翻译研究经历了从

语言学转向到文化转向的过程，并于上世纪末最终完成了翻译研究的文化转向。从上世纪末起，广泛借用各种当代文化理论对翻译进行新的阐释，探讨译入语文化语境中制约翻译和翻译结果的各种文化因素，关注翻译对译入语文学和文化的影响和作用，等等，成为当代国际翻译研究的一个主要趋势。与此同时，国际比较文学研究同样发生了一个重大转折：在经历了七十年代的理论热、八十年代的后现代主义思潮盛行并对传统文学经典进行反思和重建，到九十年代把它的研究对象越来越多地扩展到了语言文字作品之外，关注的重点也越来越多地跳出"寻求事实联系"的传统文学关系研究框架，进入到多元文化研究时代。比较文学向文化研究，尤其是向跨文化研究演进，从而呈现出三个新的发展趋势：1）运用形形色色的当代文化理论对文学、文化现象进行研究；2）把研究对象从纸质的、文字的材料扩大到非纸质的、非文字的材料，譬如对影视、卡通、动漫等作品；3）把翻译作为主要研究对象进行研究。由于翻译研究与比较文学关系最为密切，不少比较文学家都投身到翻译研究领域中去了，从而进一步促成了比较文学的翻译转向。不过有必要指出的是，比较文学的翻译转向并不意味着比较文学从此只研究翻译，而放弃传统比较文学的研究课题。恰恰相反，通过研究翻译，学者们为比较文学打开了一个新的研究层面，传统比较文学的研究课题，诸如文学的国际关系，本土文学中各种新流派的发生、发展、演变，文学创作中的外来主题、形象等，得到了比以前更为深刻、更为具体、更加显现的阐释。

关　键　词　比较文学；翻译研究；文化转向；翻译转向

作者联系地址　上海市虹口区大连西路 550 号，上海外国语大学高级翻译学院

电子邮箱　swgfxtz@163.com

13

Author: XIE Tianzhen

Title: On the Translation Turn in Comparative Literature Studies

Published in: *Journal of Peking University*, 2008 (3).

[Abstract] International translation studies moved from the linguistic turn in the 1950s to the cultural turn which was eventually accomplished at the end of the 20th century. Since then, a major trend in contemporary international translation studies has involved drawing on a variety of contemporary cultural theories to interpret translation from new perspectives, exploring the restricting cultural factors in translation and translation in the target culture(s), and focusing on the influencing roles of translation on the target language literature and culture. At the same time, there has been a critical turning point in international comparative literature research: After an upsurge of theories in the 1970s; the postmodernism in the 1980s which reflected on and reconstructed the traditional literary classics; and the research objects increasingly being extended beyond the levels of language and writing, international comparative literature research has entered the age of multicultural studies, gradually jumping out of the traditional framework of "seeking for factual links" in literary relations. Comparative literature evolves toward cultural, especially cross-cultural paradigms, showing three new trends: first, it applies various contemporary cultural theories to the study of literature and cultural phenomena; second, its research objects have expanded from paper-printed and textual materials to non-paper and non-textual ones, such as films, cartoons, animations, etc.; third, translation studies have become its main research objects. Due to the close connection between translation studies and comparative literature, many comparative literature researchers have shifted to the field of translation studies, thus further facilitating the translation turn of comparative literature. Nevertheless, it should be noted that the translation turn of comparative literature does not mean that translation is the sole object of comparative literature and traditional research topics are abandoned. On the contrary, translation studies have opened up a new horizon for comparative literature, enabling a more profound, concrete and explicit interpretation of the research topics in traditional comparative literature, such as international relations of literature, the genesis, development and evolution of various schools in local literature, and the exotic themes, images, etc. in literary works.

Key words: comparative literature; translation studies; translation turn; cultural turn

14

作　　者　辛红娟、高圣兵
标　　题　追寻老子的踪迹——《道德经》英语译本的历时描述
发表刊物　《南京农业大学学报》2008 年第 1 期

[摘　要]　《道德经》文本篇幅短小，充满意义的迷宫、语言的急流和悖论式的表达法，两千年来一直是读者索解不尽的智慧宝库。早在唐朝开国之初，道家学者就远涉高丽国讲授《道德经》，贞观二十一年，应东天竺童子王之请，高僧玄奘被任命翻译《道德经》为梵文。与中国一衣带水的日本，早在七世纪半的时候就开始了对《道德经》等道家著作的研究。明朝末年，大批西方传教士来中国传教，欧洲与中国才开始了真正意义上的文化接触与交流，《道德经》才开始了它的西方之旅。出于自身历史境遇的需要，法、德、俄、英、美等西方国家纷纷译介《道德经》并用于指导社会生活的各个层面，在哲学、文学、科学、政治等领域产生深远的影响。

在汉学研究高潮中，《道德经》成为被翻译得最频繁、发行量最大的中国典籍，现在已经有三百多个不同的英译文本。本文作者基于描述翻译学的相关成果，通过文本细读，分析了自湛约翰《老子玄学、政治与道德律之思辨》（*The Speculations on Metaphysics, Polity and Morality of "The Old Philosopher", Lau-tsze*, 1868）以来英语世界的《道德经》接受现状，以译本总数、出版频率、刊行地、刊行方式、译者性别及性别意识、译者的版本意识、译者主体情况、书名翻译及整体翻译策略为参数，对《道德经》的英语世界行旅进行分期研究，描绘了《道德经》文本在英语世界的三次翻译高潮。

关 键 词 《道德经》；历时描述；脉络图
作者联系地址 浙江省宁波市江北区风华路 818 号，宁波大学外国语学院
邮 编 315211
电子邮箱 xinhongjuan@126.com

14

Author: XIN Hongjuan & GAO Shengbing
Title: Diachronic Description of *Tao Te Ching* in the English World
Published in: *Journal of Nanjing Agricultural University*, 2008 (1).
[Abstract] *Tao Te Ching,* a book whose appeal is as broad as its meaning is deep, has drawn endless interpretation over 2000 years. Next to the Bible and the *Bhagavad Gītā*, the *Tao Te Ching* is the most translated book in the world with well over 300 different renditions of the Taoist classic have been made into English alone, not to mention the dozens in German, French, Italian, Dutch, Latin and other European languages. No other Chinese literary text has attracted as much attention and as many attempts at translation in the past hundred years or so. This survey of the *Tao Te Ching* translations identifies three historical phases characterized by different agendas. The author of this paper attempts to draw a graph illustrating 3 phases of the influential interpretations of the *Tao Te Ching*: before the end of the 19th century, the *Tao Te Ching-Bible* interpretation revealed the translators' intent to show that "the Mysteries of the Most Holy Trinity and of the Incarnate God were anciently known to the Chinese nation"; ever since the two World Wars, Western scholars adapted the Mystery of Tao to a Chinese antidote to Western problems; in the latter half of the 20th century, many scholars have focused on the text within its Chinese cultural context.
Key words: *Tao Te Ching*; diachronic description; graph of sequence

15

作　者	余文章
标　题	文学及文体翻译的重要性——以约瑟夫·康拉德的小说《黑暗的心》的中文译本为例

发表刊物　《翻译季刊》2008年第48期，第72—89页

[摘　要]　本文以康拉德的《黑暗之心》为研究对象，论述了原文写作风格对翻译所构成的问题。《黑暗之心》在文体风格上的复杂性使其在翻译时颇为不易，本文考察了康拉德艺术风格中的独特之处，包括受到作者波兰语、法语背景影响而形成的特殊语法形式，从而评估此种文体的艺术效果，对此一文本的几个中文翻译所带来的影响。通过以上论述，本文旨在重新审视语言风格对翻译的重要性。

关　键　词　文学；文体翻译；约瑟夫·康拉德；《黑暗的心》

作者联系地址　香港薄扶林，香港大学逸夫教学楼802室

电子邮箱　isaacyue@hku.hk

15

Author: Isaac YU

Title: Literature and the Importance of Stylistic Translation: A Study of the Chinese Translation of Joseph Conrad's *Heart of Darkness*

Published in: *Translation Quarterly*, 2008 (48), pp. 72-89.

[Abstract]　This paper addresses the question of style in translation, and focuses on Conrad's *Heart of Darkness*, a work whose stylistic complexity makes it especially difficult to translate. The paper examines certain distinctive features of Conrad's style, including particular forms of syntax that bear the influence of the writer's Polish/French-speaking background. It then assesses Chinese translations of the novel, and the extent to which the stylistic effects of Conrad's style have been successfully conveyed in Chinese. The paper concludes by calling for a greater awareness of "stylistic translation" and its importance.

Key words: literature; stylistic translation; Joseph Conrad; *Heart of Darkness*

16

作　　者　　张保红
标　　题　　艾米•罗厄尔汉诗英译艺术探析
发表刊物　　《翻译学报》2008年第1期

[摘　要]　庞德与罗厄尔（Amy Lowell, 1874-1925）分别是英美意象派运动前期与后期的挂帅人物，但无论在美国还是在中国，人们对罗厄尔的研究都远远不及对庞德的研究。从汉诗英译研究的视角看，这一现象同样特别明显。对庞德的翻译研究可谓汗牛充栋，而对罗厄尔的研究则门可罗雀。不仅如此，中西学者对罗厄尔的汉诗英译实践往往多持批评的态度，留给读者的印象是罗厄尔在翻译实践中随意肢解或篡改中国的文字、诗学与文化，其结果仿佛只是得到了"中国"的皮毛，而丢掉了"中国"的神髓。事实是否如此呢？这是本文探讨的问题。

本文基于艾米•罗厄尔的诗歌翻译观与创作观，从意象细节的描绘、符际转换的启示、拆解法、意象并置与多样性的节奏等方面，通过细读若干译例阐述了罗厄尔与艾思柯合译《松花笺》的翻译艺术特色。罗厄尔的翻译不仅从汉诗的诗歌艺术中吸取养分予以创新，而且还从东方诗学以及书法、绘画与雕刻艺术中获取灵感予以实践，其翻译方法灵活多样，其译作东方色彩尤其是汉文化色彩浓郁，显在地呈现出艺术上多元共存的独到个性特色，其翻译艺术之于文学创作与翻译研究以及中西文学文化交流的价值与意义值得珍视与深入发掘。

关 键 词 艾米·罗厄尔与艾思柯;《松花笺》;翻译艺术
作者联系地址 广东省广州市白云区白云大道北 2 号,广东外语外贸大学翻译学院
电子邮箱 zhangbao1969@126.com

16

Author: ZHANG Baohong

Title: A Study on Amy Lowell's Art of Translating Classical Chinese Poems into English

Published in: *Journal of Translation Studies,* 2008 (1).

[Abstract] Ezra Pound and Amy Lowell (1874-1925) are prime movers for the initial and later stages of the British-American Imagist Movement, respectively. In sharp contrast to Ezra Pound, Amy Lowell captures much less academic attention both in the United States and China. The same is also true of their Chinese-English poetry translation studies: academic publications on Ezra Pound far outnumber those on Amy Lowell. Moreover, Amy Lowell is often criticized in the current research papers as a poet-turned translator who take liberties with the Chinese characters, poetics and culture. Accordingly, how to re-evaluate Amy Lowell's poetry translation is the focus of this paper.

Based on Amy Lowell's viewpoints of poetry translation and creation, this paper outlines Amy Lowell's and Florence Ayscough's art of translating *Fir-Flower Tablets* from perspectives of description of image details, implication of intersemiotic translation, split-up, juxtaposition of images and differentiation of rhythms. It argues that Amy Lowell has made innovations in poetry translation by drawing on Chinese poetry, calligraphy, painting and carving as well as Oriental poetics; and that her poetry translation, rich in different techniques of translation, is colored with Chinese cultural elements so as to excel in coexistence of different arts; and that her art of translation provides much food for thought in the aspects of literary creation, translation studies as well as intercultural communication between China and the West.

Key words: Amy Lowell & Florence Ayscough; *Fir-Flower Tablets*; the Art of Translation

17

作　　者　陈　琳
标　　题　翻译间性与徐志摩陌生化诗歌翻译
发表刊物　《中国比较文学》2009 年第 4 期
[摘　要]　徐志摩偏异体译诗行为促使我们思考其诗歌翻译的文学审美性及其诗学意义。其翻译行为的主体间性、文本间性和话语间性等翻译间性凸显，并构成其对诗歌翻译的文学新奇性追求的哲学前提。主体间性表现为其作为新诗诗人、译者与原诗诗人、目标读者之间所发生的共同的认知和认识，促使原诗诗人的审美追求与徐志摩的新诗艺术创造力、目标读者对新诗欣赏力等主体因素共同作用，激发了他作为新诗诗人译者的各种文本经验，导致他按照陌生化翻译审美观，调节其翻译行为并反映出他对社会文化行为的态度，使其追求翻译文学新奇性成为可能。具体表现为，徐志摩作为新诗诗人，经过概念和语言符号、主体间性的参与或共同创造，抒发情志，表达感受，移情于他所翻译的诗人，影响了他对译诗诗性的追求。这一主体间性导致了其译诗互文性凸显，尤其体现在原诗与中国新诗的文本参照上，体现了其自由驾驭译文的翻译操控能力，使得互文性信号在译诗中显而易见，译诗体现出原诗话语、汉语文言诗话语和白话诗话语共现的话语间性关系，使得其译诗表现为文言诗或新格律诗。这种杂合的译诗使得他通过翻译尝试了新诗的体裁的丰富性、制造了译诗的文学新奇性，使译诗具有了相对独立的诗性。在当时白话新诗的初创时期，其译诗的"不忠"表现是其作为新诗诗人译者进行陌生化翻译使然。其译诗成为

其尝试诗歌新格律的实验地,并进一步启发其对新格律诗的摸索与创新。

关键词 翻译间性;主体间性;互文参引;话语间性;徐志摩;陌生化翻译

作者联系地址 上海市杨浦区四平路1239号,同济大学同文楼105室

邮 编 200092

电子邮箱 chenlinxt7@tongji.edu.cn

17

Author: CHEN Lin

Title: Translational Interness in Xu Zhimo's Alienizing Verse Translation

Published in: *Comparative Literature in China*, 2009 (4).

[Abstract] Xu Zhimo is noted for his deviant form in translating English poetry into Chinese, which likely implies his poetological motivation and the aesthetic values of his translational action. This paper discusses the distinctive translational interness in his verse translating, including intersubjectivity, intertexuality and interdiscursivity, the recognition of which is the philosophical motivation for his alienizing translation strategy. It thus focuses on the observation of the shared cognition and consensus between Xu as a poet-translator, the source-poem poet and the targeted readership, and the observation of the intertexual reference between his translated poems, source poems and the comparable poems in the Chinese literature as well. Those source-poem poets have exerted a tremendous influence on him in the cultivation of his sense of poetic beauty in his pursuit of poetic literariness. And this co-works with the mutual engagement and participation between him as a poet-translator and the target readership with a curiosity about the newness and freshness in translated poetry. The paper notes that his translated poems have been deliberately made new and unfamiliar by preserving the foreign or hybridizing the foreign with the indigenous features of Chinese poetry, specifically, either regulated metrical poetry in literary Chinese or *Baihua* poetry in colloquial diction. It is concluded that, as a formal mechanism, Xu's alienizing translation concerns itself with literariness, and hence, is conducive to the description of the literary significance of his deviant poetry translation instead of exclusive translation criticism about its equivalency. At the formative stage of the free verse in vernacular, his deviant form argues for his alienizing verse translation, which proves to be the experimental translation to explore the rhythm and prosody of the New Metrical Verse in vernacular and this encourages him to compose more poems.

Key words: translational interness; intersubjectivity; intertexual reference; interdiscursivity; Xu Zhimo; alienizing verse translation

18

作　者　高家萱

标　题　翻译黑倪的后现代救赎

发表刊物　《翻译季刊》2009 年第 53—54 期，第 157—186 页

［摘　要］　黑倪（Seamus Heaney, 1939-2013），二十世纪继叶芝（W. B Yeats, 1865-1939）具影响力的北爱尔兰诗人，于 1995 年获得诺贝尔文学奖。在译学上的贡献，黑倪翻译但丁（Dante Alighieri, 1265-1321）《神曲》中的 "Ugolino"，但将其再置诗集 *Field Work*（1979），作为终曲（finale）；在 1984 年，他出版"英译"中世纪的爱尔兰骑士文学《司威倪流浪记》（*Sweeney Astray*），并让此书的主角在自传 *Station Island*（1984）复活，不但创造了司威倪－黑倪（Sweeney-Heaney）二合一的新角色，更让与叶芝同名的乔艾思（James Joyce, 1882-1941）在本自传的第二部以鬼魂的方式现身。最后，黑倪以加入爱尔兰语汇于古英文史诗《贝沃夫》（*Beowulf*）译本中（1999），以传达"超过知识经验之外的神话潜力"。黑倪的译学无疑是以互文的方式，将传统的文学和文学史人物构筑于当代诗学框架之中，

所译的文本与其说是对强势文化的抗争，不如说是在历史洪流和自传脉动中，透过诗人的想象，织绘出另一股神圣和世俗的对话。基督宗教救赎议题在这样的创作理念下，透过黑倪译学诗学的镜面，新译出和平仅是残忍的信望爱。

本文分五小节。第一节以翻译和诗学了解黑倪具互文性的文学世界；第二节以历史和自传文类掌握黑倪互文的翻译策略；第三节以神圣和想象的汇流解构黑倪的神话诗学；第四节进一步了解黑倪的史诗翻译在当代时空的意义；第五节总结黑倪的后现代救赎。本文如此了解黑倪的多元文化翻译如何由今到古，由旧到新，起死回生地书写出诗人对救赎的诠释。检视黑倪由1979—1999年，这二十年的翻译"四部曲"，读者历经的并不是诗人企图推翻主流文学的后殖民意识，或附和后现代互文性理论。透过历史的脉络和文学的想象，黑倪以翻译丰富英文书写的经典，以救赎为译学思维的方向，让他在北爱尔兰所见的"血债血偿"进入"既往不咎"的新生。

关 键 词 黑倪；神话诗学；互文性；救赎

作者联系地址 台湾高雄市大寮区进学路151号应用外语系

电子邮箱 ft017@fy.edu.tw

Author: KAO Chia-hsuan

Title: Translating Seamus Heaney's Postmodern Redemption

Published in: *Translation Quarterly*, 2009 (53-54), pp. 157-186.

[Abstract] With the poetic adaptation of a few exponents of "heretical" ideas according to "Catholic" Christian standards, the literary values and religious beliefs underlying Heaney's "transgressed" translations have been taken for granted. What had been focused and discussed was his poetic authority—conscious of a sacred, religious mission (from the Christian-Druidic tradition in the Celtic Ireland) and capable of harnessing his literary discontent to the post-Joycean Ireland. In fact, Seamus Heaney's *Sweeney Astray*, "Ugolino" and *Beowulf* all revealed themselves as conflicting worldliness, but it is Heaney's mythical potency and literary imagination leading the postmodern readers to rethink the "redemption" of the mentioned medieval contexts, and though his distinction between epic and romance was by no means "generic", in the condition of the post-Yeatsian age, his translated texts should deserve more intertext-oriented studies.

Key words: Seamus Heaney; Mythopoetics; intertextuality; redemption

19

作　　者　江宝钗、罗　林、王　璟
标　　题　张爱玲笔下的自我译述以及华人全球化
发表刊物　《翻译季刊》2009 年第 53—54 期，第 73—92 页
[摘　要]　改编自中文版《金锁记》的《怨女》，是张爱玲对其中文作品所做的英文诠释，本文透过其书审视她跨语言的翻译作品，以及她作为双语作家在国际上的地位更探讨了其在中国文学全球化上的影响力。透过翻译自身的中文巨著，张氏力图在美国的文学圈里建立自己身为英语作家的一席之地。她将自身家族在中国文化剧烈动荡年代中的过往改写入自己笔下的作品中，尝试将过去的历史转变成一段对非中文读者都极具吸引力的故事，试图在二十世纪六十年代的北美文学市场中竞争。可惜的是《怨女》的出版并未达到张氏的预期。从另一方面来看，若将《怨女》翻译成中文，张氏或许可以借此重现她身为当代重要中文作家的影响力，尤其是她在全球华侨中独到的地位。因此如同塞缪尔·贝克特和弗拉基米尔·纳布可夫过去所做的尝试，张氏将自己以第二语言写成的作品，翻译成自己的母语出版。仔细检视这种不凡尝试下的成果，可以看出张氏对于华人与西方读者的态度，尤其可以了解到在她眼中来自不同文化背景读者的喜好与诉

求,这样的观点与看法都可以在其跨语言的翻译作品中所呈现的文化内涵与背景所窥见。大致上来看,中文版的《怨女》呈现了较多对于外在形象以及角色内心情感细腻的描绘。相对来说,英文版明显地迎合了西方读者对于东方文化与社会的好奇。

关 键 词 张爱玲;自我解读;文化翻译;东方异国风情;华人全球化

作者联系地址 台湾嘉义县民雄大学路168号

电子邮箱 chlbcc@ccu.edu.tw

19

Author: CHIANG Baochai, Rollins, J.B. & WANG Jing

Title: Cultural Self-Translation and Chinese Globalization: Eileen Chang's *The Rouge of the North* (Yuan nü)

Published in: *Translation Quarterly*, 2009 (53-54), pp.73-92.

[Abstract] Focusing on Eileen Chang's Chinese self-translation of *The Rouge of the North*, an English language rewriting of her earlier Chinese-language work, *Jinsuo ji* 金锁记 (*The Golden Cangue*), this paper examines some of Chang's working practices as a translingual writer as well as her position among international multilingual writers and her effect on the growing globalization of Chinese literature. Having undertaken the English rewriting of her famous Chinese masterpiece in the hope of establishing herself in the United States as an English language fiction writer, Chang labored to render her story of family intrigue in a period of vast cultural upheaval in China compelling enough to non-Chinese readers to compete successfully in the North American literary marketplace of the late 1960s. Unfortunately, *The Rouge of the North* (Yuan Nü 怨女) fell short, leaving Chang in great disappointment. On the other hand, a translation into Chinese could allow her the possibility of recapturing some of her former glory as a leading modern Chinese writer, particularly among the worldwide Chinese diaspora. Thus she undertook, like Samuel Beckett and Vladimir Nabokov, the unusual task of translating a literary piece written in her second language into her first. Close inspection of the result helps us understand some of Chang's attitudes towards her Chinese and Western readers, particularly in terms of what she felt they needed or desired to be told concerning the culture underlying the story. In general, the Chinese version includes more intricate and subtle descriptive imagery both of exterior appearances and characters' expressions and feelings than the English original. The English version, on the other hand, overtly appeals to Western curiosity about oriental exoticism.

Key words: Eileen Chang; self-translation; cultural interpretation; oriental; Chinese globalization

20

作　　者　包通法、杨　莉
标　　题　古诗歌"意境"翻译的可证性研究
发表刊物　《中国翻译》2010年第5期
[摘　要]　作为中国翻译美学研究的核心范畴之一，古典诗歌"意境"英译的研究一直受学界人士广为关注。从其研究方法看，更多的是借用西方翻译理论研究框架以及语言学的研究视角，提出意境传达的有效途径。然而，中国古典诗歌意境是根植于中华传统诗学文论的认知和审美范式的产物。诗歌意境的跨文化传输，在参照西方翻译框架和研究视角的同时，应不忘向中华典籍汲取养分。因此，本文立足中国传统文论、诗论的审美样态，着重厘清意境审美构式"情景交融、物我互为"中的"景、物"是根本实在以及"情景""物我"之间的辩证关系。在承认诗歌意境虚渺、空灵质感的同时，更探究其质感实在的一面。本文专注于辨析其情、景、人之间互为关系及其他外在因素，甄别诗歌"实象、实景"对于审美意境互为关系。本文认为，这些生命形态和物象是诗歌意境的根本，它们经由诗

人独具匠心的巧妙诗意组合，构成审美意境，创造出以景传情、情景交融的诗意境界。基于这一认识构式，本文提出诗歌意境翻译方法论——即基于发生论的可证源头，以保留源语物象为本、诗意圆融化生为用，将诗歌意境翻译置于理性可证的问题框架内。

关 键 词 意境；认知理性；可证性；诗意理性；表征
作者联系地址 江苏省无锡市江南大学外国语学院
邮　　编 214036
电子邮箱 baotongfa@163.com

20

Author: BAO Tongfa & YANG Li

Title: A Verifying Outlook on Translation of Ideo-imagery in Classical Chinese Poetry

Published in: *Chinese Translators Journal*, 2010 (5).

[Abstract] Interlingual translation of Yijing (意境)/Ideo-imagery, a unique aesthetic concept and term in classical Chinese poetics, has been a most attractive focus in translation studies for decades of years. For over 2000 years in Chinese academic circle, Yijing (意境)/Ideo-imagery is characterized by vivid images with some intangible aesthetic sense between lines in the artistic appreciation of Classical Chinese poetry. Such poetic appreciation mode actually develops from and has a close combination with the Classical Chinese Philosophy, a unique academic paradigm, thinking mode and cultural tradition different from those of the western. So it is of great significance to have a systematic probe into the interrelationship among the real thing or scene and humane emotion, and the Cognitive Subject which would be particularly beneficial to reduce the personal intuition as well as irrationality and too much of poetic enlightenment in literary appreciation and interlingual translation.

Therefore the intertwined cognitive paradigm—the integration of poetics and rationale will be bound to enhance the essence of Cognitive Rationalism in mentalist appreciation in translating performance.

Key words: ideoimagery (yijing); cognitive rationale; verification; poetic rationale; presentation

21

作　　者　关诗珮

标　　题　亲近中国？去中国化？从晚清香港"总督"的翻译到解殖民"特首"的使用

发表刊物　《编译论丛》2010年第3卷2期

［摘　要］　晚清中国既是中国史上的翻译大潮，亦是中国新词汇暴发的年代，随着西学东学进入中国知识界的视野，承载新概念的思想工具，不单有翻译语、和制汉语、外来语等新词汇，更有更多是通过"旧词汇、新思想"的转化而来。各种承载新思想的词汇更是无缝地将现代西方制度嫁接到中国固有的文化中来。

从鸦片战争英国开始管治香港到1997年香港回归中国的156年殖民历史中，港英殖民政府的政治架构中最权威最具代表性的人物，就是香港总督"港督"以及他身边代表行政立法司法最高官员及其隶属的架构，如"按察司""布政司"等。随着1997年的到来，香港旧有的殖民制度及政治架构作出了多样适时的改变。当中不少的改变，是为了适应新的政治现实而出现，譬如，1997年后以双语立法，中文同样具有法定语言地位；此外，为了达到社会及历史去殖民化，港英的政治架构同样已于基本法规定需要作出必要的修订，如第160条规定这等带有旧殖民意识的词汇"总督""总督会同行政局""布政司"及"按察司"都需作出相应改变。不少人认为这种更替只涉修改词汇，并只是属纯粹技术层面的操作而已。

然而，本文从翻译研究角度，以西方政治制度通过殖民管治移入中国的一个历史横切面,追溯 governor 成为殖民管治制度上最具权威的"总督"对译语的生成史,指出这等表面上被看成是带有殖民标志的符号,并实沿自中国传统(明清)官制。本文尝试作字源考古学,指出这种以对译语移入西方政治制度消除中西文化差异的策略,很有可能来自晚清传教士。本文带出若不审历史,不重视翻译在历史进程中担当枢纽的角色,往往可能达到相反的效果,新时代中人以为这种手段是为了达求"去殖民"的目的,并以此表达为了亲近中国的目的。然而,盲目"去殖民"却出现了相反效果,出现了"去中国"的谬误。翻译的政治性,在于分析语言承载的权力本位及来源,分析行动者(译者)如何利用翻译而达到抵抗、迎合、还是与权力共谋的微妙过程,本文通过各种早期中英字典分析 governor 的对译语,分析了译者把异文化归化于本国的过程中,如何磨平了中西管治权力及制度的差异。

关 键 词 港督;特首;后殖民;香港;回归;翻译

作者联系地址 新加坡南洋理工大学中文系,南洋道 14 号 HSS-03-13

电子邮箱 ugandakwan@ntu.edu.sg

21

Author: Uganda Sze Pui KWAN

Title: To Embrace Chinese? To De-sinicize? The Translation of the Term "Governor" in Late Qing Period and the Use of the Term "Chief Executive" in Post-colonial Hong Kong

Published in: *Compilation and Translation Review*, 2010 (Vol.3 No.2).

[Abstract] Late imperial China not only witnessed an influx of foreign literature via translation. It was also a time when new ideas germinated through lexical innovations, including loanwords, calque, *Wasei Kango* (Japanese-made Chinese words). Another subtle transformation of Chinese concepts was through the naturalization of the alien notions by appending it to the existing traditional

Chinese lexicons during the process of making the new discourse.

The transplanting of the new political system through the heterogeneous colonial space of Hong Kong in the late Imperial China demonstrates such kind of translation. The 156 years of British colonial rule (1842-1997) finally ended when the sovereignty over Hong Kong was returned to China in 1997. Since the 1980s, many new policies had been introduced in Hong Kong to smoothen handover. Some were introduced out of considerations of the new political circumstances. Others were launched with the hidden agenda of whitewashing British colonial history. The implementation of Chinese as an official language in the judicial system reflects the former, whereas the change of the Chinese titles of the government officials reflects the latter. But in fact, the Chinese titles of the major government officials in colonial Hong Kong were transplanted from those used in Imperial China, which suggests that they were markers of Chinese imperial and political history rather than British colonial history. However, for the purpose of erasing the colonial past, old-styled Chinese titles were changed to newly coined Chinese official titles that are not found in traditional Chinese language. By systematically analyzing and assessing the lexical adaptation of the Western notion of "Governor" into Chinese context through the lens of the political system of colonial regime, the paper will argue that the semantics of the term *zongdu* 总督, despite its use in the colonial history of Hong Kong for more than 156 years, fits in with the new political fact of handover better than the new nomenclature *teshou* 特首 "Chief Executive". The aim of this paper is to use this issue in translation as an example to demonstrate that in the decolonization process of Hong Kong, as in that of many other colonized countries which intend to make a clean break with the colonial past, many policies were actually self-defeating in purpose if one ignores spectrum of the politics of translations.

Key words: Governor; Chief Executive; postcolonial, Hong Kong; handover; translation

22

作　　者　蒋骁华

标　　题　典籍英译中的"东方情调化翻译倾向"研究——以英美翻译家的汉籍英译为例

发表刊物　《中国翻译》2010年第4期

[摘　要]　汉籍英译中有许多直译程度很高的译品，如，赛珍珠（P. S. Buck）的英译《水浒传》（1933）、理雅各（James Legge）的英译《中国经典》五卷本（1960）、与理雅各同时代的英国翻译家 P. J. Maclagan 的英译《道德经》、翟理斯（Herbert A. Giles）的英译《三字经》、白之（Cyril Birch）的英译《牡丹亭》（2002），等。中国译界对此类直译批评较多。以赛译为例，中国译评家对赛译主要评价是"硬译"、"歪译"、"死译"、"胡译"、"误译"、"文化陷阱"、超额翻译"、"亏损"、"失真"、"偏离"、"语用失误"等。与中国译界的贬损不同，西方译界对类似的直译在理论上进行了探讨，他们将它概括为一种"陌生化翻译策略"（defamiliarizing strategy）、"异国情调化翻译（倾向、结果、现象等）"（exoticization）、"异国情调化翻译（手段、策略、过程等）"（exoticizing），或将它描述为"充满异国情调的天空"（exotic space），等。顺着西方译界的思路，我们可以将汉籍英译中的"异国情调化翻译倾向"（exoticization）更具体地称为"东方情调化翻译倾向"（Orientalization）。本文视这种直译为一种"倾向"，因为它反映了众多译家共同的文化政治倾向、审美倾向、价值倾向、伦理倾向等。本文分析总结了"东方情调化翻译倾向"的方法与特点，从多维视角探讨了"东方情调化翻译倾向"背后的原因。

关　键　词　东方情调化翻译倾向；典籍英译；死喻"活"译；英美翻译家

作者联系地址　澳门高美士街，澳门理工学院语言暨翻译高等学校

电子邮箱　xhjiang@ipm.edu.mo

22

Author: JIANG Xiaohua

Title: "Orientalization" as Seen from Western Translators' Translations of Chinese Classics

Published in: *Chinese Translators Journal*, 2010 (4).

[Abstract] Not a few British and American translators have published literal translations of Chinese classics, on which Chinese commentators are used to slapping negative tags, such as "cultural trap", "misreading", "awkward translation", "over-translation", "under-translation", "deviation from the original", etc. Different from Chinese colleagues, Western commentators have made insightful theoretical approaches to them. This paper, based on detailed analyses of many typical examples, argues that this kind of literal translations shows the characteristics of "Orientalization".

Key words: Orientalization; English translation of Chinese classic; resurrection of dead metaphor in translation; Western translator

23

作　　者　裘禾敏
标　　题　晚清翻译小说的误读、误译与创造性误译考辨
发表刊物　《外国语》2010年第4期

［摘　要］ 论文将"创造性误译"引进文学翻译领域，着重考察了晚清翻译文学中"创造性误译"的学理价值，视代表晚清翻译文学最高成就的林译小说为个案，剖析其代表作《茶花女》。具体而言，按照"误读→误译→创造性误译"的思路阐释"创造性误译"的研究理据，借以说明"误

读、误译与创造性误译"之间的转承关系，从解构主义批评家哈罗德·布鲁姆的"误读理论"出发，论证"误读文学作品不仅是普遍的现象，而且赋予文本以崭新的生命"，进而指出"翻译是理解（阅读）与表达（解释）两个过程的结合"，证明"误译是普遍的现象"，接着界定"创造性误译"这个**关键词**的内涵，梳理林译小说里"创造性误译"的由来、特点与作用，借助历时性的描述，凭借译学的文化研究方法，将林纾的翻译活动置于当时的社会、文化背景里，并与晚清社会思潮、文化思潮相结合，以期客观公正地评价林译小说的历史价值。

译者面对一部具有异质语言与文化的文学作品，总是着眼于自身的视角理解、接受原作，因为他所处的文化范式、价值取向、译者审美观、认知能力等都给译作打上了"再创造"的烙印。而且，译者对原作的误读通常带有明显的指向性目的，并通过对"异质文化"的误读来肯定与确定自身。从接受语境看，原作跨越不同时代、民族与语言世界进入一个完全相异的语境，它必然会受到译入语语言文化规范的制约，在不同程度上异化为译入语文化形态特征，进而逐渐融入译入语文学体系里。总而言之，林译小说从文学观念、小说题材、叙事模式、人物塑造到语言表达等方面有力地促进了中国文学现代性的发生与发展，其鲜明的"创造性误译"已赋予原作以崭新的文化意义，给予原作以第二次生命。

关 键 词 晚清；翻译小说；误读；误译；创造性误译

作者联系地址 浙江省杭州市余杭区余杭塘路 2318 号，杭州师范大学外国语学院

电子邮箱 qiu8156@163.com

Author: QIU Hemin

Title: A Textual Study of Misreading, Mistranslation and Creative Mistranslation in Translated Novels in Late Qing Dynasty

Published in: *Journal of Foreign languages*, 2010 (4).

[Abstract] This paper attempts to introduce Creative Mistranslation into the translation studies and re-evaluate its academic value based on the systematic study of Lin Shu's Chinese version of *La Dame aux Camelias*, Lin's best translation in late Qing Dynasty. Clarifying the relationship among misreading, mistranslation and creative mistranslation, the author proves that misreading and mistranslation are common in literary translation with the help of relevant views from Harold Bloom. A detailed analysis of the translation of *La Dame aux Camelias* shows that Lin Shu's creative mistranslations turn to be seminal and unique in the broad cultural context of late Qing Dynasty and in the framework of comparative literature studies, all of which helped generate modern Chinese literature.

Translator tends to understand and interpret a text written in a foreign language from his own perspective regarding his cultural paradigm, outlook on value, aesthetic view and cognitive competence. As a result, both his misreading and mistranslation are intentional, and his personal marks may be found in the translated works, which are creative and individual. In summary, an elaborate analysis of Lin's novel translation may reveal that his creative mistranslation makes a great contribution to the emergence and development of the modernity of Chinese literature in terms of literary concepts, way of narration, subject matter, language structure, writing technique, literary trends and characterization. What is more, Lin's hard efforts in more than one hundred translated novels offered a new life to the source texts, which helped them gain widespread acceptance, extensive reading and steady development in the target language and target cultural system.

Key words: late Qing Dynasty; translated novels; misreading; mistranslation; creative mistranslation

24

作　　者　汪宝荣
标　　题　鲁迅小说英译历程综述
发表刊物　《翻译季刊》2010年第56期
[摘　要]　近年来，国内及西方对鲁迅小说英译本的研究颇为活跃，有大量学位论文和期刊文章问世，但这些成果大多采用规定性研究路向，且考察的鲁迅小说英译本多为后出版本，忽略了早期译本，未能展示鲁迅小说英译历程的全貌和脉络。本文在描述性翻译研究的框架下，包括埃文—佐哈尔的多元系统论、图里的起始规范理论和勒弗维尔的重写理论，聚焦于二十世纪二十年代中期至1990年出版的七个英译本，即梁社乾译本（1926）、敬隐渔与米尔斯译本（1930）、肯尼迪译本（1934/1974）、斯诺与姚克译本（1936）、王际真译本（1941）、杨宪益与戴乃迭合译本（1981）、莱尔译本（1990），尝试对近七十年间鲁迅小说英译历程进行描述性研究。具体研究方法是通过文本分析考察译者采取的基本翻译策略，从中析出译者遵循的起始翻译规范，最后结合外部制约因素和译者主体因素，试图对译者遵循的起始翻译规范做出解释。本文主要结论和观点包括：其一，总体上译文充分性逐渐提高，显示出鲁迅小说英译之旅从发端、活跃、稳定发展到成熟及学术性翻译的清晰轨迹，同时也表明鲁迅小说在目标语国家文学多元系统中的地位逐渐上升，这反过来促使后出译本更加注重充分性。其二，总体上译文可接受性也呈现出稳定上升的趋势，这有助于译作吸引更多的英语读者，扩大鲁迅的国际影响。其三，很多情况下，赞助人、意识形态、诗学观念等会影响翻译策略和译者的具体翻译选择，但译者的主体性和主观能动性不容低估，而翻译的外部操纵因素（翻译规范、赞助人、意识形态、诗学观念等）则不应过分强调，否则会滑入机械决定论的极端。
关 键 词　鲁迅小说；英译；历史综述；描述与解释；充分性与可接受性
作者联系地址　浙江省杭州市下沙高教园区学源街18号，浙江财经大学外国语学院

电子邮箱 13285815890@163.com

24

Author: WANG Baorong
Title: Lu Xun's Short Stories in English Translation: A Descriptive Study
Published in: *Translation Quarterly*, 2010 (56).
[Abstract]　In recent years, Lu Xun's fictional works in English translation have been actively studied in China as well as in the West with large quantities of degree theses and journal articles produced. However, the main approaches adopted in the previous studies are essentially prescriptive and the English versions covered are more often than not the recent ones, neglecting or giving scant attention to the earlier versions. Adopting the Descriptive Translation Studies approach, particularly Itamar Even-Zohar's polysystem theory, Gideon Toury's theory of the initial norm, and André Lefevere's rewriting theory, this paper aims to provide a historical overview of Lu Xun's fiction in English translation by focusing on seven major translations published between the mid-1920s and 1990. The translation norms and strategies employed by the translators are described and the underlying conditioning factors analyzed. The main findings and conclusions include the following: Firstly, the adequacy of these translations shows a general tendency to increase steadily, indicating that the position of Lu Xun's stories in the target literary polysystem rose gradually between mid-1920s and 1990, which in turn made the later translations more adequacy-oriented than the earlier ones. Secondly, generally speaking, the acceptability of the translations also increases steadily, which helped win a wider Western audience for Lu Xun's stories and enhance their international standing. Thirdly, although in many cases patronage, ideology, and poetics theorized by André Lefevere can influence the translation strategy and the

translatorial choices, these manipulative forces of translation should not be overemphasized as to downplay the translator's agency or the important role the translator can play in the decision-making process.

Key words: Lu Xun's short fiction; English translation; historical overview; descriptive and explanatory; adequacy and acceptability

25

作　　者　王琰
标　　题　《论语》英译与西方汉学的当代发展
发表刊物　《中国翻译》2010 年第 3 期
[摘　要]《论语》英译是在西方汉学语境中进行的一种学术性活动，翻译的过程中包括有大量的学术研究，体现了译者不同的学术诉求，进而体现了时代的学术思潮。要厘清《论语》英译的学术特点和发展脉络，进而客观评定其学术价值，就需要将其放回到西方汉学的语境中进行文本分析。当代《论语》英译发生在二战后，该时期西方汉学重心转移到美国，发生了较为深刻的变化，其整体研究趋向大致分为两个阶段：初期的外向型汉学研究阶段和后期的内向型研究阶段。受初期倾向于近现代现实研究的外向型研究趋向的影响，儒家典籍研究几乎空白，《论语》在该时期也没有新译本产出。而到后期，西方汉学界的儒学研究趋于对儒家思想内涵的探讨，原典的研究和诠释重要性突显，《论语》英译在九十年代之后出现了的高潮。同时，译本的诠释特点也与之前的译本有一定的区别，大致可归为两种诠释定向：面向理论和现实的定向与面向文本和历史的定向。以安乐哲、罗思文译本为代表的面向理论和现实的诠释定向，着眼于经典中超越时空情境的那部分特质，强调对于当下乃至未来的意义。而以白牧之、白妙子译本为代表的面向文本和历史的诠释定向，则强调经典是特定时空情境的产物，译者力图求得文本编纂者本来的意图，认为这是正确诠释文本的不二法门。当代《论语》英译的成果丰富，具有鲜明的创新性，

尽管它只属于儒学研究的一个分支,但也参与了西方汉学发展成熟的进程,其多元化的形态不仅丰富了汉学本身,还促成了汉学学科与其他相关学科的交叉,增加了汉学研究对于西方的现代意义,促进了西方汉学与中国学界的对话和交流。

关 键 词 《论语》英译;西方汉学;诠释定向

作者联系地址 北京科技大学外国语学院

电子邮箱 wyvivian@163.com

25

Author: WANG Yan

Title: Recent Renditions of *The Analects* and Their Impacts on Contemporary Development of Sinology in the West

Published in: *Chinese Translators Journal*, 2010 (3).

[Abstract] Translation of *The Analects* occupies an important position in the Western Sinology thanks to its academic contribution by numerous translators. However, there is little study on its translation as a Sinological event or an academic activity. To make an academic evaluation of the translation of *The Analects* in contemporary Western world, it is a must to make an analysis in the context of the development of contemporary Western Sinology. The Sinological studies after World War II are roughly of two approaches: external approach in the initial phase and internal approach in the later phase. Since the external approach stressed a study on the historical context of Chinese thought rather than the thought itself, there were few translations of *The Analects* during this period. As the approach turned internal, the Confucian studies in Sinology reinstated the study on Confucian thought itself. As a result, Confucian classics were interpreted frequently and translations of *The Analects* reached the climax after 1990s. The translations of *The Analects* in this period fall into two categories, i.e. philosophical interpretation and textual interpretation. The version by Roger T. Ames and Henry Rosemont, a representative of the philosophical interpretation, tries to reproduce the timeless traits of the classic, which are of significance to the present life and even the future life of human beings. As a textual and historical interpretation of *The Analects*, the version by E. Bruce Brooks and A. Taeko Brooks take the classic as a product in a specific historical time and make efforts to dig out its original look. The translations in contemporary Sinology with their own originality explore new research orientations and make their contributions to Sinology.

Key words: Translation of *The Analects*; Western Sinology; interpretation

26

作　　者　王治国
标　　题　民族志视野中的《格萨尔》史诗英译研究
发表刊物　《西北民族大学学报（哲学社会科学版）》2010年第5期
［摘　要］　在中华典籍翻译的大背景下，民族文学、口头文学的翻译研究，是中国翻译文学史的一个重要组成部分，实际上也是书写中国翻译史的一个重要篇章。《格萨（斯）尔》是我国藏族和蒙古族共同创造的一部长篇英雄史诗，藏族称为《格萨尔》，蒙古族称为《格斯尔》，本文统称《格萨尔》。史诗的诞生和传播路线是从藏族到蒙古族地区，经过长期的民间创作和流传，形成多语种史诗版本的复杂格局。

《格萨尔》史诗属于口头说唱文学，其英译则属于一类非常复杂的新的翻译领域。因此，英译研究就具有实证研究和文学翻译批评的双重性质。文章立足于民族史诗的英译研究，以《格萨尔》英译为具体对象展开个案研究，将其置身于民族志书写和跨文化阐释的视域之中，对史诗近二百多年译介传播史展开研究，包括国外翻译研究和国内翻译研究的综合考察，阐明史诗翻译的三大路线（途径），从民译、汉译、外译（英译）三个层面对众多译本进行扫描和分类。

通过《格萨尔》史诗英译多维比较研究，一方面对该史诗的多向译介和传播进行历时描写和共时比较，就其中的三个典型英译本和翻译现象进行了解释和阐发；另一方面，从翻译学角度出发，借鉴民族志诗学理论，对民族史诗翻译的类型和方法做出规划和设想，探索当前史诗翻译的可行性原则、策略和方法，为其他民族史诗翻译提供重大参考价值，从而打破单纯汉族书面文学翻译研究的一维模式，为《格萨尔》及其他口头文学翻译提供跨学科研究思路，并就民族文学翻译的学科地位和前景做出跨学科展望。

关键词 民族志诗学；史诗《格萨尔》；口头文学；民族文学翻译

作者联系地址 天津市西青区宾水西道 399 号，天津工业大学外国语学院英语系

邮 编 300387

电子邮箱 wzgjack@sina.com

26

Author: WANG Zhiguo

Title: On English Translation of Epic *Gesar* from the Perspective of Ethnopoetics

Published in: *Journal of Northwest University for Nationalities* (Philosophy and Social Science), 2010 (5).

[Abstract] Based on the context of Chinese Classics translation, this paper makes a tentative study on English translation of *Gesar*, a lengthy heroic epic created first by Tibetans and then by Mongolians. The original route of formation and dissemination of *Gesar* is from Tibetan to Mongolian regions, after long years' folk creation and circulation, forming a variety of complex multilingual versions.

Translation studies on ethnic literature and oral literature form an important part of a history of Chinese literature translation as well as an important chapter in rewriting Chinese translation history. Translation of *Gesar*, an oral ballad masterpiece, poses a new field of translation, which enjoys a dual nature of empirical research on translation and literary criticism of translation. Concepts such as "translations among minorities" "translation into Chinese" and "translations into foreign languages" will facilitate proper approaches to translate other ethnic classics as a whole.

By exploring the feasible translation principles, strategies and methods of epic translation to provide certain referential perspectives for translations of other epics, this paper makes some theoretical discussions and looks into theoretical sublimation and discipline construction of epic translation, which will be of great help in strengthening and developing a fuller concept of translation of the ethnic classics and thus benefit the rewriting of a history of China's multi-ethnic literary translation.

Key words: Ethnopoetics; Epic *Gesar*; oral literature; ethnic literature translation

27

作　者　魏家海
标　题　伯顿·沃森英译《楚辞》的描写研究
发表刊物　《北京航空航天大学学报（社会科学版）》2010年第1期
[摘　要]　中国文化"走出去"和"走进去"是中国翻译学界的热门话题，不少西方汉学家传播做出了重要贡献。《楚辞》的文学和文化价值不断受到西方汉学家的重视，美国翻译家伯顿·沃森的《楚辞》译文具有独特的文化价值和艺术价值。沃森全译了屈原的代表作《离骚》，节译了《九歌》中的四首诗——《云中君》、《河伯》、《山鬼》和《国殇》，收录在《中国诗选》

里。本文用描写的方法,分析了意象组合的特点和意象翻译的方法,并探讨了句子翻译的模式和方法,对他的译诗价值进行分析和评介,指出了其翻译合理性和局限性。研究发现,沃森的《楚辞》英译基本再现了原诗的意象组合结构和句法结构,主要使用了直译的翻译方法,其美学价值不可小觑。尽管这种方法有其不足之处,但总体上忠实于原诗,值得我们深入研究。以期为我国的典籍英译提供有益的借鉴,推进我国的对外文化传播。

关 键 词 《楚辞》;英译;传播

作者联系地址 湖北省武汉市洪山区珞喻路 1037 号,华中师范大学外国语学院

电子邮箱 wjh0063@sina.com

27

Author: WEI Jihai

Title: A Discriptive Study of Burton Watson's English Translation of *Chu Ci*

Published in: *Journal of Beijing University of Aeronautics Astronautics* (Social Science Edition), 2010 (1).

[Abstract] It is the heated-discussed topic in the circle of Chinese translation studies how Chinese culture aims at "going globally". Many Western Sinologists have made great contributions to the spreading of Chinese culture and some of them begin increasingly to focus on the literary, cultural value of *Chu Ci*. The translated version by Burton Watson the American Sinologist is of cultural, artistic value. Based on his translations of *Encountering Sorrow* and excepts of *Nine Songs* (*The Lord Among the Clouds, Lord of the River*, *The Mountain Spirit*, and *Those Who Died for their Country*), this paper analyzes the features of image combination and their corresponding translation methods, and also discusses about the modes of syntactic translation. The author of this paper points out the justification and the limitation so that the study will benefit to the English translation of Chinese classic works and their international dissemination.

Key words: *Chu Ci*; English translation; dissemination

28

作　　者　曾利沙
标　　题　论古汉诗词英译批评本体论意义阐释框架——兼论社会文化语境关联下的主题与主题倾向性融合
发表刊物　《外语教学》2010年第2期

[摘　要] 古汉语诗词翻译的批评理论研究大多数囿于音美、形美、意美等的原则性认识或主观印象式评说，尤其是针对多种译文的批评缺乏宏—中—微观理论贯通的理论体系。本文通过整合接受美学、诠释学与语篇—认知语言学理论以及有关中国古典文论，创新性地建立了一个古汉语诗词英译批评的本体论意义批评框架——历时性社会文化语境统摄下的主题与主题倾向性关联性融合。

本文研究问题：1）古汉语诗词翻译批评研究应建立何种主客观相统一的文本意义阐释的理论框架？2）为何古汉语诗词翻译批评应明确诗词的显性或隐性情态主题、主题倾向及次级主题等语篇宏观结构，与历时社会文化语境有何认知关联性？研究思路：首先，针对研究问题建构一种以目的—需求论、价值论和策略论等为核心的原则范畴；其次，建立一个宏—中—微观互动的认知关联模式，为多种译本批评的理论方法提供借鉴。主要观点：1）古汉语诗词翻译批评理论框架应力求本体论、认识论、价值论和方法论相统一；2）翻译实践批评应力求对诗词本体论意义的剖析与历时与共时并举的有理据的创译性解读。研究方法：突出可描写、可阐释、可推论、可印证、可操作性，并形成认识论结构、实践结构和方法论结构的统一；宏观理论认识能在微观（实践）层次得到印证，微观层次问题能在宏—中观层次得到原理阐发。结论：该理论框架将古汉语诗词英译批评研究纳入整体性理论框架内予以论证,为翻译学理论的拓展提供一条可行的创新途径。

关 键 词　古汉语诗词英译批评;意义阐释框架;主题与主题倾向关联;历时社会文化语境

作者联系地址　广东省广州市白云区白云大道北 2 号,广东外语外贸大学翻译学研究中心

电子邮箱　lishazen@gdufs.edu.cn

28

Author: ZENG Lisha

Title: On Constructing an Ontology-based Interpreting Framework for Criticism of Diversified English Versions of Ancient Chinese Poetry

Published in: *Foreign Language Education*, 2010 (2)

[Abstract]　The current critical studies of rendering of C-E translation of Ancient Chinese poetry (ACP) generally focus on principle-based perceptions or impressively subjective comments like beauty in sound, form and meaning. This paper, by integrating the relevant theories such as reception aesthetics, heumeneutics, textual-cognitive linguistics and classical Chinese literary notions, creatively constructs an ontology-based critical framework, "The relevant fusion of theme and theme-inclination governed by the diachronic socio-cultural context."

　　Its research questions include: 1) What theoretical framework of meaning interpretation featuring integration of subjectivity and objectivity is to be developed for critical studies of ACP? 2) Why should criticism of translation of ACP require the determination of the emotion-bound overt or covert theme of a poem with its theme-inclination and secondary themes, which is, to some extent, relevant to the diachronic socio-cultural context?

Its research procedures covers two overlapping aspects: One is to set up a problem-oriented category of principles as the core covering the principles of skopos-needs of recipients and relevant strategies; The other is to establish a cognitive-relevance mode covering the macroscopic-medium-microscopic interaction for the purpose of providing referential methods in criticism of diversified versions of ACPs.

Its major arguments can be seen as follows: A critical framework for studying translation of ACPs requires establishment of an integration of *ontology, epistemology, axiology and methodology*; while criticism of translation practice calls for motivational creative construal of the ontological meaning of ACPs from the diachronic and synchronic perspectives.

Its research methods are prominent in descriptiveness, interpretability, inferribility, demonstrativeness, manipulativeness with macroscopic theoretical perceptions verifiable at the microscopic level, and with problematical perceptions at the microscopic level elucidated and abstracted into general theories.

The paper concludes that the critical studies of diversified translation of ACP are demonstrated within a holistic theoretic framework, which shows a feasible innovative approach to the development of translotology.

Key words: critical study of diversified versions of ACP; framework of meaning construal; theme and theme-inclination; diachronic socio-cultural context

语言学与翻译

1. 接触语言学视角中的翻译——广州报章翻译现象分析　王　瑾、黄国文
2. 中国大陆与中国台湾法律翻译的对比研究　李克兴
3. 国内外语用翻译研究：回顾、述评与前瞻　李占喜
4. 计算语言学视角下的翻译研究　王金铨、王克非
5. 认知语言学的"体验性概念化"对翻译主客观性的解释力——一项基于古诗《枫桥夜泊》40篇英语译文的研究　王　寅
6. 韦努蒂"异化"理论话语的修辞分析　陈小慰
7. 小句全译语气转化研析　黄忠廉

Linguistics and Translation

1. A Contact Linguistic View on Translation: Some Examples from Four Chinese Newspapers in Guangzhou   **WANG Jin & HUANG Guowen**
2. Legal Translation between Chinese Mainland and Taiwan: A Comparative Study   **LI Kexing**
3. Pragmatics-based Translation Studies: Review, Comment and Prospect   **LI Zhanxi**
4. Translation Studies from the Perspective of Computational Linguistics   **WANG Jinquan & WANG Kefei**
5. The Interpretation of Subjectivity-Objectivity in Translation by Means of "Embodied Conceptualization" in Cognitive Linguistics—A Research Based on 40 Translations of *Night Mooring by Maple Bridge*   **WANG Yin**
6. The Rhetoric of Venuti's Conception of Foreignizing Translation   **CHEN Xiaowei**
7. Toward Mood Transformation in Full Translation of Clause   **HUANG Zhonglian**

1

作　　者　王　瑾、黄国文
标　　题　接触语言学视角中的翻译——广州报章翻译现象分析
发表刊物　《中国翻译》2006年第5期
[摘　要]　文献表明，尽管翻译研究的跨学科性已成为共识，但翻译研究从接触语言学获得的借鉴还是少之又少；而语言接触研究的触及面尽管大，鲜有研究者把翻译作为一种语言接触进行分析。文章由广州四份中文报纸《羊城晚报》、《广州日报》、《南方日报》和《南方都市报》中出现的一些语言接触现象例如英文嵌入结构出发，认为这里涉及了翻译，并通过对这些英文嵌入结构采取的翻译方法和策略如翻译对（translation couplet）和誊写（transcription）等进行分析，发现这些翻译现象与中英语言接触环境有很大的关系，受到是否存在对等成分、语言符号指涉物的唯一性、省力原则等语言因素和语言接触程度、语言态度、语言的文化优势等社会因素的影响。

　　文章认为，翻译研究者往往将原语作者和译语读者设置为两个在语言文化上不相接触的语言社团，极少考虑双语、多语或其他语言接触环境对译者和翻译方法的影响；语言接触研究者尽管关心一种语言在同另一种语言的接触中产生的语言变化，却少有考虑这种变化有可能是由翻译引起的。英语与其他语言的接触不断加强，把翻译涉及的两种语言和两个语言社团假设为不存在任何接触是不符合实际的。

　　文章最后得出结论：翻译与其他语言接触现象一样包含了两种语言的运作和碰撞，受到两种语言接触环境的影响，可能引起译语的偏离并最终产生语言变化，因而理应被视为一种语言接触现象加以研究，接触语言学也应该将翻译纳入其研究视野。

关 键 词　翻译；语言接触；接触语言学；广州中文报章
作者联系地址　（1）王瑾：广东省深圳市南山区南海大道3688号，深圳大学外国语学院；
　　　　　　　（2）黄国文：广东省广州市天河区五山路483号，华南农

业大学外国语学院

邮　　编　518060; 510642

电子邮箱　wangjinfls@szu.edu.cn（王　瑾）　flshgw@scau.edu.cn（黄国文）

1

Author: WANG Jin & HUANG Guowen

Title: A Contact Linguistic View on Translation: Some Examples from Four Chinese Newspapers in Guangzhou

Published in: *Chinese Translators Journal*, 2006 (5).

[Abstract]　While previous literature shows that on the one hand, contact linguistics has not been resorted to as an insightful perspective on translation studies, and on the other hand, the wide ranging contact linguistic research however fails to see translation as language contact phenomenon, by analyzing the way four Chinese newspapers in Guangzhou utilize translation, this article finds that the Chinese-English contact environments concerned have a strong bearing on the translational procedures being followed. How translation has been made use of by these newspapers is subject to both linguistic factors (i.e. availability of equivalence, uniqueness of the referents, and the principle of economy) and social factors (i.e. intensity of contact, language attitude, and priority in specific fields). A followed discussion shows that one reason for the detachment of translation studies and contact linguistics from each other is that researchers in translation studies tend to view source text writers and target text readers as language communities without any linguistic contact, which is unfortunately not true, especially in an age of globalization and intensive spread of the English language. On the basis of these findings, the authors argue that translation can be seen as language contact phenomenon and for its understanding and conceptualization, a contact linguistic approach should be adopted.

Key words: translation studies; language contact; contact linguistics; Chinese newspapers in Guangzhou

2

作　　者　李克兴
标　　题　中国大陆与中国台湾法律翻译的对比研究
出版单位　《翻译季刊》2007 年第 45 期

［摘　要］虽然大陆与台湾在民族属性上相同，官方语言都是汉语，但由于六十多年的分隔、两地文化交流的中断，以及意识形态上的渐行渐远，使得大陆与台湾在司法交流上越来越不顺畅。二十世纪九十年代就有两地学者和涉法人员抱怨很难读懂对方用汉语书就的法律文书，尤其是两地的法律条文。为了真正读懂、弄清两地法律文本的确切语义，笔者对台湾与大陆汉语法律文本与英文译本中的表述异同作了较系统的梳理与比较，并对造成差异的原因作了初步探索。在表述民事责任和刑事处罚方面，台湾法律的最基本句型是"……者，应 + 行为动词"，或"……者，处……刑罚"；其英译的典型句型是"Any person/a person who does sth. shall + verb (legal action) …"。而在大陆，相应的典型句型是"……的，应当 + 行为动词 / 处 / 应当……刑罚 / 处罚"，译成英文主要的句型是："Whoever does sth… shall + verb (legal action)"以及"If/where-led conditional adverbial clause + main clause (legal action)"。除此句型上的差异之外，两地的汉语法律文本在辅助动词（相当于英文中的情态动词）的使用和译法上也有较大差异；在词汇层面，台湾法律文本中仍然保留了大量的文言词用词，而在大陆法律文本中根本就没有文言文的痕迹。最后，笔者发现古旧副词、拉丁词在台湾法律译本中的使用频率远远高于大陆的法律译本。虽然两地的法律译本在文本风格上存在一定的差异，但相比中文法律文本，英文译本反倒是两地司法交流的更有效的媒介。

关　键　词　法律文本；文本比较；文体差异；句型；古旧词；民事责任；刑

事处罚

作者联系地址 香港新界马鞍山迎涛湾1座17G

电子邮箱 ctfranklu1@163.com

2

Author: LI Kexing

Title: Legal Translation between Chinese Mainland and Taiwan: A Comparative Study

Published by: *Translation Quarterly*, 2007 (45).

[Abstract] Although the mainlanders and Taiwanese are both Chinese speaking the same language, judicial exchange and communication has become more and more difficult due to the physical separation over five decades, the disruption of cultural exchanges and the widened gaps in ideology between the two places. In the 1990s, scholars and lawmakers from both places complained that it was very difficult to understand the legal documents of each other written in the same Chinese language. In order to truly understand the exact meaning of the legal texts in both places, the author systematically sorted out and compared the similarities and differences between the Chinese legal texts and the English versions of Taiwan and the mainland, and made a preliminary exploration of the causes contributing to the differences.

The most basic sentence pattern of Taiwanese law for expressing civil liability and criminal penalty is "……者，应＋行为动词", or "……者，处……刑罚"; the parallel English translation is "Any person / a person who does sth. shall + verb (legal action) … ". In the mainland, the corresponding typical sentence pattern is "……的，应当＋行为动词／处／应当……刑罚／处罚", and the prevailing English version is "Whoever does sth ... shall + verb (legal action)", and "If/where-led conditional adverbial clause + main clause (legal action) ".

Apart from the differences in sentence patterns, the Chinese legal texts in the two places also differ greatly in the usage and translation of auxiliary verbs (equivalent to modal verbs in English), Taiwanese legal texts still retain, at the generic terms level, a large number of the expressions available only in classical Chinese, but no trace of classical Chinese expressions could be found in the mainland legal texts.

Finally, the author found that the frequency of using archaic expressions and Latin words in Taiwan's legal translations is much higher than that in the mainland legal translations. Although there are some stylistic differences between legal translations in the mainland and Taiwan, the English translations of legal texts in the two places, as compared with the Chinese legal texts, are much easier to be understood and may serve as a more effective medium for judicial exchange or communication between the two places.

Key words: legal text; text comparison; stylistic differences; sentence pattern; archaic words; civil liability; criminal penalty

3

作　　者　李占喜
标　　题　国内外语用翻译研究：回顾、述评与前瞻
发表刊物　《上海翻译》2008年第1期

［摘　要］本文回顾了国内外语用翻译大约20年的研究成果，梳理其为基于语用"分相论"的翻译研究和基于关联理论或顺应理论的翻译研究，肯定了西方学者研究的贡献，指出其学术观点有待进一步丰富和发展。

本文评析国内语用翻译研究的现状，指出相关研究中存在的一些问题：1）模仿性较强，创新性不足；2）理论演绎较多，实证研究滞后；3）语用学理论与翻译研究的结合论证方面出现"不和谐的声音"；4）研究多以文学翻译为主，口译和实用文体的语用翻译研究相对滞后。并提出相应

的建议。

　　本文预测了语用翻译的发展前景：1) 以关联理论和关联翻译理论为视角的翻译研究会进一步深入化、系统化；实用文体方面的翻译研究将会突破"坚冰"，未来的研究成果会逐步出现；2) 以顺应理论为视角的语用翻译研究在国内会出现与关联翻译理论研究相类似的不断增多的局面；3) 基于语用"分相论"的翻译研究还会有一定的研究空间，但这方面的研究因这些理论的局限性、研究范围的相对狭窄性，很难构建出一个系统的翻译模式；4) 在研究方法上，语用翻译将会走向理论演绎、译例分析的定性研究和"有声思维"等实证方法相结合的研究路向。

关　键　词　语用翻译；回顾；述评；展望
作者联系地址　广东省广州市天河区五山路483号，华南农业大学外国语
　　　　　　　　学院39信箱
电子邮箱　lzx502502@hotmail.com

3

Author: LI Zhanxi

Title: Pragmatics-based Translation Studies: Review, Comment and Prospect

Published in: *Shanghai Journal of Translators*, 2008 (1).

[Abstract]　This paper intends to look back over pragmatics-based translation studies made in the past less than 20 years and classifies them into traditional pragmatics-based and Relevance Theory or Adaptation Theory-based researches. It acknowledges Gutt's contribution, and points out that some of his viewpoints require enrichment and further modification.

　　Then it makes comment on pragmatics-based translation studies in China, revealing some problems in this field: 1) more academic imitation than originality; 2) more theoretical deduction than empirical studies; 3) disharmonious integration of pragmatics theories with translation example analysis; 4) more research focus on literary translation studies than interpreting studies and nonliterary translation studies, and offer corresponding suggestions.

Finally this paper predicts the future development in this field: 1) Relevance Theory-based translation studies will be systematically made, and nonliterary translation studies will break ice; 2) Adaptation Theory-based translation studies will see a similar increase; 3) Pragmatic unit of analysis-based translation studies remain to be explored; 4) Pragmatics-based translation studies will embrace such empirical methods as think-aloud protocol.

Key words: pragmatics-based translation studies; review; comment; prospect

4

作　　者　王金铨、王克非
标　　题　计算语言学视角下的翻译研究
出版单位　《外国语》2008 年第 3 期

［摘　要］ 计算语言学（computational linguistics）是从计算的角度对语言进行研究的一门学科。计算语言学与翻译的渊源起源于二十世纪五十年代的机器翻译。随着人工智能学科的蓬勃发展，计算语言学运用自然语言处理方法对翻译研究起到了越来越重要的作用。计算语言学中运用自然语言处理方法所获得的信息可以借鉴到翻译研究之中，而惯常的翻译研究方法也可以用来指导计算语言学的自然语言处理实践，两者有很多共融共通的方面。

本研究通过对双语语料的分析，从形式和语义两方面探讨计算语言学方法对翻译研究的作用和启示。在语言形式方面，通过文本特征统计信息研究了双语文本的基本形式特征，通过赋码语料研究了双语文本的深层句法信息。在语言意义方面，运用潜语义分析方法计算语句意义间的相似度，语句计算的结果与人工评判的结果相差无几，表明计算语言学的意义分析方法十分有效，对判断多个译文间、译文与原文间的"形似"与"神似"

有重要意义。
关 键 词 翻译研究；计算语言学；语义；形式
作者联系地址 江苏省扬州市邗江区扬西路 198 号，扬州大学扬子津校区外国语学院
电子邮箱 jqwang@yzu.edu.cn

4

Author: WANG Jinquan & WANG Kefei
Title: Translation Studies from the Perspective of Computational Linguistics
Published in: *Journal of Foreign Languages,* 2008 (3).
[Abstract] The paper, focusing on language form and language meaning, introduces the theories and methodologies of computational linguistics into translation studies. In terms of language form, with the help of the statistics extracted from the texts, research can be done on both superficial formal features and deep syntactic features of the parallel texts. In terms of language meaning, semantic similarities can be computed with the help of LSA, the result of which bears a very great significance for the judgment of formal and semantic similarities between multiple source texts or between source texts and target texts.
Key words: translation studies; computational linguistics; meaning; form

5

作 者 王 寅
标 题 认知语言学的"体验性概念化"对翻译主客观性的解释力——

一项基于古诗《枫桥夜泊》40 篇英语译文的研究

发表刊物 《外语教学与研究》2008 年第 3 期

[摘　要]　本文基于体验哲学的基本原理,将认知语言学家 Langacker 的"意义概念化"修补为"体验性概念化",并尝试以此为理论基础论述翻译中的客观性和主观性。有了体验性,就可限定"读者中心论"、"译者自主论";有了"概念化"(主要是识解)就可解释翻译的主观性。本文通过"体验性概念化"或"体验性识解观"透析《枫桥夜泊》40 篇英语译文,详解翻译中既有体验性和客观性,同时揭示主观性在翻译 认知活动中的主要体现,尝试为翻译主观性的研究提供理论框架。

关　键　词　认知语言学；体验性概念化；识解；翻译；《枫桥夜泊》

作者联系地址　重庆市沙坪坝区壮志路 33 号,四川外国语大学语言哲学研究中心

电子邮箱　angloamerican@163.com

5

Author: WANG Yin

Title: The Interpretation of Subjectivity-Objectivity in Translation by Means of "Embodied Conceptualization" in Cognitive Linguistics—A Research Based on 40 Translations of *Night Mooring by Maple Bridge*

Published in: *Foreign Languages Teaching and Research*, 2008 (3).

[Abstract]　On the basis of Embodied Philosophy, this paper tries to modify Langacker's "Meaning-in-Conceptualization" into "Meaning-in-Embodied Conceptualization", which can be applied for the interpretation of objectivity and subjectivity in translation. With embodiment, we can restrain "Reader's Centralism" and "Translator's Autonomy"; With conceptualization (mainly construal), we can interpret the subjectivity in translation. The view that translation is of subjectivity has long been recognized, but it has not yet been discussed and theorized in detail. This paper attempts to analyze the 40 English translations *Night Mooring by Maple Bridge* via "Embodied Conceptualization" or "Embodied Construal", with a view to interpreting embodiment and objectivity on the one hand, and subjectivity and its detailed aspects on the other, and to exploring the rule and theoretical framework of subjectivity in translation.

Key words: cognitive linguistics; "Embodied Conceptualization"; construal; translation; *Night Mooring by Maple Bridge*

6

作　　者　陈小慰
标　　题　韦努蒂"异化"理论话语的修辞分析
发表刊物　《中国翻译》2010年第4期

[摘　要]　由劳伦斯·韦努蒂提出的"异化"翻译理论，在中国数年来备受学者们关注。本文尝试从修辞视角对其"异化"理论话语围绕动机、手段、语境、受众及重要性、关联性和实际效果等修辞要素，重新解读和认识其得失，希望借此对该理论带来新认识。文章在简要回顾"异化"翻译理论发展和探讨修辞与话语关系的基础上，重点围绕韦努蒂的主要"异化"理论话语展开讨论。本文提出：韦努蒂的"存异伦理"话语在宏观重要性和与大语境贴切度方面十分到位，在一些微观话语方面却不够全面和得体，影响了关联性与可信度；"抵抗性翻译"强调采用不"流畅"的翻译，抗击"强势翻译"和文化霸权，但对弱势文化而言，充分利用确保可读性的规范英语，尽量传达和保留自己的语言和文化特色或许更具力量；在"好的翻译是少数化的"的话语里，韦努蒂成功实现了自己强调差异的目的，但另一方面，由于没有考虑到受众接受能力和需求等文化传达中的种种问题，这一话语缺乏或然性、可信性和重要性；而在"促进译语文化更新与变化"里，韦努蒂富有修辞意味地把翻译的目的定位于促进译语文化的"更新与变化"，传达了他对主流翻译观的认可，但同时也使其观点前后不一，

缺乏对各种可能修辞语境的全面考虑,影响了它的适用性。文章提出"异化"不应使文化对立,而是要达到共同的"更新与变化"。

关 键 词 韦努蒂;异化;话语;修辞分析

作者联系地址 福建省福州市福州地区大学城学园路 2 号,福州大学外国语学院

邮 编 350118

电子邮箱 joychen@fzu.edu.cn; joychen2004@sina.com

6

Author: CHEN Xiaowei

Title: The Rhetoric of Venuti's Conception of Foreignizing Translation

Published in: *Chinese Translators Journal*, 2010 (4).

[Abstract] This paper offers a rhetorical analysis of Venuti's conception of "foreignizing translation", in an attempt to supplement and enrich the already heated scholarly discussion in China. Following a brief review of the notion's historical development and a discussion of the relationship between rhetoric and discourse, it subjects the major ideas with which Venuti defines his position on the foreignizing approach to a critical reexamination, thinking in terms of rhetorical factors such as intention, medium, context and audience as well as importance, relevance and effect, aiming to cast new light on how his theory of translation works. The paper argues that the notions of "ethics of difference", "resistant translation", "Good translation is minoritizing" and "promoting cultural innovation and change", while desirable in macro importance and in line with the broader context, do not apply when specific purpose, context and audience of translation are considered and are therefore weak in relevance and validity. It is pointed out that the one-sided emphasis on "difference", "resistance" or "minoritizing" may not turn out as better strategies than trying to preserve the original language and cultural features by using terms identified by the target audience, and the awareness of the "difference" is not to cause more division and conflict of cultures, but for the ultimate purpose of mutual progress in "cultural innovation and change".

Key words: Venuti; foreignizing; discourse; rhetorical analysis

7

作　者　黄忠廉
标　题　小句全译语气转化研析
发表刊物　《外国语》2010年第6期
[摘　要]　语气是全译表达的致句实体，全译转换以小句为中枢单位，而小句包括音节实体（语法单位）和非音节实体（句子语气）。至今为止，译界对致句实体——句子语气讨论的还很少。语气是一个重要的语用因素，语气的转化即语气的转换与求化，求化指分解语际内容与形式之间的矛盾。双语间的语气转化指在原文语义不变的基础上找到最合适的译语语气类型，以传达原作的语气。从文体看，从科技类到社科类，再到文艺类，随着情感越来越充沛，语气转换、增减、分合的频率越来越大，转化要求越来越高，翻译难度越来越大，也越发因难见巧。陈述语气占全译的绝对主体，多半如实对译；疑问语气、祈使语气和感叹语气相对较少，也可以对译。语气对译是常态，是主体，语气的转换次之，语气的增减和分合较少。语气全译的艺术尽显于陈述语气、疑问语气、祈使语气、感叹语气之间的对应、增减、转换与分合，陈述、疑问、感叹、祈使四种语气的全译转化以陈述句为主。
关 键 词　小句；全译；语气；转化
作者联系地址　广东省广州市白云区白云大道北2号，广东外语外贸大学六教A302翻译学研究中心
邮　　编　510420
电子邮箱　zlhuang1604@163.com

7

Author: HUANG Zhonglian
Title: Toward Mood Transformation in Full Translation of Clause
Published in: *Journal of Foreign Languages*, 2010 (6).

[Abstract] Mood is the entity of full translation, and the clause, which includes syllable entity (grammatical unit) and non-syllable entity (sentence mood) is the pivotal unit in the shift of full translation. Up till now, however, little attention in translation studies has been paid to the mood in clause. Mood is an important element in language use and the transformation of mood covers both the shift and the sublimation. The sublimation solves the contradiction between the content and form of two languages. In order to convey the original mood in the source text, the transformation of mood between the two languages is to find out the most appropriate type of mood in the target language with the original meaning in the source text unchanged.

From the perspective of stylistics, the emotion becomes richer and richer from technological texts to social sciences texts and then to literary texts, which makes the frequency of using translation techniques such as shift, amplification, omission, division and combination and the demand of transformation higher and higher, and the difficulty of translation bigger and bigger. Thus, sophisticated techniques should be used in translation. In full translation, the mood transformation most frequently appears in declarative sentences, which needs correspondence technique to convey the original mood in most cases. The correspondence technique employed in the transformation of moods in interrogative, imperative and exclamatory sentences is less used compared with the declarative sentence. Generally speaking, for the transformation of mood, the correspondence technique is most frequently used, with the shift technique less used, and such techniques as amplification, omission, division and combination the least employed. It is concluded that the art of mood transformation in full translation is featured with the correspondence, amplification, omission, shift, division and combination in the declarative, interrogative, imperative and exclamatory sentence.

Key words: clause; full translation; mood; transformation

学科与应用翻译研究

1. 中国世界自然文化遗产对外宣传解说翻译失误分析　　许明武、王明静
2. 外宣翻译中"认同"的建立　　陈小慰
3. 重写：科普文体翻译的一个实验——以《时间简史》（普及版）为例　　郭建中
4. 中医古典文献中"阴阳"的源流与翻译　　兰凤利
5. 批评性话语分析视角下的新闻翻译分析——以转述话语的翻译为例　黄勤
6. 对官方口号翻译有效性的实证研究　　窦卫霖、祝　平
7. 法律全球化与法律起草和法律翻译——中国知识产权法的法律术语和技术词语使用情况　　陈可欣
8. 论法律翻译的静态对等策略　　李克兴
9. 组织控制与新闻专业自主的互动——以台湾报纸国际新闻编译为例　罗彦杰、刘嘉薇、叶长城
10. 英汉"低碳"新词翻译以及生成机制的认知阐释　　邵　斌、黎昌抱

Applied Translation Studies

1. Error Analysis for the English Translation of the Interpretations of China's World Cultural and Natural Heritage   **XU Mingwu & WANG Mingjing**
2. Identification as a Principle in Translating Materials for International Publicity   **CHEN Xiaowei**
3. Rewriting: An Experiment of Translating Popular Science Writings with the Translation of Hawking's *A Briefer History of Time* as an Example   **GUO Jianzhong**
4. The Origin of *Yin* and *Yang* as Chinese Medical Terms and Their Translation   **LAN Fengli**
5. Translation of News from the Perspective of Critical Discourse Analysis—A Case Study of the Translation of Reported Discourse   **HUANG Qin**
6. A Survey on the Translation Efficiency of Chinese Official Slogans   **DOU Weilin & ZHU Ping**
7. Legal Globalization and Law Drafting and Translation: Use of Legal Terms and Technical Words in Intellectual Property Laws of the People's Republic of China   **CHAN Ho-yan Clara**
8. On Static Equivalence for Legal Translation   **LI Kexing**
9. Interaction Between Organizational Control and News Professional Autonomy: International News Editor/Translators at Taiwanese Newspapers   **LO Yen-chieh, LIU Jiawei & YE Changcheng**
10. Translation of New Expressions about "Low Carbon" and Cognitive Perspective on Their Formation   **SHAO Bin & LI Changbao**

1

作　　者　许明武、王明静
标　　题　中国世界自然文化遗产对外宣传解说翻译失误分析
发表刊物　《中国翻译》2006年第2期
[摘　要]　随着中国对外开放程度的加深和旅游事业的蓬勃发展，中国的壮美河山及悠久灿烂的历史文化吸引了越来越多的外国游客，特别是那些被联合国教科文组织列为"世界自然文化遗产"的30处景点（截止到2005年）更为广受青睐。遗产解说词的英译文对帮助外国游客更好地了解这些世界遗产资源乃至整个中国文化都起到了至关重要的作用。本文试图对我国世界自然文化遗产旅游解说词的英译文本中出现的翻译错误进行归纳总结，并提出可行的翻译策略。

　　作者首先通过网络收集并建立中文解说词库（约3.5万字）及其英语翻译库（约2.5万词）和美国英文解说词库（约1.8万词）。分析中文解说词库和美国英文解说词库，证明两者存在功能上的本质差异。中文遗产解说文风华美正式，除信息功能之外，特别突出表情功能。而英文遗产解说以事实服人，文辞简洁，主要以传达信息为目的。作者认为东西方人民的审美差异导致了写作习惯的差异，从而进一步造成了中英文遗产解说功能的差异，翻译中必须予以充分考虑。

　　按照功能学派对翻译失误的定义和分类，作者对遗产解说英译文中出现较多的语言翻译失误和文化翻译失误进行了收集、筛选和分类，并在充分咨询英语本族语相关专家意见的基础上，对翻译失误部分给出了英译建议，在此基础上提出了相应的景点解说词翻译的改进方法和翻译策略。
关 键 词　世界自然文化遗产；解说；翻译失误
作者联系地址　湖北省武汉市洪山区珞喻路1037号，华中科技大学外国语学院
邮　　编　430074

电子邮箱 xumingwu@hust.edu.cn

1

Author: XU Mingwu & WANG Mingjing

Title: Error Analysis for the English Translation of the Interpretations of China's World Cultural and Natural Heritage

Published in: *Chinese Translators Journal*, 2006 (2).

[Abstract] With China's reform and opening to the outside world, its gorgeous landscapes, splendid culture and age-long history have attracted more and more overseas tourists. The sceneries inscribed on the World Cultural and Natural Heritage List by UNESCO are especially favored by both Chinese and foreign visitors. The Chinese-English translation of the heritage interpretation therefore plays a very important role in helping foreigners know better about these heritage resources as well as the Chinese culture. The paper attempts to summarize all kinds of errors in the C-E translation of heritage interpretations and suggest effective translation techniques.

The authors established three corpus, namely, 1) Chinese interpretations of China's World Cultural and Natural Heritage; 2) the English translation of it; 3) English interpretations of some American famous scenic spots. Many features of the Chinese and English heritage interpretations provide solid evidences that a great disparity exists between their functions. The Chinese heritage interpretation is formal and refined, stressing expressive function besides the dominant informative function. While its English counterpart impresses readers as a typical informative text type, which is based on concrete facts and features plain language. In the authors' opinion, different aesthetic values of Chinese and Westerners give rise to different writing conventions, which in turn result in their different functions. In the process of translating, such differences should be fully taken into consideration.

Based on the functionalist definition and classification of translation errors, with the help of some native speakers' suggestions, the authors analyze the common linguistic translation errors and cultural translation errors and suggest improved translations and relevant techniques.

Key words: world cultural and natural heritage; interpretation; translation error

2

作　　者　陈小慰
标　　题　外宣翻译中"认同"的建立
发表刊物　《中国翻译》2007年第1期

[摘　要]"认同"（identification）是当代西方修辞学中一个影响深远的重要观点，由美国著名修辞学家肯尼斯·伯克（Kenneth Burke）提出。根据伯克的定义，修辞指"人们运用语言表明态度或诱导他人完成某种行为"；它以语言的基本功能为基础，其关键在于'认同'。在伯克看来，人类作为生物学上独立的个体生存在世上，为了克服隔离感，始终在通过交际追求认同。以翻译为主要渠道的对外宣传，作为面对西方受众的跨语言、跨文化的交际活动，可以视为一个现代说服行为，一种修辞活动。从这个角度出发，"认同"说可以给我们极大的启示。

　　成功的对外宣传，是要让外国受众真正了解中国，获得对其发展状况、成就、独特的文化等事实的认识，在国际上树立和维护中国的良好形象，为改革开放和现代化建设创造良好的国际舆论环境。而这些事实最终能否被接受。能否产生积极正面的影响，很大程度上取决于宣传内容和手段是否在受众可以认同、接受的范围内。受众若是不认同，宣传也就难以达到目的。在存在巨大语言文化鸿沟的东西方之间，事实难以做到不言自明，只有在受众认可其为事实时才成其为事实。因此，外宣翻译要想获得成功，需要在翻译过程中与受众建立"认同"，采用他们喜闻乐见的话语方式，赢得其善意，从而获得受众的认同，实现对其施加有效影响的对外宣传目的。文章将"认同"说引入外宣翻译的探讨，围绕建立"认同"的必要性、基础及如何建立，从理论和实例两方面说明外宣翻译中"认同"的建立，是实现对外宣传目的、获得最终理解认同的有效保证。

关 键 词 认同；受众；翻译；外宣翻译

作者联系地址 福建省福州市福州地区大学城学园路2号，福州大学外国语学院

邮　　编 350116

电子邮箱 joychen@fzu.edu.cn；joychen2004@sina.com

2

Author: CHEN Xiaowei

Title: Identification as a Principle in Translating Materials for International Publicity

Published in: *Chinese Translators Journal*, 2007 (1).

[Abstract] A key concept in Western rhetoric, K. Burke's notion of "identification" stipulates that the success of persuasion depends on causing the audience to identify himself/herself with the speaker, both in what he says and how he says it, which requires that the rhetor identifies with the audience in what it accepts as true, probable, or desirable. This is because, according to Burke, whatever form rhetoric takes, it is 'rooted in an essential function of language itself, the use of language as a symbolic means of inducing cooperation in beings that by nature respond to symbols.' (Burke 1969:41, 43) Rhetoric is an attempt to bridge the conditions of estrangement that are natural and inevitable. The Chinese-English translation of materials for international publicity, which is a cross-language and cross-cultural act of communication with western receptors as the target audience, also has to uphold the principle of identification in order to achieve its intended purpose. Applying Burke's insights to this special genre of translation, the paper discusses the necessity, the prerequisites and the methods for invoking a sense of consensus in the targeted international audience. The principle provides valuable insights into solution of the perennial problem of poor quality of translation of publicity for international audience.

Key words: identification; audience; translation; international publicity

3

作　　者　郭建中

标　　题　重写：科普文体翻译的一个实验——以《时间简史》（普及版）为例

发表刊物　《中国科技翻译》2007年第5期

[摘　要]　可读性是科普作品的重要特征之一。因此，科普翻译也应保留这一特点。笔者在阅读霍金的科普著作《时间简史》（普及版）时，感到译本中的不少句子翻译腔严重。笔者对照英语原著，发现问题在于译作过分信守原作的句法结构和表达方式。众所周知，英语句法和表达方式与汉语差异甚大。在英汉/汉英翻译中，译者必须调整原作的句法结构和表达方式，使之符合目的语的行文习惯，从而使译作读起来像目的语中的原创作品一样流畅。要避免翻译腔，一个有效的方法是在目的语中重写原作。这里，我们所说的"重写"，是指在不改变原文意义和内容的前提下，译者在语言层面的操控。这种重写与勒菲弗尔所主张的重写是不同的。勒氏的重写，是指为适应目的语文化和意识形态对原作进行的改写。因此，在汉语中，我们必须区分这两种不同的rewriting。我们把前者称之为"重写"，因为译者并没有改变原作的意思和内容；我们称后者为"改写"，因为译者改变了原作的文化和意识形态。

基于上述理论和方法，笔者做了一个实验，把《时间简史》（普及版）

译作中一些明显的翻译腔的句子进行了重写。实验的目的是使科普译作读起来像目的语中的原创作品一样流畅，至少要避免翻译腔。实验的结果表明，我们不仅可以避免翻译腔，更可能使译文在不改变原作的意思和内容的前提下，读起来像目的语中的原创作品一样通顺流畅。

这种重写也是目的论理论应用的一个实例，即考虑了作者意图、翻译目的、读者对象和文本类型等诸因素。

本文的意义是把英语的rewriting在汉语中区分为"重写"和"改写"，并用实验证明了翻译中"重写"的必要性和可能性。

关　键　词　科普作品；科普翻译；重写；改写；文体
作者联系地址　浙江省杭州市西湖区嘉绿西苑 15-1-401
电子邮箱　gjz1938@126.com

3

Author: GUO Jianzhong

Title: Rewriting: An Experiment of Translating Popular Science Writings with the Translation of Hawking's *A Briefer History of Time* as an Example

Published in: *Chinese Science & Technology Translators Journal*, 2007 (5).

[Abstract]　Readability is one of the distinctive features of popular science writing. So the translation of the genre should maintain this feature. While reading the translation of Hawking's *A Briefer History of Time*, the author is deeply impressed by its translationese though generally speaking the translation of the book is tolerably readable. So I began to read the original and found that the problem of the translation lies in the translator who unduly adhered to the original sentence structures and ways of expressions. As is known to all, there are wide differences between English and Chinese in syntax and ways of expression. It is entirely necessary to change sentence structures and ways of expressions in C-E/E-C translation, more so than the translation between

Indo-European languages. To avoid translationese, one of the effective ways is to rewrite the original text in the target language so that the translation will read like an original composition. That is a method advocated by many distinguished translators and translation theorists both at home and abroad. Here rewriting is defined as the translator's manipulation in the linguistic aspects without changes of meaning and content of the original. It is different from the rewriting advocated by Lefevere. His rewriting is regarded as the translator's manipulation in the cultural and ideological aspects with changes of meaning and content of the original so as to be adapted to the culture and ideology of the target language. So in Chinese, we can distinguish between the two kinds of rewriting: the former may be called *chongxie*（重写）while the latter *gaixie*（改写）.

Based on the above-mentioned theories and methods, the author made an experiment of rewriting some of the translationese sentences in the translated text of Hawking's *A Briefer History of Time*, which are either unreadable or block comprehension. The objective of the experiment is to make the translation read like an original composition of a piece of popular science writing, or at least, to try to avoid distinct translationese. The result of the experiment shows that it is not only possible to avoid translationese, but also possible to make the translation read like an original composition without changes of meanings and content of the original. The translator's task is to change the English sentence structures and ways of expressions so as to conform to the style or manner of Chinese writing. The rewritten sentences read smoothly and are easy for comprehension.

The translation strategies and methods the translator adopts depend on the objective of the original author, the aim of the translation, the reader of the translation and types of the text. The translation should have the distinctive features of the original popular science readings, which is written in plain, vivid and clear language. For this purpose, the author holds that rewriting by the translator's manipulation in the linguistic aspects should be recommended as an effective translation strategy and method for the translation of popular science writing.

It is significant to distinguish two kinds of rewriting that are different in nature. And the experiment gives eloquent proof of the feasibility and necessity of "rewriting" in linguistic aspects as an effective translation strategy and method. The experiment is also an example of applying Scopos theory to translation.

Key words: popular science writing; translation of popular science writing; rewriting; style

4

作　　者　兰凤利
标　　题　中医古典文献中"阴阳"的源流与翻译
发表刊物　《中国翻译》2007年第4期
[摘　要]　中医学继承、发挥了《周易》的阴阳思想。中医古典文献中的"阴阳"主要是指哲学意义上的"阴阳",又有具体的医学所指,如指男女、性生活、阴经阳经、阴邪阳邪、阴气阳气等等。"阴阳"含义的确定是高度依赖于语境的。"阴阳"的翻译亦应视其具体的含义而定,不可一概音译为 *yin* and *yang*。如：

A《黄帝内经素问·上古天真论》：二八,肾气盛,天癸至,精气溢泻,**阴阳**和,故能有子。

英译：At the age of 16, the Kidney *Qi* becomes abundant, the *tian gui* or sex-stimulating essence matures, he begins to secrete semen; if at this point **the female and male** unite in harmony, a child may be conceived.

B《诸病源候论·妇人杂病诸候·带下候》：**阴阳**过度,则伤胞络。

英译：If **sex** is in excess, uterine collaterals may be injured.

C《黄帝内经素问·疏五过论》：粗工治之,亟刺**阴阳**……

英译：A careless doctor treats it by pricking ***yin* and *yang* meridians** time and again …

D《神农本草经卷三·中品》：蘗木,味苦,寒。主治……**阴阳伤**；蚀疮。

英译: Phellodendri Cortex (Huang Bai), bitter in flavor and cold in property. Indications: ... **hyper-sexuality**; sores resistant to healing.

E《伤寒论》：<u>阴阳</u>相搏，名曰动。<u>阴</u>动则汗出，<u>阴</u>动则发热。

英译: When **_yin qi_ and _yang qi_** wrestle with each other, the pulse is throbbing. When **the _cun_ pulse** is throbbing, sweating results; when **the _chi_ pulse** is throbbing, fever ensues.

关 键 词　阴阳；源流；中医学；古典文献；翻译

作者联系地址　上海市罗阳路 255 弄 39 号 202 室

邮　　编　201100

电子邮箱　fengli.lan@163.com

4

Author: LAN Fengli

Title: The Origin of *Yin* and *Yang* as Chinese Medical Terms and Their Translation

Published in: *Chinese Translators Journal*, 2007 (4).

[Abstract]　Chinese medicine inherits and develops the concepts of *yin* and *yang* from the *Book of Changes*. While this pair of terms is used in ancient Chinese medical texts primarily for their philosophical senses, within specific contexts they could also signify concrete medical meanings, such as female and male, sex or sexual activity, *yin* meridians and *yang* meridians, *yin* pathogens and *yang* pathogens, *yin qi* and *yang qi*, etc. Since the specific meanings of yin and *yang* depend highly upon the linguistic context in which they appear, it is ill-advised to consistently use their pinyin transliterations in rendering the two concepts into other languages. To be adequate, their translation should accord with the actual contextual meanings they have acquired. Examples:

A《黄帝内经素问·上古天真论》：二八，肾气盛，天癸至，精气溢泻，阴阳和，故能有子。

Translation: At the age of 16, the Kidney *Qi* becomes abundant, the *tian gui* or sex-stimulating essence matures, he begins to secrete semen; if at this point **the female and male** unite in harmony, a child may be conceived.

B《诸病源候论·妇人杂病诸候·带下候》：阴阳过度，则伤胞络。

Translation: If **sex** is in excess, uterine collaterals may be injured.

C《黄帝内经素问·疏五过论》：粗工治之，亟刺阴阳……

Translation: A careless doctor treats it by pricking **yin and yang meridians** time and again …

D《神农本草经卷三·中品》：蘖木，味苦，寒。主治……阴阳伤；蚀疮。

Translation: Phellodendri Cortex (Huang Bai), bitter in flavor and cold in property. Indications: … **hyper-sexuality**; sores resistant to healing.

E《伤寒论》：阴阳相搏，名曰动。阳动则汗出，阴动则发热。

Translation: When **yin qi and yang qi** wrestle with each other, the pulse is throbbing. When **the cun pulse** is throbbing, sweating results; when **the chi pulse** is throbbing, fever ensues.

Key words: *yin; yang*; origin; Chinese medicine; ancient texts; translation

5

作　者　黄　勤

标　题　批评性话语分析视角下的新闻翻译分析——以转述话语的翻译为例

发表刊物　《外语与外语教学》2008年第3期

［摘　要］　批评语言学（Critical Linguistics）这一术语由英国语言学家Roger Fowler于1979年首次提出，在不到三十年的时间里，批评语言学呈现出方兴未艾之势。但迄今为止，对于批评性话语分析的运用主要限于单语语篇的话语分析。本文尝试着以新闻报道中的转述话语这一互文性表

现形式为具体分析对象，将批评性话语分析运用于新闻翻译这一双语语境下的话语分析中，试图阐明意识形态是如何影响原文本和译文本的话语实践。文章选取《纽约时报》上关于美国侦察机撞毁中国战机事件是否影响北京申奥成功的一篇报道和《参考消息》对该篇报道的翻译为目标语料，分别从消息来源、转述形式和内容以及转述动词三个方面对比分析转述话语在两语篇中所行使的不同语篇和语用功能，同时考察译者如何运用翻译策略来表现自己的立场与观点。文章发现，转述话语是报道者进行意识形态操控的重要方面。报道者通过有目的、有选择地援引不同利益集团的典型话语，向读者再现和强化自己需要的声音，并进一步选择为自己需要的转述方式。在翻译中，译者有必要在新的语境下对原文中的转述话语的方式、内容等进行一些取舍与调整，以适应于目的语主流意识形态。

关 键 词 批评性话语分析；新闻语篇；转述话语；意识形态；翻译
作者联系地址 湖北省武汉市洪山区珞瑜路1037号，华中科技大学外国语学院
邮 编 430074
电子邮箱 huangqin@hust.edu.cn

5

Author: HUANG Qin

Title: Translation of News from the Perspective of Critical Discourse Analysis—A Case Study of the Translation of Reported Discourse

Published in: *Foreign Languages and Their Teaching*, 2008 (3).

[Abstract] The term 'Critical Linguistics' was first introduced by British linguist Roger Fowler in his work *Language Control* in 1979. Over the last three decades, Critical Linguistics has been thriving. The employment of which, however, has been confined to monolingual discourse analysis. Drawing on critical discourse analysis, this paper attempts to make a comparative study of the reported discourse both in the source news text and the target news text, scrutinizing how ideology could exert influence on them. The study extracts a piece of news report from New York Times and its Chinese translation in Cankaoxiaoxi and analyzes the textual and pragmatic functions performed by reported discourse in both texts through news sources, reporting forms and contents as well as reporting verbs, with an eye on how the translators manipulates translation strategies to represent their ideological stances. It is found that reported discourse is an effective approach of ideology manipulation. Reporters purposefully cite the representative discourse from different interest groups to amplify the voice they need. Translators shall rearrange the reporting forms and contents to adapt to the mainstream ideology in the target culture.

Key words: critical discourse analysis; news; reported discourse; ideology; translation

6

作　　者　窦卫霖、祝　平
标　　题　对官方口号翻译有效性的实证研究
发表刊物　《中国翻译》2009 年第 5 期
［摘　要］　中国官方口号是宣传政治理念和主张的有效形式，其英语翻译能否被外国读者理解，直接关系到外宣效果。本文通过对母语为英语的外国读者进行问卷调查和后续访谈，探讨我国近三十年政府重要口号翻译的有效性。通过对英语读者对这些翻译理解正误偏差情况的研究，笔者发现，外国人对中国官方口号的理解度高低首先跟口号所涉社会实践和文化理念在多大程度上是中国特有的相关，所涉越是我国特有的事物和观念，就越难被外国人所理解。由"独特性造成的误解"首先与意识形态和社会文化有关，其次也有语言的原因。因此，为了达到其宣传的有效性，官方口号的翻译需要注意三个要点：把握本质、顾及全面、注意修饰。即口号翻译

有效性的前提是准确地把握口号的本质，力争使口号的翻译在不同的文化语境中都能真实地传递我们想要表达的信息；在把握本质的前提下，考虑到译文读者所欠缺的语境知识，有时需要提供口号的隐含内容；为了更全面准确地传递口号的含义，还应该注意英语的表达习惯和逻辑思维特点，选词要精确，句子结构尽量体现口号简洁、易懂、方便记忆、朗朗上口、对称押韵等修饰特点。简而言之，中国口号的翻译应该以翻译有效性作为基本原则。

关　键　词　官方口号；翻译有效性；英语读者；实证研究
作者联系地址　上海市闵行区东川路 500 号，华东师范大学（闵行校区）
电子邮箱　wldou@english.ecnu.edu.cn

6

Author: DOU Weilin & ZHU Ping
Title: A Survey on the Translation Efficiency of Chinese Official Slogans
Published in: *Chinese Translators Journal*, 2009 (5).

[Abstract] Proper translation of Chinese official slogans is of vital importance in foreign publicity. This paper aims to study the efficiency of existing translations of Chinese official slogans by way of questionnaire and follow-up interviews among and with English native speakers (including Englishmen, Americans, and Australians). The survey shows that while a majority of the slogans makes sense to the native speakers, misunderstanding and failures of understanding still exist. Foreigners' understanding of Chinese official slogans is primarily influenced by the extent to which these slogans are culturally-related, in other words, whether these slogans convey Chinese characteristics. The closer they are related to unique Chinese culture and ideas, the harder they are for foreigners to understand. The "misunderstanding caused by uniqueness" is first of all a product of ideological differences, and it also has to do with cultural differences. Last but not least, language itself constitutes a barrier to understanding. Therefore, the authors point out that the translation of Chinese slogans should be practiced on a basic standard of acceptability, i.e. the translation should effectively serve the Skoposi, or purposes, of Chinese official slogans. In order to achieve this, the translation of slogans should be guided by three principles: faithfulness, comprehensiveness, and linguistic accuracy and modification.

Key words: official slogans; translation efficiency; English readers; survey

7

作　　者　　陈可欣

标　　题　　法律全球化与法律起草和法律翻译——中国知识产权法的法律术语和技术词语使用情况

发表刊物　　《翻译季刊》2010 年第 58 期

［摘　要］　本文旨在分析法律条文与国际条约中一些重要的法律术语及技术词语，比较其使用和翻译的异同，以探讨中国近年在全球化的趋势下，积极改革法律制度，务求与国际标准接轨所带来的转变，以及本土化一直以来的影响。在经济全球化大趋势下，一方面不少国际法成为国家法，另一方面不少国家采纳世界各国法律使用，形成法律全球化的局面。文中探讨的法律术语包括"copyright"（"著作权" vs."版权"）、"copyright owners"（"著作权人"vs."版权所有权人"）；技术词语则包括"fix/fixation"（"录制"vs."固定"）以及"broadcasting"（"播放"vs."广播"）。作者期望，法律起草者和翻译者能多参考大中华区内不同的英汉和汉英法律文本，借以提高法律术语的使用和翻译质量。本文讨论主要分为"法律术语"与"技术词语"两部分，所选取的法律术语及技术词语均来自中国《著作权法》（2001）和《与贸易有关的知识产权协议》[即世界贸易组织的"Agreement on Trade-Related Aspects of Intellectual Property Rights"(TRIPS) 汉译版本]，参照文本主要为香港《版权法》（《香港法例》第 528 章）。

关 键 词　全球化；法律起草；法律翻译；法律术语；知识产权法；中华人民共和国

作者联系地址　广东省深圳市龙岗区龙翔大道 2001 号，香港中文大学（深圳）人文社科学院

邮　　编　518172

电子邮箱　clarachan@cuhk.edu.cn

7

Author: CHAN Ho-yan Clara

Title: Legal Globalization and Law Drafting and Translation: Use of Legal Terms and Technical Words in Intellectual Property Laws of the People's Republic of China

Published in: *Translation Quarterly*, 2010 (58).

[Abstract]　To meet the general requirement for term consistency and equivalence in legal translation, the study compares the lexis of two Chinese intellectual property law statutes and an international agreement and describes differences in the use and translation of legal terms and technical words that arise from the respective influences of globalization and localization, as China attempts to connect its legal system to the international standard under the trend towards globalization. The legal terms under investigation include "copyright" (*zhuzuoquan* 著作权 vs. *banquan* 版权) and "copyright owners" (*zhuzuoquanren* 著作权人 vs. *banquan suoyouquanren* 版权所有权人), while the technical words include "fix/fixation" (*luzhi* 录制 vs. *guding* 固定) and "broadcasting" (*bofang* 播放 vs. *guangbo* 广播). The study attempts to enhance the translation of all lexical items by promoting the use of "cross-examination" of Chinese-English translation and English-Chinese translation. This process demonstrates that legal drafters and legal translators can be more sensitive to each other's diction amid the trend towards local laws being globalized and international laws being localized. The discussion is divided into "legal terms" and "technical terms and words". The data is taken from two laws, namely the Copyright Law 2001 of the People's Republic of China, and Agreement on Trade-Related Aspects of Intellectual Property Rights (TRIPS), with reference to Hong Kong's Copyright Ordinance (Chapter 528).

Key words: Globalization; legal drafting; legal translation; legal term; intellectual property law; People's Republic of China

8

作　者　李克兴
标　题　论法律翻译的静态对等策略
发表刊物　《外语教学与研究》2010年第1期
[摘　要]　在翻译实践中，相同的文本，采用不同的翻译策略，出产的目标语文本迥然不同。广为译者所知的翻译策略不下十余种。究竟哪一种策略最适合法律文本的翻译呢？为寻找合适的法律翻译策略，笔者首先对法律文本的目的和语言特点进行了确切的界定，发现法律文本虽然属呼唤型（vocative），但在多数情形下还是为了传意，即把立法者或法律文本制作人的意旨或意图传达给有关人士。为了达到精确传意的目的，不但要求译者把文本的表层意思、深层意思、语言结构、风格、语域和格式原原本本地转换成目标语，还要求译文最大限度地再现原文作者的每一个写作意图——这也是笔者对静态对等翻译的界定。译文若能达此境界，便是静态对等的文本，即使将译文回译成源语，回译文本与原文本不会有任何本质上的差异。

采用现有的相关翻译策略——"动态／功能对等""异化"或"归化"、"功能主义""语义翻译"和"传意／交际翻译"等等，能否使译文达到上文描述的境界呢？笔者将这些现成的主要翻译策略放在法律文本的语境中逐一进行了检验和论证,发现这些策略均有各自的局限性,不适用法律翻译,只有笔者发明的静态对等翻译策略才可胜此重任。笔者还发现法律语言的特点为静态对等翻译提供了充足的客观条件:法律文本不但修辞手段单调、语言模式化、格式化、语域程度高,而且文本目标读者群也非常单一,因此,法律语言本质上是静态语言。所以,笔者将相应的静态对等翻译确立为法律翻译的专用策略。

关 键 词 静态对等;动态对等;异化;归化;功能主义;语义翻译;传意／交际翻译;模式化语言;回译

作者联系地址 香港新界马鞍山迎涛湾 1 座 17G

电子邮箱 ctfranklu1@163.com

8

Author: LI Kexing

Title: On Static Equivalence for Legal Translation

Published in: *Foreign Language Teaching and Research*, 2010 (1).

[Abstract] In translation practice, the target language products would be very much different for the same piece of source text when different translation strategies are used. There are no fewer than ten translation strategies available to contemporary translators. What kind of strategy is most suitable for translation of legal texts? To find a suitable legal translation strategy, the author starts the mission by defining the purpose of legal texts and identifying the linguistic features of legal language. He finds that legal texts fall into information-based vocative text-type and the purpose of legal writing is to communicate or to convey the message or intent of the legal writer to the persons or parties concerned.

For effective and accurate communication, a legal translator is required not only to translate the surface meaning, in-depth meaning, proper sentence pattern, style, register as well as format of the text into target language, but also to reproduce every intent of the source text writer to the utmost extent. This is also the author's definition of static equivalence translation. If a translation can achieve all these features, it must be a statically equivalent translation. Even if it is back-translated into its source language, there will be no discrepancy between the translated text and the original text.

Can we accomplish a static equivalence by applying the main existing translation strategies such as "dynamic/functional equivalence", "foreignization or domestication translation" "functionalism" "semantic or communicative translation"? The author tested one by one all these mentioned strategies in legal contexts and found that they all have their own limitations in one way or another and are not suitable for legal translation. The only approach which can achieve the mission is the static equivalence strategy developed by the author. He also found that the unique features of legal language provide necessary conditions for static equivalent translation. He observed that legal texts are basically written in a static and rigid language with formal registers, patterned structures, formulaic expressions, fixed formats and a few rhetoric devices. Besides, the target readership of a legal text is very specific and pre-defined. Therefore, legal language is in essence a static language and the corresponding static equivalence approach is most appropriate for legal translation.

Key words: static equivalence; dynamic equivalence; foreignization; domestication; functionalism; semantic translation, communicative translation; patterned language; back-translation

9

作　者　罗彦杰、刘嘉薇、叶长城
标　题　组织控制与新闻专业自主的互动——以台湾报纸国际新闻编译为例

发表刊物 《新闻学研究》2010年第102期，第113—149页

[摘　要]　由于以英文为主要语言的国际通讯社长期以来垄断国际新闻的资讯流通，台湾具一定规模之报社除在重要国家派遣驻外特派员外，均设有编译人员，负责翻译与编撰国际新闻外电稿件。本研究即在探讨台湾报纸国际新闻组织控制与编译人员专业自主之间的互动关系。国际新闻以往被认为不易存在组织控制，编译专业自主权也高于记者。然而根据作者对台湾四家报纸国际新闻编译进行深度访谈及参与观察台湾报纸之国际新闻内容产制实务，发现编译实际上仍无可避免受到组织控制，且受控制程度更甚于记者。编译面临的组织控制包括报业所有权人、报社科层制度与新闻产制流程，形成三种互动关系。在后两者的具体表现上，国际新闻迥异于国内新闻，而且其特有的科层制度与产制流程更不利于编译人员争取专业自主。作者发现，编译个人背景条件的不同，确实在对组织控制的认知或享有的专业自主权方面，有程度上的差别。资深编译、明星编译及具有新闻传播科系背景的编译，对组织控制认知较高或享有较多的自主权；资浅编译、非明星编译及不具有新闻传播科系背景的编译，则对组织控制认知较低或享有较少的自主权。整体而言，编译享有的报道自主权不如翻译自主权，但若要抗拒组织控制、争取国际新闻产制的自主空间，仍须从"综合报道"类新闻着手，其因在于"综合报道"需要多元取材与丰富叙事内容，所以编译有机会借此还原新闻事件背后的脉络意义，稀释组织控制的影响力。至于资浅编译虽不如资深编译有较多捍卫专业自主权的筹码，但可运用其擅长网路搜寻资料的优势，回避组织控制的压力。

关　键　词　组织控制；专业自主；国际新闻；编译
作者联系地址　台湾台北市阳明山华冈路55号，中国文化大学新闻学系
电子邮箱　inging@ms15.hinet.net

9

Author: LO Yen-chieh, LIU Jiawei & YE Changcheng

Title: Interaction Between Organizational Control and News Professional Autonomy: International News Editor/Translators at Taiwanese Newspapers

Published in: *Mass Communication Research*, 2010 (102), pp. 113-149.

[Abstract] This paper is aimed to explore the interactive relationships between the international news' organizational control and editor/translators' professional autonomy. International desks of the newspapers in Taiwan had been supposed to be the units where organizational control exists much less, and editor/translators should have enjoyed more professional autonomy than reporters. In practice, however, editor/translators face more organizational control than reporters. The organizational control of international news comes from newspaper owners, the bureaucracy and news-making process that disadvantage editor/translators in exerting professional autonomy, leading to three kinds of interactive relationships. The authors found that editor/translators with different background performed differently in exerting professional autonomy. Senior, star and journalism/communications-educated editor/translators enjoy more autonomy than junior, non-star and nonjournalism/communications-educated ones. As a whole, editor/translators enjoy reporting autonomy less than translating one. But if they want to resist organizational control, "wrap-up" reports can help. Compared to senior ones, junior editor/translators can use their advantages of Internet search to avoid the organizational control.

Key words: organizational control; professional autonomy; international news; editor/translator

10

作　者　邵　斌、黎昌抱
标　题　英汉"低碳"新词翻译以及生成机制的认知阐释
发表刊物　《中国翻译》2010年第4期
［摘　要］　随着人们对全球气候变化的关注,"低碳经济"已经成为全球关注的焦点。英汉语中随之涌现出一系列有关"低碳"的新词语,其翻译也成了译界的热门话题。本文追踪了近年来出现的"低碳"新词,通过实证探讨其翻译策略,并从认知语言学的角度解读其生成机制。
关　键　词　低碳；新词语；翻译；认知语言学
作者联系地址　浙江省杭州市下沙高教园区学源街18号,浙江财经大学外国语学院
电子邮箱　seesky1978@163.com

10

Author: SHAO Bin & LI Changbao

Title: Translation of New Expressions about "Low Carbon" and Cognitive Perspective on Their Formation

Published in: *Chinese Translators Journal*, 2010 (4).

[Abstract]　The "Low Carbon Economy" has been given greater prominence globally due to international concern over climate change. Consequently, the recent years have witnessed a series of new expressions about "Low Carbon" both in English and Chinese, whose translation has become a hot topic in the translation field. After a detailed investigation of these new expressions, this paper attempts to explore their translation approaches, and then analyze their formation from the perspective of cognitive linguistics.

Key words: low carbon; new expressions; translation; cognitive linguistics

翻译教学

1. 翻译测试及其评分问题　穆　雷
2. 任务型教学法运用于口译教学的实验研究　文　军、刘　威
3. 语义"匹配"与翻译教学　罗选民、徐莉娜
4. 再谈翻译教学体系的构建　刘和平
5. 建设完整的翻译教学体系　穆　雷
6. 中国翻译教学研究 50 年（1951—2005）回眸　文　军、张金陵
7. 翻译专业：正名过程及正名之后　杨晓荣
8. 翻译教学的发展与 TOT 计划的实施　任　文
9. 翻译教学中的主体心理关注与多维导向教学模式构建　张瑞娥
10. 关于开放型语料库翻译教学的思考　罗选民、刘　彬
11. 教授翻译科技的新课程：以教授翻译项目科目作为个案研究　陈善伟
12. 基于语料库学习者汉英翻译省译策略的研究　潘鸣威
13. 发展性翻译教学评价模式　王树槐、王卫平
14. 翻译过程中翻译策略的实证性研究——基于英语专业大学生的有声思维调查　文　军、殷　玲
15. 学术性·职业性·趣味性——"影视翻译"课程教学探索　肖维青

Teaching of Translation

1. Translation Testing and Grading   **MU Lei**
2. An Empirical Study on the Application of Task-based Instruction in Interpreting Teaching   **WEN Jun & LIU Wei**
3. A Semantic Matchmaking Approach to Translation-related Teaching   **LUO Xuanmin & XU Lina**
4. Rethinking the Construction of a Pedagogical System for Translation Teaching   **LIU Heping**
5. Conceptualizing a System of Translation Pedagogy   **MU Lei**
6. A Review of the Study of Chinese Translation Teaching for 50 years (1951-2005)   **WEN Jun & ZHANG Jinling**
7. Translation as a Major: Being Specialized Institutionally   **YANG Xiaorong**
8. Development of Professional Translation/Interpreting Education and Implementation of the TOT Project   **REN Wen**
9. On Students' Psychology Care and the Construction of Multi-orientation Translation Teaching Model   **ZHANG Rui'e**
10. Open-style Corpus-driven Translation Teaching: Some Thoughts   **LUO Xuanmin & LIU Bin**
11. A New Curriculum for the Teaching of Translation Technology: The Teaching of a Translation Project Course as a Case Study   **CHAN Sin-wai**
12. A Corpus-based Study on the Omission Strategy in EFL Learners' Chinese-English Translation   **PAN Mingwei**
13. Translation Teaching Assessment: A Developmental Model   **WANG Shu-**

huai & WANG Weiping
14. Translation Strategies of Chinese English Majors: An Investigation Based on Think Aloud Protocols   **WEN Jun & YIN Lin**
15. Pedagogical Reflections on the Design of a Course in Audiovisual Translation   **XIAO Weiqing**

1

作　　者　穆　雷
标　　题　翻译测试及其评分问题
发表刊物　《外语教学与研究》2006 年第 6 期
[摘　要]　本文主要探讨翻译测试的几个核心问题，包括翻译测试的本质与类别、翻译测试与语言测试的区别、翻译测试的评分方式和评分标准，并提出未来翻译测试研究应注意的问题。

翻译测试根据测试目的可以分为翻译课程测试、学生遴选测试、翻译竞赛测试和职业培训测试；根据测试方式又可以分为客观性测试和主观性测试。

翻译测试与语言测试最主要的差异在于，语言测试注重测试语言能力及语言交际能力，翻译测试则在此基础上进一步考察翻译能力及对待处理两种文化的态度与能力。单用语言测试的内容与方法来进行翻译测试是不够的，翻译测试应有自己独立并超出语言测试之外的内容和方法。

翻译测试的评分方式和评分标准当前研究较为欠缺，本文通过调研国内外高校发现：1）中国内地较多高校翻译教师在教学测试中并没有很明确的评分标准，中国香港部分高校的评分标准包括准确/流畅/主题知识或理解/翻译/技术等维度或参数，中国台湾部分高校的评分标准包括理解/表达正确度、词汇灵活度、语法正确度和文体/风格表达度几项参数，中译外和外译中的评分参数相同而分值各异；2）英国高校的评分标准体现出差异化特征，有的笼统灵活，有的遵从传统翻译标准，有的比较具体便于参考；3）美国部分高校的评分标准采用五分制，评分方式选择三位评分者同时独立评判取其平均值。

翻译测试研究主要是为翻译教学服务，未来翻译测试研究应当从翻译理论和测试理论出发，研究作为一门独立学科的翻译学的教学及其测试问题。

关 键 词　翻译测试，测试方法，评分方式

作者联系地址 广东省广州市白云区白云大道北 2 号，广东外语外贸大学第四教学楼高级翻译学院 405 室
邮　　编　510420
电子邮箱　mulei2002@139.com

1

Author: MU Lei
Title: Translation Testing and Grading
Published in: *Foreign Language Teaching and Research*, 2006 (6).
[Abstract] The article discusses several key issues of translation testing, including its categorization, features different from language testing, methods and marking scales, and future research directions.

Translation testing, according to its different purposes, can be categorized into testing for translation teaching, testing for translator screening, testing for translation competition and testing for vocational translation training courses. It can also be classified into objective translation testing and subjective translation testing.

What makes translation testing significantly different from language testing is that the latter focuses merely on language competence and language communication competence, while the former not only tests these competences but goes further by testing translation competence and translators' attitudes and competences of dealing with two different cultures. So it is not sufficient to merely adopt the methods of language testing in translation testing, which should have its own distinctive testing methods.

Few studies up to now have touched upon translation testing methods and marking scales. Based on a survey of global translation education, the paper finds that: 1) many teachers in China's mainland do not have specific marking scales in their translation teaching; translation testing in some Hong Kong universities includes such parameters as accurateness, fluency and subject knowledge, or such dimensions as apprehension, transferring and technology use; translation testing in some Taiwan universities adopts uniform parameters but allocates different weights to the parameters for testing translation from Chinese and translation into Chinese; 2) translation testing in British universities tends to follow different pedagogical traditions; 3) translation testing in some American universities adopts the five-point marking scale.

Future research on translation testing should mainly be contributed to translation teaching under the independent discipline of Translation Studies, and be suggested to refer to both translation theories and testing theories.

Key words: translation testing, testing methods, marking scales

2

作　　者　文　军、刘　威
标　　题　任务型教学法运用于口译教学的实验研究
发表刊物　《中国翻译》2007年第4期
[摘　要]　进入二十一世纪以来，中国和世界各国之间的交流与合作都在迅速增长。因此，市场对于翻译从业人员，尤其是口译人员的需求量也越来越大。这也使得口译技能的教学与培训在近年来受到了越来越多的关注。本文所要探讨的问题是如何将任务型教学法应用到口译教学当中。作者在总结前人研究成果的基础上，为任务性教学法在口译教学中的应用提供理论依据。同时，通过实验设计，证明了任务型教学法在口译教学中的适用性与可行性。
关 键 词　任务型教学法；口译教学；动机；兴趣
作者联系地址　北京市海淀区学院路37号，北京航空航天大学外语学院
邮　　编　1000000

电子邮箱　junwen@vip.163.com

2

Author: WEN Jun & LIU Wei

Title: An Empirical Study on the Application of Task-based Instruction in Interpreting Teaching

Published in: *Chinese Translators Journal*, 2007 (4).

[Abstract]　Nowadays, the communication and cooperation between China and other countries are increasing rapidly, which calls for a large demand of translators especially interpreters. Thus in recent years, the study of interpretation teaching and training has drawn much more attention than before. The author of this paper intends to discuss the application of task-based instruction to interpretation teaching. On the basis of relevant study fruits, the author tests the practicability of task-based instruction in interpretation teaching.

Key words: task-based instruction; interpretation teaching; motivation; interest

3

作　　者　罗选民、徐莉娜

标　　题　语义"匹配"与翻译教学

发表刊物　《外语教学与研究》2007年第5期

［摘　要］　一种语言的习得在"匹配"中完成并存入长时程记忆，进入长时程记忆的"语义关系结构模式"一经语音打包处理，行为主体就可以自由使用现成语块进行交际。基于这样的语言习得理论，本文通过分析

语义匹配和句法框架的关系来讨论教学翻译与翻译教学问题。翻译过程中，如果源语表达方式与译者从长时记忆中检索出的语义关系结构模式一致，译者就会迅速给出与原文语义内容相同的译文，这是"完全匹配"状态下的"无标记翻译过程"。然而，当源语表达方式在译者的长时记忆中找不到匹配的语义关系结构模式时，就会带来翻译障碍，甚至导致翻译失败。在这种情况下，译者需要重新进行"匹配评价"，调整理解和表达的视点，直至"匹配"成功。因为只有获得"匹配"的语义关系模式才能作为可互换语块进入"语义关系模式库"，这是"不完全匹配"状态下的"有标记翻译过程"。本文认为，翻译教学旨在让学生学会在双语无标记转换失败的情况下有意识并积极地完成信息加工任务，寻找合适的"不完全匹配"；而教学翻译所触及的大多是语法翻译和现成"匹配"，缺乏应有的语义感知过程。换言之，作为教学工具的翻译一般是一种被动的双语转换行为或者说是无标记的"匹配"行为，而翻译教学关注的重点是培养学生积极处理有标记信息的能力，即语义匹配的能力。这两种不同的教学形式并不是完全对立，而是相互接应，互为补充。如能在两者中充分有效地运用双语语义匹配的训练，可以培养学生的翻译能力，增强其认知力和创造性。

关 键 词 教学翻译；翻译教学；语义匹配；语义知觉

作者联系地址 广东省广州市白云区白云大道北 2 号，广东外语外贸大学六教 205 室外语研究与语言服务协同创新中心

邮 编 510420

电子邮箱 luoxm@tsinghua.edu.cn

3

Author: LUO Xuanmin & XU Lina
Title: A Semantic Matchmaking Approach to Translation-related Teaching
Published in: *Foreign Language Teaching and Research*, 2007 (5).

[Abstract] Learning a language usually involves semantic match-making and storage of the semantic matches in long-term memory. When this is successfully done and the sound articulation of the corresponding syntactic frames is ready, a learner can freely use the language chunks for communicative purposes. Based on this theoretical position in language acquisition research, this paper proceeds to examine the teaching of translation through the analysis of semantic match-making and syntactic frames. It recognizes that complete semantic matches between the source and the target languages will result in quick unmarked translation process, while incomplete semantic matches between the two languages will cause translation barrier or failure. In the latter circumstance, the translator needs to make adjustments to the points of view he or she takes in analyzing the original or in representing the syntactic frames of the original in the target language. Only when he or she manages to make matches in syntactic frames in certain senses can exchanges between the chunks of two languages happen in marked translation process. Accordingly, a justifiable distinction between teaching translation and translation teaching can be provided. In teaching translation learners are exposed to more grammar translation and matched chunks than to semantic processing as expected in translation teaching class, where active and conscious involvements in processing mis-matched chunks are necessary. This process is problem-solving in nature. The two kinds of teaching are not mutually exclusive, but complementing. The application of semantic match-making in the both kinds of teaching can strengthen students' cognitive power and creative performance significantly.

Key words: teaching translation; translation teaching; semantic match-making; semantic awareness

4

作　者　刘和平
标　题　再谈翻译教学体系的构建
发表刊物　《中国翻译》2008年第3期
[摘　要]　本文主要就教学翻译和翻译教学的差异能否作为翻译教学体系构建的理论基础进行思考。教学翻译作为一种教学手段和方法，在外语教学中发挥着积极作用，但不能因此成为翻译教学的一个层次。翻译教学通常指职业翻译教学，是一种专门的技能训练。按照认知心理学理论，学员对技能的掌握通常可分为基础、中等和高等。因此，无论是外语专业的口笔译课程，还是本科翻译专业课程，或是硕士层次的翻译课程，其区别在于技能训练的内容和学员掌握技能的程度，故划分翻译教学层次应以此为基础。本文第一次对各层级翻译教学进行定义并对其教学对象、内容、方法等作出分析。
关 键 词　翻译教学体系；认知特点；技能训练；程序化
作者联系地址　北京市海淀区学院路15号，北京语言大学
电子邮箱　hepingliu@hotmail.com

4

Author: LIU Heping

Title: Rethinking the Construction of a Pedagogical System for Translation Teaching

Published in: *Chinese Translators Journal*, 2008 (3).

[Abstract]　This paper distinguishes between "teaching foreign languages through translation" and "teaching translation for its own sake", maintaining that since the latter is devoted to professional training on practical translation skills only, the former ought not to be taken for one of its components. Drawing from cognitive psychology's insight that mastery of skills could be achieved for foreign languages majors, for undergraduate majors in translation, and for master students of translation should be differentiated primarily on the basis of: 1) the contents of skills training, and 2) the targeted level of mastery.

Key words: translation teaching system; cognitive psychology; skills training; sequencing

5

作　　者 穆　雷
标　　题 建设完整的翻译教学体系
发表刊物 《中国翻译》2008 年第 1 期
[摘　要] 翻译教学在中国内地迅速发展，短短几年，一些高校相继成立翻译学院或翻译系。目前，中国内地已有 20 多所高校培养翻译学 / 方向博士生，约 150 所高校培养翻译学 / 方向硕士生，7 所高校培养翻译专业本科生，约 900 所高校拥有英语本科专业，开设英汉汉英翻译课程，甚至设有翻译方向。中国内地已经建立起了较为完整的翻译教学体系。然而，在这一过程中，也存在诸多不容忽视的问题，如：各层次培养目标不清、教学内容重复、层次之间缺乏衔接等。因此，从翻译教学理论出发，研究各层次翻译教学的本质、探索符合中国国情的翻译教学体系十分必要。本文所讨论的核心问题即如何设计出符合我国国情的翻译教学体系，明确各层次翻译教学的培养目标、教学大纲与课程设置等问题。文章首先从学理层面区分了"教学翻译"与"翻译教学"的概念，明确了"翻译教学"的培养目标与要求；其次，对现行翻译教学层次作出区分。最后，在广泛调研我国语言服务行业及企业需求、翻译教学实际情况的基础之上，考察并借鉴国外翻译教学人才培养经验，提出了中国翻译教学体系

的整体架构。文中提出：1)"教学翻译"和"翻译教学"在学科定位、教学目的、教学重点和培养目标方面均有显著区别；2)现行教育体制下的翻译教学层次应对外语专业高年级翻译课、外语专业翻译方向、翻译专业（本科）作出明确区分，在课程时数、培养目标、学生基础及教学性质方面，三者均有明显区别；3)中国的翻译教学体系应该包括翻译学博士、翻译学硕士、翻译硕士专业学位（MTI）、翻译专业文学学士、笔译/口译硕士培训证书、笔译/口译培训证书等不同层次。本文是对我国翻译教学体系的思考与规划设计，有助于推动我国翻译教学体系的完善以及翻译学学科的发展。

关 键 词 翻译教学；学位层次；培养目标

作者联系地址 广东省广州市白云区白云大道北2号，广东外语外贸大学四教405

电子邮箱 mulei2002@139.com

5

Author: MU Lei

Title: Conceptualizing a System of Translation Pedagogy

Published in: *Chinese Translators journal*, 2008 (1).

[Abstract] Translation teaching in mainland China has experienced a rapid development and some colleges and universities have set up school/college/department of translation just within a few years. Up to now, there are more than 20 colleges and universities cultivating doctoral students in translation studies, about 150 colleges and universities cultivating master students in translation studies, 7 colleges and universities undergraduate students in translation, and about 900 colleges and universities have English undergraduates taking courses in translation. At present, a relatively complete translation teaching system has been established. However, there are also some problems that can't be ignored, for example: the unclear training goal at different levels, the repetition of teaching content and the lack of convergence among various levels. Thus, it is necessary to study the nature of translation teaching at all levels and explore the translation teaching system which conforms to China's national conditions. This paper discusses how to design a complete translation teaching system and clarifies the training objectives, syllabus and curriculum at all levels. It first distinguishes the concept of "teaching translation" and "translation teaching"; secondly, it distinguishes the current levels of translation teaching. Finally, on the basis of extensive research on China's language service industry and the actual situation of translation teaching, by examining and drawing lessons from foreign translation teaching programs, it puts forward the overall structure of Chinese translation teaching system. This paper is an overall reflection, planning and design of the translation teaching system in mainland China, which is helpful to promote the perfection of China's translation teaching system and the development of the translation discipline.

Key words: translation teaching; degree level; training objectives

6

作　　者　文　军、张金陵
标　　题　中国翻译教学研究 50 年（1951—2005）回眸
发表刊物　《上海翻译》2008 年第 2 期

[摘　要]　本文系依据笔者主编的《中国翻译教学五十年回眸》一书，对中国五十余年来翻译教学研究进行的统计与分析。本文依据此书，对已有研究成果进行了分类及分析，依据这些统计分析，本文提出了研究中值得注意的几个问题。

关 键 词　翻译教学；统计分析；回眸

作者联系地址　北京市海淀区学院路37号，北京航空航天大学外语学院
邮　　编　1000000
电子邮箱　junwen@vip.163.com

6

Author: WEN Jun & ZHANG Jinling

Title: A Review of the Study of Chinese Translation Teaching for 50 years (1951-2005)

Published in: *Shanghai Journal of Translators,* 2008 (2).

[Abstract]　This paper is based on the author's " *A Review of the Study of Chinese Translation Teaching for 50 years* (1951-2005)," a book devoted to the statistics and analysis of Chinese translation teaching for 50 years from 1951-2005. This paper classifies and analyzes the existing research results. Based on these statistical analysis, this paper presents several issues worth noting in such a research field.

Key words: translation teaching; statistical analysis; review

7

作　　者　杨晓荣
标　　题　翻译专业：正名过程及正名之后
发表刊物　《中国翻译》2008年第3期
［摘　要］　自2006年前后起，我国高校翻译专业的建立成了一个引人注目的事件。本文核查有关信息，梳理了翻译专业"正名"的过程及其教学体系形成的过程。据查，自1979年以专业名义开始招收硕士生，至2007

年应用型专业硕士学位建立，我国高教体制中的翻译专业初具规模，形成了从本科到硕博士研究生、从学术型到应用型、从学历教育到非学历教育的比较完整的教学体系。这是外部形势发展、内部学科建设加上行政支持共同作用的结果。翻译专业以体制为标记的名已初立，但还有一些问题需要进一步研究并有针对性地做出努力，方可真正实至名归：1）对翻译专业的疑虑：需要翻译专业在实践中做出回答，同时提供新的理论支撑；2）学位体制的改进：目前只是初步形成，每个层级的定位等还需要进一步研究验证；3）学科地位问题：翻译学的综合性跨学科特点事实上已经得到学界广泛承认，但由于自身理论建设还比较弱，加上多年形成的思维惯性，学术界对其独立地位仍有疑虑，需要翻译学界加强学科理论建设，在解决自己问题的同时，获取更高程度的认可；4）翻译教学基础理论研究：一是有些领域还没有涉及，二是原理探究还不够深，而只有解决了原理问题，才能减少翻译教学的主观随意性。

关 键 词 翻译专业；翻译学科；教学体制；教学研究

作者联系地址 江苏省南京市建邺区水西门大街 356-2-603

邮 编 210017

电子邮箱 yxrongcn@163.com

7

Author: YANG Xiaorong

Title: Translation as a Major: Being Specialized Institutionally

Published in: *Chinese Translators Journal,* 2008 (3).

[Abstract]　Since around 2006, the set-up of translation as a major in China's universities has become an eye-catching event. In fact, this is a part of the process of institutionalization of this major, marked by setting up academic degrees, innovating specialized departments/institutes and organizing nation-wide examinations for professional qualification certificate.

Such a process is gradual but clear, starting significantly from 1979 up to 2007, when the establishment of the whole system was roughly completed, covering all the higher education levels including degree-aimed courses for BA, MA, MTI, PHD and non-degree professional training. This is mainly a natural result of three factors: outwardly, the rising need for more qualified translators and interpreters; inwardly, the academic perseverance to build up translation studies as a relatively independent discipline in various dimensions; the support of policy-makers, which was also won through persistent efforts. Nevertheless, there are still problems to be taken seriously, including: 1) Remaining doubt over the necessity of separating translation from, say, English major, which is in essence a doubt over translation as a special competence other than language competence in general; 2) Similar doubt over translation studies as an independent discipline either theoretically or in public awareness; 3) Necessity for further improvement of the freshly established levels; 4) Necessity for further research on the fundamentals of teaching or training of translating and interpreting, which is still often conducted on the basis of personal experience only instead of theoretical and experimental support.

Key words: translation major; translation studies; education institutionalized; pedagogical studies

8

作　　者　任　文
标　　题　翻译教学的发展与 TOT 计划的实施
发表刊物　《中国翻译》2009 年第 2 期
［摘　要］近年来，本科翻译专业和翻译硕士专业学位在越来越多的高校获准设立。然而，由于不少老师欠缺口笔译实战经验和口笔译教学法培训，

在面临从教学翻译向翻译教学的转型时难免力不从心。鉴于此,本文拟探究:1. 从事应用型口笔译教学的老师可能面临哪些问题? 2. 这些问题可通过什么样的"培训者培训"计划得以解决?笔者通过文献研究以及担任翻译师资培训的经历发现,转型期老师的问题体现在理念和行为两方面,包括:1)尚未形成正确的教学观念,分不清教学翻译与翻译教学的区别;2)相关教学法知识较欠缺,教学管理能力较弱;3)教学方式不当,不能开展基于情境的技能培训;4)教学内容单一陈旧,不能很好利用现代信息技术和鲜活实用的教学素材;5)考核评估方式欠妥。

TOT 属成人教育模式,基于成人学习者拥有的能力、需要、动机和负责任的学习态度展开,目的是使学员在较短时间获得观念变革、知识更新和技能发展,从而掌握日后向他人提供培训的"工具箱"以及使用"工具"的能力。基于成人教育理论,理想的翻译教学 TOT 计划应由国内外在翻译教学领域卓有建树、口笔译实战经验丰富、对翻译教学研究颇有心得的专家团队来策划和实施,具体包括:1)培训需求分析;2)培训对象分析;3)培训目标、课程和步骤设计;4)前期准备;5)培训活动实施;6)培训效果评估。成功的 TOT 计划可使学员产生翻译教学观念、态度和行为的改变,获得相关知识和技能的增长,并能将习得的知识技能作为工具放进"工具箱",在日后的教学工作中"为我所用"。只有翻译教学队伍的整体素质提高了,翻译教育事业才能得到更好发展。

关 键 词 翻译教学;"培训者培训计划";成人学习

作者联系地址 重庆市沙坪坝区壮志路 33 号,四川大学外国语学院

电子邮箱 wenrensu@hotmail.com

8

Author: REN Wen

Title: Development of Professional Translation/Interpreting Education and Implementation of the TOT Project

Published in: *Chinese Translators Journal*, 2009 (2)

[Abstract] Recent years have seen more and more professional translation and interpreting programs set up at the undergraduate and graduate levels in Chinese universities. However, a considerable number of teachers shifted to these new programs lack either practical T/I experience or knowledge of T/I pedagogy, or both. This paper purports to address two questions: First, what are the difficulties and problems faced by these teachers when placed in the new programs? Second, how can these problems be resolved through a TOT (Training of Trainers) project designed specifically for them?

Literature study and the author's own experience of teaching at a TOT program indicated that these teachers often do not distinguish between translation in foreign language teaching and translation teaching for professional purposes nor conduct contextualized skill-oriented teaching. Based on the andragogical theories and adult learning principles proposed by Kroehner (1995) and Knowles (1980), a TOT project designed and implemented by a group of expert trainers who are experienced in T/I practice, professional translators/interpreters training, and T/I pedagogy research will be conducive to inducing conceptual, attitudinal and behavioural changes among these teachers.

Key words: professional T/I teaching; "TOT project"; adult learning

9

作　　者　张瑞娥
标　　题　翻译教学中的主体心理关注与多维导向教学模式构建
发表刊物　《外语界》2009年第2期
[摘　要] 以翻译行为理论为理论基础，结合社会心理学的图式理论，重视学生翻译行为发生时的环境与心理表现。文章以翻译主体为中心，关注

翻译教学中的主客体关系及主体间的社会性；以时间为纬度，对学生在翻译过程中各阶段的心理表现做了描写性研究。最后提出构建以翻译过程、环境、社会关系和能力等为导向的多维导向教学模式以及倡导心理关注的教学策略。

扭转以往翻译教学中只关注翻译客体而忽视主体、只关注翻译产品而忽视产品产生过程的做法，给予翻译主体和翻译过程以充分的重视和关注，在此基础上聚焦于学生在翻译过程中的心理表现，做到与翻译和翻译学习的交际性、社会性和过程性等特点相契合，从而全面系统地分析问题产生的原因，并能对症下药地解决问题。

本文的意义在于：1）在教学中充分关注过程可使我们既能从宏观上把握教学方向，又能从微观上把握教学细节，防止问题的发生或者明确问题发生的原因；2）对学生翻译过程中的心理进行关注能够帮助教师找到问题产生的根源，从而有的放矢地解决问题。3）多维导向教学模式的建构能够在很大程度上保障学生翻译能力的提高，确保教学目标的实现。

关　键　词　翻译行为；心理关注；多维导向；教学模式
作者联系地址　安徽省凤阳县东华路9号，安徽科技学院
邮　　　编　233100
电子邮箱　ruiezhang@163.com

9

Author: ZHANG Rui'e

Title: On Students' Psychology Care and the Construction of Multi-orientation Translation Teaching Model

Published in: *Foreign Language World*, 2009 (2).

[Abstract]　Based on the theory of translational action, this paper attaches importance to the translation context in which students do their translations. Centering on the translating subject, it pays close attention to the subject-object relation and the subject-subject interaction. And taking the translating stages as the latitudinal reference, it explores students' inner world in the translation process, and puts forward a multi-orientation teaching model and teaching strategies that enhance psychology care.

To change the custom of stressing the translational object and product but neglecting the subject and process in translation teaching, it attaches importance to the latter two, especially the students' inner world in the translation process so as to comply with the communicative, social and progressive attributes of translation and translation learning.

Key words: translational action; psychology care; multi-orientation; teaching model

10

作　　者　罗选民、刘　彬
标　　题　关于开放型语料库翻译教学的思考
发表刊物　《外语教学》2009 年第 6 期
[摘　要]　本文提出引入语料库，建立以学生为中心，数据驱动的开放型大学翻译教学模式。这一教学模式能更好地适应新教学大纲的要求，它的提出首先是基于对语料库可提供大量真实（双语）语料、可避免教师知识存贮不足等优势的分析，其次是基于对当前大学翻译教学中存在的诸多问题的反思，如以教师为中心，缺少高质量教材和师资，不重视对翻译文本语境的考察。这一新的教学模式的核心在于开放性，主要体现在四个方面：一是思想和理论的开放性，即专业化的翻译理论、不同类型的翻译现象、不同专业的语料与翻译实例等都可以开放地带入课堂，打破固化的观念和思维定式，敢于创新，勇于实践；二是教学平台的开放性，教师在利用语料库进行教学时，不局限于大型汉英平行语料库，也可借用 CAT 软件，利用好其中的翻译语料库、习语词库，并可以思考研

发软件的开放性共同升级路径，拓展翻译教学可利用的平台和资源；三是数据驱动学习的开放性，即在开放式的学习环境中，大学翻译学习者主动利用词语索引软件寻找并最终确定自己所需的语料，总结归纳相关的翻译规律，完成学习任务，整个学习过程都是以学生自主和开放探索为特征的；四是翻译文本评测机制的开放性，可借鉴机译软件的"匹配阈值"方法，评测体系将学生译文与答案自动匹配，从而给出较客观的评价。开放型语料库大学翻译教学可以为老师和学生提供许多的便利，它也给老师提出了更高的要求，充分发挥开放型语料库翻译教学的功用应得到鼓励。

关 键 词 大学翻译教学；语料库；开放式教学

作者联系地址 广东省广州市白云区白云大道北 2 号，广东外语外贸大学外语研究与语言服务协同创新中心

邮　　编 510420

电子邮箱 luoxm@tsinghua.edu.cn

10

Author: LUO Xuanmin, LIU Bin

Title: Open-style Corpus-driven Translation Teaching: Some Thoughts

Published in: *Foreign Language Teaching*, 2009 (6).

[Abstract] This paper proposes to use corpus in establishing student-centered, data-driven, open-style translation teaching, which can better fulfill the requirements of the new national curriculum guidelines. Our proposal of this teaching model is based firstly on considerations of the advantages corpus-driven teaching has in terms of authentic material and infinite memory capacity, and secondly on observation of current problems in teacher-centered college translation teaching. The most salient feature of this new model of teaching is its openness, manifesting in the following four respects: First, being open to different theories and ways of thinking, that is, to bring in varying translation theories, translation phenomena and translation materials to the classroom, and to encourage innovations and new forms of practices to replace traditional ideas and modes of thinking. Second, being open in the use of teaching platform, which means that the teacher can use many teaching platforms apart from big Chinese-English parallel corpus, for example, the translation corpus in CAT software. He or she is also encouraged to seek for ways to allow its users to add new data or corpus in and thereby collaboratively update the CAT software. Third, being open in data-driven learning. Learners look for needed data in corpus, and from there they acquire the techniques and laws of translation. The whole learning process is autonomous and open. Fourth, being open in translation assessment. It is suggested the "matching threshold" in machine translation be borrow to build up a system of automatic translation assessment. Students can submit their translations to it and get objective quality assessment at any time. Open-style corpus-driven translation teaching is useful, yet has higher demands to the teacher. We should promote its full uses in translation teaching.

Key words: college translation teaching; corpus; open-style teaching

11

作　　者　　陈善伟
标　　题　　教授翻译科技的新课程：以教授翻译项目科目作为个案研究
发表刊物　　《翻译学报》2010 年 13 卷第 1—2 期
［摘　要］本篇论文检视香港中文大学翻译科技引进新教学课程的过程，以翻译项目科目作为个案研究以显示课程改革所带来的正面效果。翻译科技的训练可以各种不同形式进行，其中以学院教学最为正式与全面。论文上半部交代 2002 年至 2008 年管理电脑辅助翻译硕士课程的经验，下半部

介绍实际教授翻译项目科目的情况,包括项目所使用的系统及学生所选用的文本。

关 键 词 翻译科技教学;翻译项目科目

作者联系地址 广东省深圳市龙岗区龙翔大道2001号,香港中文大学人文社科学院

电子邮箱 chansinwai@cuhk.edu.cn

11

Author: CHAN Sin-wai

Title: A New Curriculum for the Teaching of Translation Technology: The Teaching of a Translation Project Course as a Case Study

Published in: *Journal of Translation Studies*, 2010 (Vol.13 No.1-2).

[Abstract] This paper looks at the process whereby a new curriculum for the teaching of translation technology was introduced at The Chinese University of Hong Kong, using the translation project course as a case study to reveal the good results of such a change. Training of transaltion technology is offered in various forms, with the academic environment as the most formal and comprehensive. The first part of this paper gives an account of the experience of running the Master of Arts in Computer-aided Translation programme from 2002 to 2008, while the second part of this paper describes the experience of actually teaching the translation project course, including the system used for the project and the texts the students used in the course.

Key words: the teaching of translation technology; translation project course

12

作　　者　潘鸣威
标　　题　基于语料库学习者汉英翻译省译策略的研究
发表刊物　《外语研究》2010 年第 5 期
[摘　要]　省译策略是汉英翻译中的一种重要技巧，其目的是为了使译文简洁，符合目标语的表达习惯和修辞特点。现行的许多翻译研究和教材对这种技巧的运用和研究众多。这些研究采取的视角有所不同，有冗余信息理论的角度，有英汉语言对比角度，有文化研究的角度，亦有译文体裁特征的角度。然而，对于省译技巧在学习者翻译中的具体使用情况却鲜有大量的观察和研究。

本文以中国英语专业学习者语料库（Corpus for English Majors）中的翻译子库作为研究对象，从定量和定性两个角度考察了学生对汉英翻译中冗余信息的处理，细致分析了学习者运用省译策略的情况。研究主要得到了三个方面的发现。第一，学生在对冗余信息的处理上，总体使用省译策略不多，往往依靠逐字逐句的翻译在译文中还原原文。其中的原因可能与冗余部分的信息量、显性度等原文的因素，也可能与考试环境下的焦虑等多重因素有关。第二，学生在不同种类冗余信息处理上，对修辞修饰以及隐性重复冗余的处理上困难最大，极少使用省译的策略。这可能与汉英两种语言本身的差异有关，使得学生在语言转换过程中未有这方面的意识。第三，从学生译文的具体表现来看，省译策略的运用与其整体译文的表现存在一定的相关，但是不同水平组之间的差异并不明显。

最后，在本研究结论的基础上，本文就汉英翻译的测试提出了一些思考。特别是对于汉英测试的评分量表而言，英语专业八级汉英测试的评分在描述语上还相对笼统，操作性有待加强。

关 键 词　省译；冗余；汉英翻译；学习者语料库
作者联系地址　广东省广州市白云区白云大道北 2 号，广东外语外贸大学英文学院
电子邮箱　mwpan@oamail.gdufs.edu.cn

12

Author: PAN Mingwei

Title: A Corpus-based Study on the Omission Strategy in EFL Learners' Chinese-English Translation

Published in: *Foreign Language Research*, 2010 (5).

[Abstract] As an important strategy in Chinese-English (C-E) translation, omission achieves brevity, idiomaticity and rhetoric features of the target language. Although there is an extant literature contributing to the employment of this strategy, the perspectives vary, ranging from redundant information processing, C-E contrastive studies, culture studies, to genre theory. However, how omission is employed in EFL learners' translation seems scant.

Gearing the sub-corpus of Corpus for English Majors as the research target, this paper quantitatively and qualitatively probes into how learners deal with the redundancy in C-E translation. The main findings can be unfolded in three aspects. First, learners generally do not employ omission, where word-by-word translation prevails instead. This could be partly attributable to the information load and its visibility in the source texts, and partly to learners' anxiety in assessment settings. Second, learners are most obstructed with redundant information with rhetorical device(s) and implicitness. This may be caused by the discrepancies between the two languages, which might downplay learners' awareness in code-switching. Third, it is found that language proficiency somehow correlates with the employment of omission, yet the inter-group differences seem rather subtle.

In the end, based on the research findings, this paper yields some thoughts on Chinese-English translation. Particularly, the descriptors for Chinese-English translation scoring criteria seem too holistic, with more efforts to be made on their practicality.

Key words: omission; redundancy; C-E translation; learner corpus

13

作　　者　王树槐、王卫平
标　　题　发展性翻译教学评价模式
发表刊物　《解放军外国语学院学报》2010 年第 5 期

[摘　要]　翻译教学评价以一定的教学目标为导向，对学生的翻译结果以及行为和心理过程做出价值判断，并不断完善、改进翻译教学。我们提出的"发展性翻译教学评价模式"，包括结果评价和过程评价。在结果领域教学中，教学和评价的重心分为三个阶段。第一阶段是语言结构对比与转化评价；第二阶段是语篇生产评价；第三阶段是翻译功能实现评价与美学表现评价。每一阶段我们都陈述了评价范畴与阶段目标、错误分析。过程领域的评价依序分为三个阶段：翻译策略评价、翻译人格评价、翻译学习风格评价。其中，第一阶段评价的是表层的、与文本相关的心理策略因素有关，第二阶段评价的是中层的、与"知、情、意"相关的人格特征因素有关，第三阶段评价的是深层的、与"认知与价值"相关的创造性因素有关，这是一个不断深入的过程。每一阶段我们也都陈述了评价范畴和评价要点。

"发展性翻译教学评价模式"的心理学基础兼涉了教育领域的三大心理学流派：行为主义、认知主义、人本主义。它强调以目标调控教学过程，重视反馈、掌握和达标，注重翻译习惯的养成（行为主义），要求了解并利用学生的最近发展区超越现有发展水平，主张学生掌握翻译心理过程中的加工策略（认知主义），同时强调培养良好翻译人格和真诚的人际关系，对学生潜能持乐观信念，对学生个体差异特征作出甄别、导引（人本主义）。"发展性翻译教学评价模式"的实质有二：1）强调阶段性的循序发展；2）以评价带动教学，使学生在认知、行为、人格上得到和谐发展。

关　键　词　发展性翻译教学评价模式；结果评价；过程评价

作者联系地址　湖北省武汉市洪山区珞瑜路 1037 号，华中科技大学外国语学院

电子邮箱　wangshh@hust.edu.cn

13

Author: WANG Shuhuai & WANG Weiping
Title: Translation Teaching Assessment: A Developmental Model
Published in: *Journal of PLA Foreign Studies University*, 2010 (5).

[Abstract]　Translation teaching assessment plays an important role as the goal-orientor, controller and manager of the teaching system. In this paper, the co-authors put up "the developmental model of translation teaching assessment". It consists of two aspects: product assessment and process assessment. The product assessment comprises "language structure contrast and conversion assessment", "text producing assessment" and "translation function realization assessment and aesthetic reproduction assessment", in every stage the elements of assessment and error analysis are described. The process assessment comprises "translation strategies assessment", "translation personality assessment" and "translation leaning style assessment", in every stage the elements of assessment are described.

The psychological basis of the developmental model of translation teaching assessment involves behaviorism, cognitivism, and humanism. The aim of the model is to guide and further translation teaching through the top-down teaching approach, and to promote the progressive and harmonious developments in terms of students' cognition, behavior and personality.

Key words: the developmental model of translation teaching assessment; product assessment; process assessment

14

作　　者	文　军、殷　玲
标　　题	翻译过程中翻译策略的实证性研究——基于英语专业大学生的有声思维调查
发表刊物	《解放军外国语学院学报》2010年第4期

[摘　要] 本文运用有声思维法，选取二十名母语为汉语的英语专业三年级学生为研究对象，研究他们在翻译过程中对于翻译策略的运用情况。研究发现包括：受试者在英译汉过程中使用最多的两种策略为"监控目标语文本的准确性"和"自我修改"；而在汉译英过程中使用最多的五种策略是："接受内在的解决办法""发现问题""汉英词典查询""直觉判断"和"释义源语文本"。翻译策略使用的多少与受试者对源语和目的语的掌握程度及在翻译培训中获得的翻译经验有关。

关 键 词　翻译过程；翻译策略；有声思维

作者联系地址　北京市海淀区学院路37号，北京航空航天大学外语学院

邮　　编　1000000

电子邮箱　junwen@vip.163.com

14

Author: WEN Jun & YIN Lin

Title: Translation Strategies of Chinese English Majors: An Investigation Based on Think Aloud Protocols

Published in: *Journal of PLA University of Foreign Languages*, 2010 (4).

[Abstract]　This study is concerned with the translation strategies employed by twenty Chinese subjects when they fulfill both E-C and C-E translation tasks. A think aloud method was used to elicit the subjects' self-report of their translating processes. Sixteen protocols proved to be reliable and valid for analysis. The TAPs data were then coded according to the set principles. Combined with questionnaires, the data were analyzed both qualitatively and quantitatively, with focus on the frequency and distribution of translation strategies exhibited in the translating process.

Key words: translation process; translation strategies; think aloud method

15

作　　者　　肖维青
标　　题　　学术性·职业性·趣味性——"影视翻译"课程教学探索
发表刊物　　《外语教学理论与实践》2010年第3期

[摘　要]　本文是上海外国语大学英语学院翻译专业开设"影视翻译"课程的教学思考和经验总结。课程面向本科二年级下学期的翻译专业学生开设，从理论讲解到实际操练，主要由几个板块构成：影视翻译研究概览、配音翻译、字幕翻译、戏剧翻译等，其中配音和字幕翻译是教学重点。

影视翻译为广义的文学翻译的一部分，故与一般文学翻译有共通之处，但是影视翻译在很多方面它又与传统的纯文学（小说、散文、戏剧、诗歌）翻译不同，具有很大的特殊性。影视翻译所面对的并非是单一的文字文本，而是由图像、画面、声音、色彩等特殊的表意符号所融合而成的多重符号文本，受到传播中空间和时间的制约，影视语言具有听觉性、视觉性、瞬时性、大众性和无注性的特点，因而对影视翻译就有了特殊的要求。这是"影视翻译"课程要向学生传递的一个最基本的信息。

今天翻译行业正在实现从传统的、手工作坊式的翻译流程和运作模式到现代化、信息化、商业化的翻译流程和运作模式的转变，因此，我们在教学理念上应该做出相应的调整和更新，在传统学术性的基础上，更注重职业性，兼顾趣味性。不仅教学内容要不断更新，而且翻译辅助技术也要与时俱进。作者认为，上好专业性较强的翻译选修课必须在教学理念、资源利用以及师资培养等方面转变观念：突出学生的主体角色，充分利用网络资源，加强与市场的联系，加快与国内外高校的交流。以师资培养为例，以下几个路径都可以改善影视翻译教学师资短缺的现状：加强校内院系合作、寻求业界支援、加快港澳台合作以及充分利用海外高校的教学资源。在翻译教学改革方面，"引进来，走出去"战略对于加快国际融合度、优化资源配置具有重要意义。

关　键　词　影视翻译；翻译教学；学术性；职业性

作者联系地址　上海市松江区文翔路 1550 号，上海外国语大学英语学院翻译系

电子邮箱　wqxiao@shisu.edu.cn

15

Author: XIAO Weiqing

Title: Pedagogical Reflections on the Design of a Course in Audiovisual Translation

Published in: *Foreign Language Learning Theory and Practice*, 2010 (3).

[Abstract]　The study and teaching of screen translation is still a relatively uncommon academic pursuit, but interest is growing rapidly. This paper reflects on the teaching of a course in Audiovisual Translation (AVT) at Shanghai International Studies University for the past two years. Integrating theory and practice, this course has as its teaching modules a historical review of audiovisual translation, principles for dubbing and subtitling, theatrical translation, AVT workshop and so on. By sharing the design of the course with colleagues in the field, the author points out that working practices in audiovisual translation are experiencing fundamental changes. In the case of subtitling, technology plays a crucial role and this has been particularly so since the launch of software equipment designed exclusively for the production of subtitles. With this change in mind, universities must play an essential role in training these new professionals. For example, students must be able to work in groups and under pressure, with very stringent deadlines; they must be familiar with software packages and the internet and they must have an insight into the inner workings of the professional world, not only view it from inside the academic cocoon. To this end, universities need more resources and must show more initiative in curricular development and research carried out in the field.

Key words: audiovisual translation; translation teaching; academic nature; professionalism

语料库、翻译技术与机器（辅助）翻译

1. 基于本体的专业机器翻译术语词典研究　黄河燕、张克亮、张孝飞
2. 机器翻译相关之对比研究：学生翻译过程之模块化　史宗玲
3. 英汉翻译中人称代词主语的显化——基于语料库的考察　黄立波
4. 口译的神经心理语言学研究——连续传译"过程"模式的构建　刘绍龙、仲伟合
5. 机器翻译之生产及消费——由解构主义观点论析　史宗玲
6. 对翻译小说语法标记显化的语料库研究　胡显耀、曾佳
7. 《红楼梦》叙事标记语及其英译——基于语料库的对比分析　刘泽权、田璐
8. N元组和翻译单位对英译汉自动评分作用的比较研究　江进林、文秋芳
9. 基于语料库的译者风格与翻译策略研究——以《红楼梦》中报道动词及英译为例　刘泽权、闫继苗
10. 系统功能语言学翻译质量评估模式的实证与反思　吕桂
11. 英译汉翻译语言的结构容量：基于多译本语料库的研究　秦洪武
12. 国内外机器自动评分系统评述——兼论对中国学生翻译自动评分系统的启示　王金铨、文秋芳

Corpus, Translation Technology and Machine (Aided) Translation

1. A Study on Ontology-based Technical Lexicons for Specialty Machine Translation   HUANG Heyan, ZHANG Keliang & ZHANG Xiaofei
2. Mapping Out Students' Translation Process: An MT-specific Comparative Study   SHIH Chungling
3. Explicitation of Personal Pronoun Subjects in English-Chinese Translation—A Corpus-based Investigation   HUANG Libo
4. Researching the Process Model of Consecutive Interpreting   LIU Shaolong & ZHONG Weihe
5. The Production and Consumption of Machine Translation: A Deconstructionist Perspective   SHIH Chungling
6. A Corpus-based Study of the Explicitation of Grammatical Markers in Chinese Translated Fiction   HU Xianyao & ZENG Jia
7. Narrative Markers in *Hong Lou Meng* and Their Translations—A Corpus-based Study   LIU Zequan & TIAN Lu
8. A Comparative Study of Ngram and Translation Unit Alignment in Automated Scoring of Students' English-Chinese Translation   JIANG Jinlin & WEN Qiufang
9. Translator Choice and Translator Style: A Corpus-based Study of the English Translations of Reporting Verbs in *Hong Lou Meng*   LIU Zequan, YAN Jimiao
10. Revisiting the Translation Quality Assessment Model Based on Systemic-

    Functional Linguistics: A Case Study   **LV Gui**
11. Load Capacity of Constructions in Translational Chinese: A Multi-version Corpus-based Study   **QIN Hongwu**
12. Review and Implications of Existing Automated Scoring Systems—From the Perspective of the Computer-assisted Scoring Model of the Chinese EFL Learners' Translation   **WANG Jinquan & WEN Qiufang**

1

作　　者　黄河燕、张克亮、张孝飞
标　　题　基于本体的专业机器翻译术语词典研究
发表刊物　《中文信息学报》2007年第1期
[摘　要]　在专业机器翻译（MT）系统的设计和实现中，要解决的一个关键问题是如何有效地组织面向不同专业领域的专业术语，以及如何根据当前所处理的文本选择相应的术语定义。本文首先分析现有专业机器翻译系统在术语词典组织和建设方面存在的主要问题，以及基于本体（Ontology）的领域知识概念体系的特点；其次，探讨面向专业机器翻译的术语词典研究的几个重要方面，包括通用领域本体的设计、专业术语的描述和向本体的映射、双语或多语 MT 专业词库的组织和应用等；最后，介绍我们初步已完成的工作，主要包括机器翻译专业领域分类系统设计、专业词典向专业分类系统的映射、国际标准分类系统（ICS）标准向专业领域分类系统的映射等。映射实验结果表明，专业领域分类系统对于机器翻译专业词典具有良好的覆盖性。有关本体的理论研究还很不成熟，应用研究则处于起步阶段。建立一个符合机器翻译系统需求的完整本体的工作量是极为庞大的，本文尝试建立一个面向机器翻译术语学研究的任务本体，希望这一新方法能够提高机器翻译系统的语义处理能力，解决在特定领域机器翻译系统研发中遇到的一些实际问题。
关 键 词　人工智能；机器翻译；本体；术语词典
作者联系地址　黄河燕：北京市海淀区中关村南大街 5 号院，北京理工大学计算机学院
邮　　编　100081
电子邮箱　hhy63@bit.edu.cn

1

Author: HUANG Heyan, ZHANG Keliang & ZHANG Xiaofei

Title: A Study on Ontology-based Technical Lexicons for Specialty Machine Translation

Published in: *Journal of Chinese Information Processing*, 2007 (1).

[Abstract] In machine translation systems, the organization and selection of domain-specific technical terms is crucial. This paper begins with an analysis of some problems ubiquitous in technical lexicons for specialty MT systems and a brief introduction to the features of ontology-based domain-specific conceptual systems. Some important aspects of specialty MT-oriented technical lexicons are then studied, including the design of general-purpose specialty ontology, the description of technical terms and their mapping to specialty ontology, the organization and application of bilingual or multilingual MT domain-specific lexicons. Last, the paper presents some of the experimental work, covering the design of a draft MT-oriented specialty classification system, the mapping from technical lexicons to specialty classification system, and the mapping from ICS (International Classification System) to the MT specialty classification system. The results of the mapping experiments prove that the classification system conducted by the paper has a desirable coverage over MT technical lexicons.

Key words: artificial intelligence; specialty machine translation; ontology; technical lexicon

2

作　　者　史宗玲
标　　题　机器翻译相关之对比研究：学生翻译过程之模块化
发表刊物　《翻译学研究集刊》2007 年第 10 期
［摘　要］　人们将翻译视为问题解决的活动，而后机器翻译编辑乃是找出机器译文错误，然后修正这些错误，故我们可将后机译编辑视为一种翻译活动。然而，后机译编辑者可参考机器译文大意，而人工译者则无此优势，此两种不同的翻译方式会间接地影响到翻译过程，导致不同的翻译表现。鉴于此，我们决定执行一项机译相关之研究，以比较学生使用与无使用机器翻译的过程，并了解人工辅助机译（man-aided machine translation）与全人工翻译（pure human translation）之差异。我们提出一些议题作为调查指标，包括：后机译学生编辑者是否比学生译者使用较小的翻译单位（translation unit）、是否花费更少时间完成工作、是否有较少的翻译错误、是否他们使用不同的翻译策略及何者更具信心。我们采用统计调查（statistical survey）及非正式访谈方法（informal interview），来调查学生的翻译错误、翻译单位及翻译时间。

结果发现因为后机译编辑学生偏用逐字翻译策略，非以句子或语群为翻译单位，故后机译学生编辑者使用的翻译单位比学生译者较小，造成较不通顺的翻译风格。此外，因为前者参考机器译文大意及特制的专业翻译字典，所以其翻译错误率及花费时间比后者稍低些。统计结果发现前者平均有 0.4 个漏译、1.4 个语义错误、0.1 个语法错误、0.9 个语用错误，但后者分别是 1 个漏译、1.9 个语译错误、0.3 个语法错误、1.2 个语用错误；另前者全文翻译平均花费 37.1 分，而后者花费 38.9 分。除了统计测量外，从非正式访谈中我们得知学生使用机译工具比不使用时，其心情更为安稳及自信，此显示机器翻译工具对于学生在心理层面所造成之正面影响（positive affective contribution）。虽然本研究之设计并非很周全，但其调查结果已显示学生使用及不使用机译工具之翻译过程各有其优、缺点，故于过程导向翻译研究中，该实证研究模块可作为放声思考方法 (think-aloud protocol) 的另一个替代方案。

关 键 词　机器翻译相关之对比研究；翻译过程；翻译错误；翻译单位；翻译时间

作者联系地址　台湾高雄市燕巢区大学路 1 号，国立高雄科技大学应英系暨口笔译硕士班

电子邮箱　clshih@nkfust.edu.tw

2

Author: SHIH Chungling

Title: Mapping Out Students' Translation Process: An MT-specific Comparative Study

Published in: *Studies of Translation and Interpretation,* 2007 (10).

[Abstract]　Translation has been viewed as a problem-solving activity, so post-machine-translation (post-MT) editing, which attempts to identify translation errors and then to solve them, can be defined as an alternative way of translation. Nevertheless, post-MT editing has gist translation for reference while human translation (HT) has nothing at hand for consultation. These different situations affect the translation process, so we administered an MT-specific comparative project to compare two tests with and without MT use. Research questions to guide investigation include whether post-MT student editors use smaller translation units, spend less time and have fewer translation errors than student translators, whether both groups use different translation strategies and which group has more confidence. A statistical survey and an informal interview were conducted to investigate students' translation errors, translation units and time. The findings show that the translation unit tends to be smaller in the translation with the MT use than without the MT use because students translate word-by-word rather than sentence-by-sentence or group- by-group in post-MT editing. Time takes less in the translation with the MT use than without the MT use because students can consult MT-produced translations of specialized terms. Students produce fewer semantic errors with the MT use because they interpret the text based on the gist translation. Students also produce fewer pragmatic errors with the MT use than without the MT use because the MT system, after being tailored to the specialized dictionary, provides a register-specific translation for student reference. The results of informal interview suggest that students feel more comfortable and more confident in the translation with the MT use than without the MT use. Despite the inadequate experimental design, this empirical research has revealed the strength and weakness of students' translation process with and without the help of the MT system, so it can be treated as an alternative approach to the typical think-aloud protocols (TAP) methods that are often used in the process-oriented translation studies.

Key words: post-MT editing; translation errors; translation units; time; the translation process

3

作　　者　黄立波
标　　题　英汉翻译中人称代词主语的显化——基于语料库的考察
发表刊物　《外语教学与研究》2008年第6期
［摘　要］人称代词"隐去"是汉语的一个特点，汉英、英汉翻译中一个比较突出的表现就是主语的显化和隐化现象。由于在构句层面汉、英两种语言对人称代词的依赖程度不同，汉英、英汉翻译中的人称代词转换也表现出一定特点。本文借助双语平行语料库，对人称代词主语在汉英和英汉两个翻译方向、文学和非文学两种文体类型中数量、频次和转换类型三方面考察发现：1) 从数量上，汉译英时，文学与非文学文本均呈现人称代

词主语数量和频次增加；英译汉时，文学与非文学文本中人称代词主语数量和频次均减少，初步表明英语对人称代词主语的依赖程度要高于汉语，这一点还需类比语料加以确认；2）从转换类型看，汉英翻译中均呈现人称代词主语语际显化的趋势，语际隐化不突出；英汉翻译中人称代词主语以对应关系为主，语际显化和语际隐化均不大明显；3）就类比显化看，英汉翻译中，汉语翻译文本人称代词主语的频次要比汉语非翻译文本频次高，即表现出类比显化的趋势；而汉英翻译中，英语翻译文本人称代词主语比英语非翻译文本中频次低，即类比显化不明显。作者指出，英汉翻译中，人称代词主语语际以对应关系为主，抛开译者语言能力因素，表现出英语作为强势语言在译语文本中的迁移，造成译语中的冗余现象；与原创汉语文本相比，汉语翻译文本表现出类比显化的趋势。倘若将对人称代词的依赖程度作为语言形式化程度的一个参数，那么由形式化程度高的语言向形式化程度低的语言翻译时，类比显化突出，即翻译文本在形式上比译语中的非翻译文本显性程度高；从文体类型上，文学与非文学文本翻译中的类比显化表现均比较突出。研究结果进一步说明语言形式化程度是影响翻译转换中形式方面显化与否的重要因素。

关　键　词　人称代词主语；语际显化；语际隐化；类比显化

作者联系地址　陕西省西安市长安区文苑南路1号，西安外国语大学英文学院

电子邮箱　huanglibo@xisu.edu.cn

3

Author: HUANG Libo

Title: Explicitation of Personal Pronoun Subjects in English-Chinese Translation
　　　　— A Corpus-based Investigation

Published in: *Foreign Language Teaching and Research*, 2008 (6).

[Abstract]　The sentence structuring in English relies more heavily on the use of pronouns compared with its counterpart in Chinese. The transfer of pronoun in both directions between Chinese and English demonstrate some regularity. With the help of parallel corpora, this paper investigates the rendering of personal pronoun subjects in literary and non-literary E-C translation in terms of absolute number, frequency and transferring types. The study shows:1) Both the absolute number and the frequency of personal pronoun subjects in literary and non-literary E-C translation are reduced; 2) In terms of transferring types, there are more correspondences between English and Chinese; 3) Compared with non-translated Chinese texts, translated Chinese texts tend to contain more personal pronoun subjects. The results indicate that interlingual correspondence is the main type of personal pronoun subject transferring from English into Chinese. With no regard for the translators' linguistic competence, the English source language interference takes place in the transfer owing to English's dominance as a lingua franca and it leads to the wordiness in the target texts. Compared with non-translated Chinese, translated Chinese is characterized by remarkable comparable explicitation. If the reliance on pronouns is taken as one of the parameters of degree of formalization in language, explicitation is more remarkable when the transference is from the more formalized language to the less formalized one. In other words, the translated language is more explicit compared with the non-translated language with the same language.

Key words: personal pronoun subject; interlingual explicitation; interlingual implication; comparable explicitation

4

作　　者　刘绍龙、仲伟合
标　　题　口译的神经心理语言学研究——连续传译"过程"模式的构建
发表刊物　《外国语（上海外国语大学学报）》2008年第4期

[摘 要] 国内外关于连续传译的研究可以被归纳为以下几种类型：连续传译分项技能研究、连续传译本质研究和连续传译教学研究。但从研究视角和研究内容来看，学者们似乎更加关注对翻译产品或译品的描写和探讨。作为一项理论构模研究，本文聚焦会议传译中的连续传译，并通过借鉴神经语言学、心理语言学的相关理论和研究成果探索连续传译的神经心理语言学模型。

连续传译作为一个特殊的元交际过程有着其特殊的神经心理机制、运作环节和信息加工内容。连续传译的内在过程可分解为言语理解机制、记忆系统、中介系统和言语生成机制等四个环节。连续传译的神经心理语言学模型的第一部分——言语理解机制是由语音感知、词汇识别、句法分析、意义分析和语用推导等构成。记忆系统构成了连续传译神经心理模型的核心，是连接源语输入和译语输出并使两者得以生效的信息加工场或中心环节，它由长时记忆和工作记忆两部分组成。模型第三部分由言语理解和言语生成的"中介系统"组成，其主要环节是概念表征，它具有相对的独立性和抽象性，是一个抽象、普遍的概念和关系集。模型的最后一个部分是"言语生成"机制，其主要环节有语义初迹、句法合成、词汇合成、内部言语及语音生成。

该模型的突出特点体现在五个方面：1. 记忆系统的中心地位、纽带作用和两种记忆的合理分工；2. 输入、输出过程的环节性、回溯性、实虚/强弱分明性；3. 中介环节的突显性和连接性；4. 模型图式的直观性和简明性；5. 信息流程的连续性和动态性。

关 键 词 连续传译；理解/生成机制；概念表征；神经心理语言学模式

作者联系地址 （1）刘绍龙：浙江省杭州市留和路288号，浙江工业大学外国语学院英语系

（2）仲伟合：广东省广州市白云区白云大道北2号，广东外语外贸大学高级翻译学院

邮 编 310023; 510420

电子邮箱 huanglibo@xisu.edu.cn

4

Authors: LIU Shaolong & ZHONG Weihe
Title: Researching the Process Model of Consecutive Interpreting
Published in: *Journal of Foreign Languages,* 2008 (4).

[Abstract]   The present paper is much indebted to the achievements of neuro-linguistic and psycholinguistic research, on the basis of which the authors have designed a tentative "process model" of consecutive interpreting (CI). The process model distinguishes itself in its suggested component parts comprising the model, and five unique features characterizing the cognitive process of consecutive interpreting.

Firstly, the authors aim at making general claims involving the necessary component parts of the model and cognitive process in CI: 1) Consecutive interpreting as a form of meta-communication enjoys special neuro-psychological mechanisms, operating stages and information processing content; 2) Its internal process is made up of speech comprehension mechanism, memory system, intermediary system (esp., featured by semantic representation) and speech production mechanism. Then the authors go ahead to make individual analyses of the neuro-psycholinguistic model of consecutive interpreting in terms of the above four component parts: 1) Speech comprehension mechanism is composed of phonetic perception, lexical identification, syntactic analysis, meaning analysis and pragmatic inference, etc.; 2) Memory system (made of long-term and short-term memories) becomes core of the neuro-psycholinguistic model of CI, connecting source language input and target language output, and making both work effectively; 3) The intermediary system as featured by semantic representation appears to be relatively independent and abstract, forming a general concept-and-relation set; 4) Speech production mechanism is characterized by such five stages as semantic trace, syntactic synthesis, lexical synthesis, internal speech and articulation.

Finally, the authors have summarized five unique features characterizing the CI process model: 1) non-linearity of interpreting process, 2) highlighted memory system, 3) intermediary deverbalization by sematic representation, 4) dynamic information processing, and 5) brevity of schematized illustration. These unique features as well as the seventeen specific concepts contained in them differentiate the model from the ones of its kinds as more CI oriented and related.

Key words: consecutive interpreting; comprehension/production mechanism; deverbalized (semantic) representation; neuro-psycholinguistic model

5

作　　者　史宗玲
标　　题　机器翻译之生产及消费——由解构主义观点论析
发表刊物　《编译论丛》2008 年第 1 期

［摘　要］　在人类历史中，解构主义的语言革命及机器翻译的翻译革命，扮演着颠覆传统的角色。解构主义企图推翻西方真理和形而上理论，而机器翻译系统则努力为人类找寻另类的翻译模式，试图取代人工译者，并提升翻译产业的效率与产能。此两项革命分别从语言及翻译的传统包袱解放而出，寻求差异及多元的价值，故本文试图从解构主义"去中心论"及"差异之操弄"之观点来探讨机器翻译生产及消费过程，同时针对其正反面解构现象，提出个人评论。本文采用质化分析方法来探究一些机器翻译相关议题，包括机译的主体性、机译的编修过程、机器译文生产过程、机器翻译应用之内涵及机器翻译生产与消费之间的关系。首先，作者引用解构主义"作者之主体性消解"的概念来讨论"机器译者之权威性泯灭"的类比

现象,此意味着 MT 系统之译者只是语言转换之中介者,并不呈现任何个人风格,或仅能呈现一种机械化风格。此外,由于机器译文经过不同使用/消费者解读、加工及改制后,就如同解构主义形容文本经由不同读者诠释后,其形式及意义将产生更迭或"延异"(différance)之现象。再者,机器译文之生产可透过借用已库存译文及其他使用者/译者补充译文之过程,突显其翻译之"互文本性"及开放结束之现象,也呼应了解构主义之"书写文本"概念,并打破作品之独立完整性。谈及机器翻译之正反面效益时,作者由机器翻译系统置放于网络上供大众免费使用之现象,以揭橥其自主参与、差异追求及多元开放之正面解构观;另一方面因为机器翻译之诞生衍生了前机器翻译编辑之控制性语言及后机器翻译编辑之翻译腔语言、大众科技迷思及翻译著作版权等议题,为我们带来语言混乱、角色错置及责任归属等负面之解构观。至此,试问机器翻译是近代翻译史上的福音(boon)或诅咒(doom)?恐怕在浮动开放的解构空间里,只能找到暂时回避及暂时休止的"分号"(;),但同时却也留下更多延异及令人质疑的"问号"(?)。

关 键 词 机器翻译;解构主义;非主体性;延异;互文本性;正反面影响

作者联系地址 台湾高雄市燕巢区大学路 1 号,国立高雄科技大学应英系暨口笔译硕士班

电子邮箱 clshih@nkfust.edu.tw

5

Author: SHIH Chungling

Title: The Production and Consumption of Machine Translation: A Deconstructionist Perspective

Published in: *Compilation and Translation Review*, 2008 (1)

[Abstract] This paper probes and identifies the deconstructionist features of machine translation (MT) because deconstructionism and machine translation share a reformative role in seeking a breakthrough from the traditional concepts of language and translation in human history. A qualitative analysis method was adopted to discuss some MT issues, including the subjectivity of MT, the process of editing MT outputs, the production of MT outputs, the implications of MT use and the relationship between the production and consumption of MT. The discussions show that the MT system has no authority like the author has no subjectivity in the process of writing from the deconstructionist perspective. In addition, the MT system creates multiple versions of the end product through user/consumer appropriation, revision and editing. The behavior of the transformation of the original MT text concurs with Derrida's concept of différance, suggesting the generation of multiple textual meanings as the result of different readers' interpretations. MT's retrieval of data from existing translated texts and supplementary user-edited texts reflects the feature of inter-texuality, breaking from the traditional concept of unique, complete text and translation. Meanwhile, the positive and negative impacts of MT use are explored. In the positive sense, the free online MT systems are open to diverse users/consumers for different purposes, revealing the spirit of diversity and democracy. Nevertheless, MT use initiates the production of new languages such as controlled language (pre-MT editing) and post-MT edited language. The long-term use of these languages could make it difficult to distinguish between natural/formal and artificial/informal languages. Also on the negative side, some MT users mistakenly identify MT as a potential substitute for human translators and MT use involves certain copyright problems. Whether MT is boon or doom remains a riddle with no definite answer, but we need to face the reality that MT is already there and can't be easily banished from our daily life in the foreseeable future.

Key words: machine translation; deconstructionism; de-subjectivity; différance; inter-textuality; positive/negative impacts

6

作　　者	胡显耀、曾　佳
标　　题	对翻译小说语法标记显化的语料库研究
发表刊物	《外语研究》2009 年第 5 期

[摘　要]　本文是一项基于语料库对当代汉语翻译小说中语法标记词的实证研究。本研究发现：一、当代汉语翻译小说中各类语法标记词的使用频率明显高于非翻译小说；二、翻译小说中定语标记明显增多，而时体标记减少；三、一些语法标记词的增减在客观上起到了口语化或简化的效果。我们认为，语法标记显化是汉语翻译小说的重要特征之一。与原创小说相比，汉语翻译小说的语法明确程度显著提高，该特征一方面可能旨在通过明确语法关系增强译本的可接受性，但另一方面却使汉语译文在一定程度上偏离了现代汉语的倾向于较少使用语法标记的总体规范，呈现出句法形式的陌生化或异化倾向。本研究所揭示的汉语翻译小说中语法标记显化现象对汉语文学翻译规范和翻译共性研究具有重要的价值。

关 键 词　汉语翻译小说；语料库；语法标记；显化
作者联系地址　重庆市北碚区天生路 2 号，西南大学外国语学院
邮　　编　400715
电子邮箱　huxyao@swu.edu.cn; scarletjia@hotmail.com

6

Author: HU Xianyao & ZENG Jia

Title: A Corpus-based Study of the Explicitation of Grammatical Markers in Chinese Translated Fiction

Published in: *Foreign Languages Research*, 2009 (5).

[Abstract] This paper investigates the explicitation of grammatical markers in contemporary Chinese translated fiction based on the contrastive studies of the translated and non-translated corpora. These explicit features of the Chinese translated novels are discussed in detail and supported with corpus linguistic data: 1) the translated Chinese fiction has higher general usage frequencies of most grammatical markers, 2) larger amount of attributive markers with a noticeable decrease of the markers of tense and aspect, and 3) more colloquial effect of some markers, etc. It is believed that the tendency toward syntactic explicitation is one of the most significant features of the fiction translated into Chinese, which tends to comply with the grammatical norms of source languages, mostly European languages, while deviating from the Chinese grammatical norms and leading to the foreignization of the translated texts. These findings on grammatical explicitation of translated Chinese are supportive to the discussions of translation universals and norms of translation.

Key words: Chinese translated fiction; corpus; grammatical markers; explicitation

7

作　　者　刘泽权、田　璐
标　　题　《红楼梦》叙事标记语及其英译——基于语料库的对比分析
发表刊物　《外语学刊》2009年第1期

[摘　要]　章回小说是中国古典长篇小说的一种主要形式。受说书传统的影响，章回小说保留了大量具有拟书场特征的叙事标记语。这些模式化、雷同化的标记语在语篇连贯上具有重要作用，从而成为章回小说独具特色的叙事标记。然而，对古典文学的英译本是否充分体现了叙事标记语的文体特色及功能尚鲜有研究。

本文首先根据叙事语篇的宏观结构模式，结合《红楼梦》中叙事标记语的语篇功能，对叙事标记语进行分类与定义。根据其在叙事中的作用，将叙事标记语分为起始标记语、发展标记语和结束标记语。根据其在文中出现的位置，起始标记语和结束标记语又分为章回标记语和局部标记语。根据事件的缘起，发展标记语分为表示动作结束、言语打断、感官侵入和叙述人现身等叙事标记语。

借助《红楼梦》中英文平行语料库的检索结果及语料库统计工具，以系统功能语法为评价手段，本文对《红楼梦》叙事标记语中的章回标记语及其在三个英译本（霍译、杨译、乔译）中的体现进行检索和对比分析。通过定量与定性研究相结合，发现《红楼梦》的叙事标记语体现了章回小说所特有的拟书场特征。然而，其英译本（尤其是霍译和杨译）为了保证文本顺畅，对这些标记语进行了大幅的忽略和变通，大大削弱了原文拟书场的语言特色，未能体现章回体的语言特色。乔译对叙事标记语基本上进行了保留，但译文过于冗赘，与原文简练的语言风格不甚相符。最后，文章提出在处理《红楼梦》叙事标记语的英译时，可参照其他章回小说的英译情况，考虑采用固定的表达方式，以凸现章回小说的特色。本文的研究结果对于典籍外译具有一定的启示和借鉴作用。

关 键 词 《红楼梦》；叙事标记语；翻译；语料库

作者联系地址 （1）刘泽权：河南省开封市顺河区明伦街85号，河南大学外国语学院；

（2）田璐：广东省广州市白云区白云大道北2号，广东外语外贸大学高级翻译学院

电子邮箱 zeqliu@163.com; ivytianlu@gdufs.edu.cn

7

Author: LIU Zequan & TIAN Lu

Title: Narrative Markers in *Hong Lou Meng* and Their Translations—A Corpus-based Study

Published in: *Foreign Language Research*, 2009 (1).

[Abstract] Noted for its significance in language and culture, *Hong Lou Meng* (*A Dream of the Red Mansions*) is known as a masterpiece of Chinese classical literature. Influenced by the storytelling narrative feature of Chinese full-length vernacular fictions, *Hong Lou Meng* is embedded with a series of narrative markers simulating an oral performance situation. These seemingly dispensable clichés are in effect crucial narrative devices for connecting episodes and indicating the involvement of the narrator. Nevertheless, there seldom have been any studies evaluated the preservation of such narrative features in the English versions.

In this paper, narrative markers are firstly defined and categorized into beginning markers, ending markers and turning markers. According to the positions they appear, the first two categories are further divided into global markers and local markers. Within the framework of Systemic Functional Grammar and with the help of corpus tools, this paper carries out a quantitative and qualitative comparative study of the use and functions of global narrative markers in *Hong Lou Meng* and its three English translations. It is found that global narrative markers are largely omitted or altered in Yang's and Hawkes' English versions, thus losing the storytelling narrative feature of Chinese full-length vernacular fictions. Joly's version retains most of the narrative markers, but the rather lengthy expressions are inconsistent with the conciseness of the original text in language style. The findings of the study may shed light on the translation of classical Chinese literature.

Key words: *Hong Lou Meng (A Dream of the Red Mansions)*; narrative marker; translation; corpus

8

作　者　江进林、文秋芳
标　题　N元组和翻译单位对英译汉自动评分作用的比较研究

发表刊物 《现代外语》2010 年第 2 期

[摘　要] N 元组匹配是评价机器翻译质量的主要方法，即通过检索待评译文与参考译文中相同 N 元组的数量来考察译文质量。该方法也已用于人工译文的自动评分。不过，其不足之处非常明显。首先，N 元组以单个或多个词的自然序列为单位，没有充分考虑语境因素。并且，N 元组忽略了译者的翻译过程，因为译者通常从意义出发，将多个词作为整体来考虑。

与 N 元组匹配不同，文秋芳等（2009）提出人工译文质量评价可采用翻译单位对齐技术。该研究采用的翻译单位概念由双语语料库研究者提出，它一般由多词组成、符合句法规则、具有完整、单一的意义。与 N 元组相比，其优势在于能够关注语言的语法性、连贯性与地道性，但难以顾及学生译文中一两个字或词与参考译文匹配的数量。

在人工译文质量评价中，我们能否用翻译单位取代 N 元组，还是将两种方法有机结合？本文采用 320 篇学生英译汉译文探讨了这一问题。本研究比较了 N 元组匹配数量和翻译单位对齐数量与人工对译文语义、形式、总评分的相关性，并采用多元回归考察了它们对译文质量的解释力。结果表明：1) 翻译单位对齐数量与人工评分的相关度高于绝大多数词 - 和字 -N 元组匹配数量；2) 与 N 元组匹配数量的整体作用相比，翻译单位对齐数量对语义评分的解释力稍高，对形式和总评分的解释力稍低；3) 与仅以 N 元组匹配数量或翻译单位对齐数量为自变量的模型相比，词 - 一元组和翻译单位对齐数量结合产生的模型对人工评分的解释力更强，模型评分与人工评分的相关度和一致性也更高。这表明词 - 一元组匹配与翻译单位对齐互为补充，两者结合对译文质量的预测效果最佳。

关 键 词　英译汉；自动评分；N 元组；翻译单位
作者联系地址　北京市朝阳区惠新东街 10 号，对外经济贸易大学英语学院
电子邮箱　jiangjinlin2014@163.com

8

Author: JIANG Jinlin & WEN Qiufang

Title: A Comparative Study of Ngram and Translation Unit Alignment in Automated Scoring of Students' English-Chinese Translation

Published in: *Modern Foreign Languages*, 2010 (2).

[Abstract]　As a widely adopted quality predictor of machine translation, Ngram, a linear sequence of single or multiple words, does not attach due importance to the linguistic context and ignores the translating process when evaluating human translation. Wen et al. (2009) proposed translation unit (TU) alignment instead. As a concept from bilingual corpus studies, TU is a monosemous multi-word unit with complete meaning and conforms to grammatical rules. TU can better evaluate grammaticality, coherence and idiomaticity than Ngram. But as multi-word unit, it cannot capture the consistency of one or two Chinese characters between human translation and reference translation.

This study uses 320 students' English-Chinese translations to explore whether TU can replace Ngram. It compares the correlations between the number of matched Ngram and human scorings of meaning, form, and overall translation quality with those between the number of aligned TUs and scorings. It further explores the predicting power of matched Ngrams and aligned TUs with multiple regression analysis. Research indicates that the number of aligned TUs has higher explanatory power for meaning scoring than overall Ngrams, but lower explanatory power for form and overall scoring. In addition, models with the number of word-based unigrams and aligned TUs as independent variables explain more scorings than those with Ngrams, and their calculated scores are more consistent with human scorings. Therefore, the combination of word-based unigram and aligned TU number has the best predicting effect of human translated texts.

Key words: English-Chinese translation; Automated scoring; Ngram; TU alignment

9

作　　者　刘泽权、闫继苗
标　　题　基于语料库的译者风格与翻译策略研究——以《红楼梦》中报道动词及英译为例
发表刊物　《解放军外国语学院学报》2010年第4期
［摘　要］　中国古典小说《红楼梦》汉英平行语料库的创建为典籍翻译研究提供了一种观察和分析翻译语言选择和应用的直观平台。本文借助语料库工具把之前未受关注的报道动词的翻译中作为考察对象，对《红楼梦》前56回的报道动词及其三个英译本（霍译、杨译、乔译）的翻译选择进行描述性研究，通过"道"的最频繁报道形式"（某人）道"的翻译对比，以窥探三位译者的翻译风格和策略异同。

研究发现，译者们对报道动词"道"的翻译确有规律可循，其选择不仅受到源语和译入语习惯的影响，而且体现了译者各自的风格，呈现出明显的显化特征。首先，三译者对报道动词的选择均不同程度受到源语单一报道方式"道"的影响：霍译最为明显，几乎统一为 said，杨译次之，多省略，乔译最不明显。其次，译者结合语境选择解释性的报道动词对报道小句进行明晰化处理，乔译尤为突出，使用的报道动词种类最多，显示了较强的译者主动性。再次，译文均受到译入语表达习惯的影响，报道小句多采用倒装形式和扩展结构：霍译和杨译表现较为明显，乔译更拘泥于源语报道的语序，即顺序叙述。上述考察表明，译者的共性在三文本中得到彰显，验证了语际显化现象。同时，通过与非翻译文本对比，发现翻译文本的类比显化明显。

关 键 词　《红楼梦》；翻译；语料库；报道动词；道
作者联系地址　河南省开封市顺河区明伦街85号，河南大学外国语学院

邮　　编　475004
电子邮箱　zqliu@163.com

9

Author: LIU Zequan & YAN Jimiao

Title: Translator Choice and Translator Style: A Corpus-based Study of the English Translations of Reporting Verbs in *Hong Lou Meng*

Published in: *Journal of PLA University of Foreign Languages*, 2010 (4).

[Abstract] The compilation of "The *Hong Lou Meng* (*A Dream of the Red Mansions*) Chinese-English parallel corpus" provides an objective platform for the observation and analysis of the linguistic choices in the English translations of the Chinese vernacular classical novel. With the help of corpus-query tools, this present study set out for a descriptive analysis of the choices the three translations made with reference to the typical reporting verb in the first 56 chapters of the novel, i.e., *DAO* ("say").

　　The findings of the study provide evidence of translation explicitation: they indicate conspicuous patterns of regularity as a result of the dual influence of both the source and target languages, and register distinctive translator style. 1) The frequent use of the monosyllabic Chinese reporting verb in the source text left some imprints on the choices of the three translators: Hawkes' was most recognizable in that almost all of his choices fell on "said"; the Yang's followed him with some omissions; Joly seemed least explicit. 2) The translators resorted more to the English manner of "speech" by means of explicit reporting verbs rather than merely "say", which is truer of Joly than the other two translators. 3) English structure became the normative choice insofar as the whole reporting clause is concerned, i.e. the inverted verb+speaker sequence and the extended (added) reporting clause were employed to mark "who said something to whom."

Key words: *Hong Lou Meng* (*A Dream of the Red Mansions*); translations; corpus-based, reporting verbs; *DAO* ("say")

10

作　　者 吕　桂
标　　题 系统功能语言学翻译质量评估模式的实证与反思
发表刊物 《外语研究》2010 年第 2 期
［摘　要］ 在黄国文系统功能语言学研究古诗词英译的分析和评价之后，国内有学者基于系统功能语言学构建了翻译质量评估模式。

该翻译质量评估模式的实证不充分。实证研究涉及小说《孔乙己》、科普短文"蟑"和几则广告的英译本，虽涵盖了"信息（informative）文本""表情（expressive）文本"和"感染（operative）文本"，但数量极其单薄。

这一翻译质量评估模式，其环节和参数是基于集合意义的语篇而设定的，对语篇大类的下一级语篇翻译的评估缺乏针对性。具体而言，多数文本都是以某一功能为主导的复合文本，其功能侧重面不同，同一大类之下的各文本都有着自己的个性；故该模式各环节的必要性、参数的权重大小在实际运用中需进行调整。

基于此，本文应用该模式评估《故都的秋》英译（张培基译）质量。都是文学语篇，同属表情文本，但情景交融的"悲秋"散文和以二十世纪辛亥革命前后的中国社会为背景的白话小说《孔乙己》相比，有着不同的情景语境因素。

本文在应用系统功能语言学翻译质量评估模式评估《故都的秋》的实证过程中，进一步丰富了对该模式的认识，认为对小文本的译文评估而言，该模式相对较为实用，操作性也较强；它为人们理解和欣赏原文语篇提供了一个新的纬度；对译文语篇概念意义、人际意义的建构进行一些描述和解释，为翻译提供了一个描述而非规定的框架或参数；为翻译批评提供了一个解释和预测的参数；本文对建立更具针对性的次级语篇——散文翻译质量评估模式给出了有益的探索。同时，本研究也进一步彰显了功能语言学理论对翻译研究的启示以及在翻译研究中的可应用性和可操作性。

关 键 词　翻译质量；评估；概念功能；人际功能；散文英译

作者联系地址　广东省广州市白云区沙太南路 1023 号，南方医科大学外国语学院

电子邮箱　lglgq@126.com

10

Author: LV Gui

Title: Revisiting the Translation Quality Assessment Model Based on Systemic-Functional Linguistics: A Case Study

Published in: *Foreign Languages Research*, 2010 (2).

[Abstract]　After Huang Guowen analyzes and evaluates the Chinese-English translation of ancient poems in the light of systemic-functional linguistics, a translation quality assessment model based on systematic-functional linguistics is constructed.

This translation quality assessment model is not widely applied in practice although it has been used to assess Chinese-English translation of the novel *Kong Yi-ji*, the popular scientific essay and several advertisements, which are categorized under "expressive text" "informative text" and "operative text" respectively.

The steps and parameters in this model are based on text types of "informative text", "expressive text" and "operative text"; therefore the model is not applicable for those sub-types categorized under "informative text", "expressive text" or "operative text". To put it more precise, most of the texts has various functions with certain one predominant. Each text categorized under certain text type has its own features. Therefore, the steps and parameters in this assessment model need to be adjusted in actual use.

Based on this, the paper uses this model to assess translation of *Autumn in Old Capital* (translated by ZHANG Peiji). Both are literary works and expressive text; however, the essay of *Autumn in Old Capital* is different with the vernacular novel *Kong Yi-ji* written in the background of the Chinese society around the 1911 Revolution.

This paper further enriches our understanding of this translation quality assessment model in evaluating the translation of *Autumn in Old Capital*. We hold that this model is feasible for evaluating translation of small texts. First, it is insightful for us to understand and appreciate the original texts. Second, this model provides a descriptive framework for translation by describing and explaining ideational meaning and interpersonal meaning of the translated version. Third, it provides a framework for interpretation and prediction for translation criticism. This paper is useful for establishing a translation quality assessment model targeted upon essay, a subtype of expressive texts. At the same time, this paper further demonstrates the enlightenment of systemic-functional linguistics to translation studies and its applicability and operability in translation studies.

Key words: translation quality; assessment; ideational function; interpersonal function; Chinese-English translation of essay

11

作　　者　秦洪武
标　　题　英译汉翻译语言的结构容量：基于多译本语料库的研究
发表刊物　《外国语》2010年第4期
［摘　要］句子长度是探讨翻译简化现象的重要指标，即译文中句子平均长度低于原创文本。但这一假设只是在报刊文本中得到验证，是否适用于

文学翻译还没有研究,是否适用于汉语更是无从知晓。本文基于多译本文学翻译语料库探讨了影响汉语翻译文本语言运用质量的两个因素:句段长度和结构容量。研究发现,影响翻译语言运用质量的不是句子长度而是句段长度,且句段长度与结构容量正相关,后者可以反映佳译和普通译文在语言运用质量上的差异。语料库研究中常用的句长分析不能完全适用于汉语翻译语言的描写。研究还发现,考虑到汉语本身的非形态和意合性质,句段长度和结构容量方面的分析更能反映汉语翻译语言的个性特征;汉语翻译文本之间在句段长度和结构容量上差异较大,而汉语原创文本正好相反,这说明汉语翻译语言在结构容量上偏离了目的语汉语的规范。研究指出,结构容量对翻译质量有重要影响,具体表现为:佳译文本擅长使用非前置手段避免容量过度扩张,译文的结构容量较小;对比译文本过多依赖修饰成分前置来铺排句式,导致结构容量偏大。容量过大会降低句段的易读性,进而降低句子的可接受程度。因此,运用积极的语言手段调控结构容量既是汉语翻译语言运用质量的重要保障,又是翻译从业人员需要掌握的技能。研究认为,目前常用的句长分析解释力有限,而句段长度和结构容量更能反映汉语翻译语言的个性特征;鉴于此,结构容量应成为汉语翻译语言质量评估的对象,也应是翻译技能训练的重要内容。

关　键　词　多译本语料库;佳译;句段长度;结构容量
作者联系地址　山东省济宁市曲阜市静轩西路57号,曲阜师范大学外国语学院
电子邮箱　qinhongwu@163.com

11

Author: QIN Hongwu

Title: Load Capacity of Constructions in Translational Chinese: A Multi-version Corpus-based Study

Published in: *Foreign Languages*, 2010 (4).

[Abstract] It has been well-argumented that sentence length is an important index in talking about simplification in translation, which argues that the average sentence length of translated texts is smaller than that of the source texts. The hypothesis is proved to be true in the translation of journalism, however, it remains unknown whether it is applicable to literary translation with Chinese being the target language. Based on an E-C literary multi-version corpus, the study attempts an adequate description and analysis of sentence segment length (SSL) and constructions' load capacity (COC) characterizing translational Chinese. It finds that a simplistic sentence length calculation is less reliable than SSL and COC account in describing translational Chinese, and that it is SSL but not sentence length that affects the quality of language use. According to the statistic analysis, the good translations typically is adept at using non-prepositioning in order to avoid the over-expanding of the construction's load capacity, and they are characterized by appropriate control over load capacity. Considering overloading may reduce readability, the positive readjustment of construction's load capacity is crucial to the quality of language use in translation. It also finds that SSL can be defined by COC which can reflect difference between good translations and less recognized ones in language use. The paper concludes that load capacity of construction should fall within the scope of translation quality assessment, and translator training as well.

Key words: multi-version corpus; good translation; sentence segment length; load capacity of construction

12

作　者　王金铨、文秋芳
标　题　国内外机器自动评分系统评述——兼论对中国学生翻译自动评分系统的启示

发表刊物 《外语界》2010 年第 1 期

[摘 要] 计算机技术在语言测试中已经得到广泛运用,客观题自不待言,随着技术的不断进步,主观题测试也纳入了自动评分的视野。作文自动评分技术从 1966 年问世以来,日臻成熟,美国教育考试处(ETS)研制的 E-rater 目前已经完全商业化,被正式用于 GMAT 等大规模语言测试中(Marina 2005:104)。国内,梁茂成(2005)对中国学生英语作文自动评分进行了有益的尝试,并取得了初步成果。然而,翻译自动评分技术仍处于探索阶段,目前国内外尚无成熟的人工译文自动评分系统。本研究回顾了国内外机器自动评分系统的现状、内容和特点,并探讨了现有自动评分技术对中国学生翻译自动评分系统的借鉴和启示,在总结前人成功经验的基础之上,将语料库技术、自然处理技术和统计技术结合起来,深入挖掘能够反映译文质量的文本预测变量,建成具有中国特色的翻译自动评分系统应该为期不远。

关 键 词 自动评分系统;机器翻译自动评价;翻译自动评分系统

作者联系地址 江苏省扬州市邗江区华扬西路 196 号,扬州大学扬子津西校区外国语学院

电子邮箱 jqwang@yzu.edu.cn

12

Author: WANG Jinquan & WEN Qiufang

Title: Review and Implications of Existing Automated Scoring Systems—From the Perspective of the Computer-assisted Scoring Model of the Chinese EFL Learners' Translation

Published in: *Foreign Language World*, 2010 (1).

[**Abstract**] This paper reviews the contents and characteristics of the existing automated scoring systems and summarizes the insights and revelations for the construction of the computer-assisted scoring model of the Chinese EFL learners' translation. With the integration of corpus linguistics, natural language processing and statistics, more effective predictors, besides those found in the literature, can be located and the construction of the computer-assisted translation scoring model is not far away.

Key words: automated scoring systems, automatic machine translation evaluation, computer-assisted translation scoring system

口译研究

1. 关系语用学的三元关系在口译中的互动研究　莫爱屏、蒋清凤
2. 从话语分析的角度重识口译人员的角色　任　文、蒋莉华
3. 台湾口译研究现况之探讨　廖柏森
4. 反省法对于同声传译研究适用性探析——兼论口译研究的学科独立性　马志刚
5. 口译质量与控制　王东志、王立弟
6. 口译研究的路径与方法——回顾与前瞻　王斌华、穆　雷
7. 国内口译研究的发展及研究走向——基于三十年期刊论文、著作和历届口译大会论文的分析　穆　雷、王斌华
8. 同声传译中的视译记忆实验研究　王建华
9. 基于语料库的口译研究：回顾与展望　李　婧、李德超
10. 口译中译员主体性意识的语用研究　莫爱屏

Interpreting Studies

1. Interaction among the Triadic Relations of Relational Pragmatics in Interpreting **MO Aiping & JIANG Qingfeng**
2. Reinterpreting the Interpreter's Role: A Discourse Analytical Perspective **REN Wen & JIANG Lihua**
3. The Review of Current Interpretation Research Publications in Taiwan **LIAO Posen**
4. A Preliminary Analysis of the Applicability of Retrospection to Simultaneous Interpreting Research: On the Independence of Interpreting Research **MA Zhigang**
5. The Quality of Interpreting and Its Control **WANG Dongzhi & WANG Lidi**
6. Approaches and Methods of Interpreting Studies: Retrospect and Prospect **WANG Binhua & MU Lei**
7. Interpreting Studies in China: A Journal Articles-based Analytical Survey **MU Lei & WANG Binhua**
8. Empirical Study on Summarization Memory Models for Simul-or-Sight-interpreters **WANG Jianhua**
9. Corpus-based Interpreting Studies: The State of the Art **LI Jing & LI Dechao**
10. The Pragmatics of the Interpreter's Subjective Awareness in Interpreting **MO Aiping**

1

作　　者　莫爱屏、蒋清凤
标　　题　关系语用学的三元关系在口译中的互动研究
发表刊物　《外语研究》2006 年第 6 期
［摘　要］　关系语用学和口译研究因涉及交际者、语言、语境等主要研究对象而相互联系，但又因各自的研究方法与侧重点的不同而相互区别。关系语用学主要研究构成语用体系各构成成分之间的关系，即交际者、语言和语境三者之间的关系。口译研究则在此基础上强调两种语言间传译过程中各种制约因素之间的互动。本文首先从关系语用学的角度阐述言语交际中交际者、语言和语境三者之间的关系；然后探讨这三者在口译过程中的互动。本文认为，弄清关系语用学中的三元关系，不仅可以使译员从理性思考的高度来认识它们，而且还可以在实际运用中，把握和利用这三者之间的互动关系。口译是语言使用的一种特例，将关系语用学和口译有机地结合起来研究，有助于揭示言语交际中复杂的语用过程，其交叉研究的成果对其他研究领域亦有极大的启示。
关 键 词　关系语用学；口译；三元关系；互动研究
作者联系地址　广东省广州市白云区白云大道北 2 号，广东外语外贸大学翻译学研究中心
邮　　编　510420
电子邮箱　moaiping@gdufs.edu.cn

1

Author: MO Aiping & JIANG Qingfeng

Title: Interaction among the Triadic Relations of Relational Pragmatics in

Interpreting

Published in: *Foreign Language Research*, 2006 (6).

[Abstract] Relational pragmatics and interpreting studies are two closely related branches of the linguistic science. Both of them take interactants, language and context as their own objects of study, but differ in research methods and perspectives. The former focuses on the relationship among various components in pragmatics, i.e. interactants, language and context, while the latter emphasize the interactional relationships and the pragmatic constraints involved in the transference of meaning from one language into another. This paper first elaborates on the relationships among the three different elements from a relational pragmatic perspective, and then explores into the dynamic and interactional process of this triadic relationship. It argues that a clear understanding of the above mentioned triadic relationship can not only enable the interpreter to take such a relationship rationally, but also help them grasp and use these elements in actual practice. The paper concludes that the application of relational pragmatics theory in interpreting (a special form of language use) is conducive to unveiling the complicated pragmatic processes, which in turn has great implications for some other related research in verbal communication.

Key words: relational pragmatics; interpreting; triadic relations; interaction

2

作　　者　任　文、蒋莉华
标　　题　从话语分析的角度重识口译人员的角色
发表刊物　《中国翻译》2006年第2期
［摘　要］　长期以来，译员被认为是跨语跨文化交际活动中的被动参与者，只负责准确传达讲者意义，严守中立，不应当对谈话的内容、观点、进程等发表看法或提出建议；合格的译员应当是"透明的"、"隐形的"，

让人几乎感觉不到他／她的存在。本文从微观话语分析的角度出发，将日常对话口译看作是由不同话语系统的人通过口译员所进行的一个面对面的口头交际活动，一个特殊的话语过程，进而运用话语分析中的"话轮转换机制"解析真实生活中的口译活动，通过观察谈话过程中各方的参与方式和话轮的走向，考察译员的话语角色以及对谈话活动可能带来的影响。

通过从真实口译活动中取证，我们发现，译员不仅仅只是讲话人话语的翻译者，有时还会根据现场情况和自己的判断，在谈话的某些节点上通过语言、副语言和非语言行为参与到交流过程，甚至影响话轮的走向。比如通过身体和面部朝向、眼神等方式进行话轮传递或话轮交还；在长时间无人讲话出现沉默时为避免尴尬主动制造话轮，让谈话继续；在当事双方出现重叠话轮时打断或忽略某个话轮，或者当译员自己与某个当事人出现重叠话轮时选择放弃话轮或继续持有话轮；在预测到讲者的话语可能会让听者感到尴尬时选择暂不翻译，而是主动接受讲者话轮与其直接交流等等，从而证明了 Roy (2000) 提出的观点：在三方共同参与的口译话语过程中，译员与谈话各方一道影响甚至决定着交际活动的方向和结果。

本文的意义在于：一、对对话口译过程进行跨学科（社会语言学）考察；二、通过实证研究解构了视译员为"传声筒"、"隐形人"的传统偏见，证明译员是交际活动主动参与者和共同建构者。

关　键　词　谈话口译；话语分析；话轮；转换；译员角色
作者联系地址　四川省成都市武侯区科华街路 3 号川大花园
邮　　　编　610041
电子邮箱　wenrensu@hotmail.com

2

Author: REN Wen & JIANG Lihua
Title: Reinterpreting the Interpreter's Role: A Discourse Analytical Perspective
Published in: *Chinese Translators Journal*, 2006 (2).

[Abstract] Interpreters have long been viewed as passive participants in interlingual and intercultural communication, responsible for accurately conveying interlocutors' message only. It is believed that a qualified interpreter should be neutral, transparent and invisible, and should not give advice to either party or comment on the talk on whatever grounds. By taking a micro discourse analytical approach, the authors of this paper endeavor to observe the interpreter's role by a close look at the turn-taking mechanism in an interpreter-mediated conversation, a special discourse process in which the primary interlocutors coming from different linguistic and cultural systems interact face-to-face with one another through an interpreter.

Through empirical studies on real-life cases, the authors find that interpreters were not just translators of the interlocutors' speech. At certain point in time, they also tended to manage the flow of talk through verbal, non-verbal and paralinguistic means based on specific situations. For instance, an interpreter may distribute a turn by way of body/face direction or eye contact to seek response from a certain participant, create a turn when nobody speaks for a relatively long period of time to avoid lengthy silence, interrupt or ignore a turn when overlapping talks occur, or accept a turn directly when the listener is likely to be embarrassed if the speaker's utterance is directly translated, thus confirming Roy's claim (2000) that interpreters work together with the primary interlocutors to influence or sometimes even determine the direction and outcome of the interaction. The traditional notions of interpreters being "microphone personality" and "invisible persons" are thus deconstructed. Interpreters (re)grain their status as co-constructors of the conversation in a multi-party interaction.

Key words: interpreter-mediated conversation; discourse analysis; turn; turn-taking; interpreters' role

3

作　　者　廖柏森
标　　题　台湾口译研究现况之探讨
发表刊物　《翻译学研究集刊》2007 年第 10 期

［摘　要］　台湾社会近年来相当重视口译专业，各大专院校亦大量开设口译课程以训练学生口译技能。一个新兴学科能在短短十几年间广受学界和各大专院校的青睐，实属罕见。目前口译教学与研究的风潮虽然大兴，但其现况仍缺乏较翔实的描述和检验。口译研究是门新兴学科，相对缺乏坚实的学术研究传统。然而，台湾目前的口译研究成果当中究竟透显了何种面貌和质量？现今大势和未来趋向又如何？应该是口译学界加以重视的课题。因此，本研究旨在回顾探讨台湾口译研究过去十余年在学术期刊、研讨会和学位论文上发表口译研究的成果，利用内容分析法（content analysis）对口译研究的主题、研究方法、研究语种等向度作一有系统的检视和概括，以呈显口译此一新兴学科目前的发展情况和研究成果，并提出口译学科继续向前推展的依据和建议。主要研究结果指出，目前台湾口译研究团队人数不足，有待生力军加入；台湾口译研究的语种虽有七种之多，但绝大多数是处理中英和中日两种语言组合间的口译活动；撰写口译研究的语文现时仍以中文为主，硕博生用外文写作比例高；口译研究的主题偏重于口译课程规划和教材教法，其后依序为口译理论或现象之探讨、口译相关的实务议题、口译技巧或策略之分析与口译质量或错误之评量；口译研究的方法则以语篇分析为主，其次依序为个案研究、论证法、问卷调查、实验法、访谈法、观察法，其中定性研究数量明显高于定量研究。期望本文能对台湾口译研究提供一全面而有系统的回顾，有助了解口译学界目前的研究走向，未来亦可采取具体步骤，使用新的研究方法，探索新的研究问题，以有效增进口译研究质量，确立口译学科的学术定位。

关 键 词　口译研究；口译研究分类；口译研究方法
作者联系地址　台湾台北市和平东路一段 162 号，台湾师范大学翻译研

究所

电子邮箱　posen@ntnu.edu.tw

3

Author: LIAO Posen

Title: The Review of Current Interpretation Research Publications in Taiwan

Published in: *Studies of Translation and Interpretation*, 2007 (10).

[Abstract]　Over the past decade, the profession of interpretation has received considerable attention, and interpretation training activity has been increasing sharply around Taiwan. There has also been a dramatic increase in the number of research publications on interpretation as well. In view of such a rapid popularity of the new academic discipline in recent years, nevertheless, research focusing on the examination and reflection on the current state of interpretation research is still very scarce. Thus, the purpose of this paper is to review a large number of research papers devoted to this area in order to determine key issues the academic community has been concerned about in interpretation research. In order to review the literature devoted to interpretation, content analysis was conducted on journal articles, conference proceedings, and Master theses on interpretation, all of which were read, analyzed, encoded, and lastly put into different categories based on their research themes, research methods, languages studied, and other categories. By reflecting on the research literature, the researcher seeks to identify the research issues that are most frequently written about, to report on major trends in established research of interpretation, and then to make suggestions for local researchers to address new or promising research directions in the future. The major results showed that most papers dealt with Chinese-English and Chinese-Japanese interpretation issues; the topics researched were mostly related to interpretation pedagogy; the most frequently used research method was discourse analysis. It is hoped that, through the findings of this study, interpretation researchers may gain a better understanding of the present state of interpretation research and to explore new questions.

Key words: interpretation studies; research categories; research methods

4

作　　者	马志刚
标　　题	反省法对于同声传译研究适用性探析——兼论口译研究的学科独立性
发表刊物	《外语与外语教学》2007 年第 11 期

［摘　要］　翻译方法研究讨论的核心议题之一是其他学科常用的研究范式是否适用于不同模态的翻译研究。作为国际正式场合中主要的信息传递模式，同声传译的研究方法日益呈现多元化的趋势。基于文献解析，本文探讨心理学和语言习得研究中经常采用的口头报告法对于同声传译研究中的适用性。通过文献解读和评述得出以下结论：口头报告法中仅有反省法适用于同声传译的研究；其研究方案的设计须在研究焦点、受试选择、实验材料、实验条件和结果解释等方面遵循同声传译的本质要求。 如果能够结合言语输入和输出的相关理论对所得资料加以解释，反省法有助于揭示同声传译员的认知变化过程。文章力图说明，同声传译研究乃至任何形式的口译研究都必须着眼于提出科学的研究问题并作出合理的理论假设，然后采用适切的研究方法，进而得出较为切实的研究结论。同时，将同声传译以及连续传译等其他口译模式均纳入心理学研究中的常态范式有助于引导相关研究领域进一步科学化和实证化。文章还指出，未来的同声传译研究还应该基于心理学原理加强研究设计的内在逻辑，提高研究方案的信度、效度并增强其创造性。

关 键 词　反省法；同声传译；研究设计

作者联系地址　广东省广州市白云区白云大道北 2 号，外语外贸大学外国语言学及应用语言学研究中心
邮　　编　510420
电子邮箱　vm111222@126.com

4

Author: MA Zhigang

Title: A Preliminary Analysis of the Applicability of Retrospection to Simultaneous Interpreting Research: On the Independence of Interpreting Research

Published in: *Foreign Languages and Their Teaching*, 2007 (11).

[Abstract]　One of the key topics in translation studies is to explore the applicability of research paradigms in other fields to the various modes of translation studies. As a major mode of information transmission on international occasions, research methods for Simultaneous Interpreting (SI) tend to be of multi-dimension. This paper, based on the review of selected literature, analyzes the applicability of verbal-reporting methods, which are frequently employed in psychological and linguistic studies, to the research of Simultaneous Interpreting. Literature review and in-depth analysis reveal that, retrospection is the only verbal-reporting method applicable in SI research. However, its effectiveness is highly dependent upon well-thought research design, which, as required by SI, poses specifications, upon research focal point, subject selection, research materials, experimental conditions and results interpretation. If the obtained results can be interpreted in terms of theories concerning speech input and output, retrospection is potentially to be effective in revealing cognitive processes in SI. This paper seeks to illustrate that, SI research, together with any modes of interpreting, must first focus on raising scientific research questions with reasonable research hypotheses, and then, by employing appropriate research methods, arrive at scientific conclusions. Meanwhile, putting SI and consecutive interpreting under the canonical research paradigms of psychological studies is conducive to leading relevant studies to be more empirical and scientific. In addition, this paper emphasizes the internal logic of research design with the psychological principles as its basis, thereby enhancing the reliability, validity and originality of SI research.

Key words: retrospection; Simultaneous Interpreting; research design

5

作　　者　王东志、王立弟
标　　题　口译质量与控制
发表刊物　《中国翻译》2007年第4期

[摘　要] 随着社会发展对口译人才需求量的不断扩大，国内的口译培训开展得如火如荼。特别是，近年来各高校纷纷开设了MTI课程，力求培养职业化口译人才。那么，到底要培养什么标准的译员以及如何培养，就成了培训工作必须要面对的问题。口译质量评价一直是口译培训的重要内容，与课程设置和培训效果息息相关。但现实中口译评估过程往往存在多重标准，且不同主体对口译质量的要求也不尽相同。为此，本文首先通过横向对比联合国、欧盟、AIIC、中国译协（TAC）等国内外主要职业机构的行业标准，并结合八十年代以来有关口译质量的典型性研究成果（Bühler, 1986; Kurz, 1989; Kopczynski, 1994; Moser, 1995），提炼出了影响口译质量的共识因素：忠实准确、表达清晰、术语正确。在此基础上，结合过往的研究和实践经验提出了确保中译英口译质量的三策略：1）语义优先，即理解发言人主张要义、表达灵活自如；2）结构解析，做到"得意忘形"，不受语言形式拘束；3）词语简化，发挥口语表达简洁直白的特性，提高信息传达效率。当然，在实际操作中保障口译质量的策略绝不止

这三种，还存在其他变通和补偿的手段，但这三种是最常用的方法。运用得当，口译就会变得轻松自如、游刃有余、保质保量。本研究对口译培训具有直接指导意义，通过对比分析、归纳总结首次厘清了口译质量标准的共识因素，为职业化培训构建起目标体系。此外，提出来的口译质量保障三策略也为培训课程设置、训练内容以及评估测试提供了参考依据。

关 键 词 口译；质量；要素；策略

作者联系地址 （1）王东志：北京市朝阳区惠新东街10号，对外经济贸易大学；

（2）王立弟：中国香港新界沙田，香港中文大学人文社科学院

电子邮箱 wangdongzhi@uibe.edu.cn; wanglidi@cuhk.edu.cn

5

Author: WANG Dongzhi & WANG Lidi

Title: The Quality of Interpreting and Its Control

Published in: *Chinese Translators Journal,* 2007 (4).

[Abstract] Nowadays the demand for conference interpreter is growing as the result of increasing cross-border exchanges. Therefore, interpreter training in China is booming, as evidenced by the fact that MTI program mushrooms in universities aiming to train professional interpreters. But what are the qualities a professional interpreter should have and how to build them up through training? This is a fundamental question for any interpreter training program. As we know, interpreting performance assessment is an integral part of a training program, closely related to curriculum design and training result. But in practice, such assessment involves multiple criteria and performance judgment is highly subjective. To address this problem, this paper purports to identify some shared criteria for interpreting performance judgment by examining the professional standards proposed by key institutions like the United Nations, the European Union, AIIC and the Translators Association of China, and by reviewing some major research findings (Bühler, 1986; Kurz, 1989; Kopczynski, 1994; Moser, 1995). The shared criteria include meaning-based fidelity, consistent expression, and correct terminology. Based on that, the paper proposes three strategies to assure interpreting quality: a) Sense-driven translation – grasping speaker's intention instead of slavishly following the form; b) De-construction – reformulating to make your own speech; c) Simplification – using plain language to maximize delivery efficiency. This paper may serve as a reference for pedagogical orientation, curriculum development, exercise design, and performance judgment in a training program.

Key words: interpreting; quality; criteria; strategy

6

作　　者　王斌华、穆　雷
标　　题　口译研究的路径与方法——回顾与前瞻
发表刊物　《中国外语》2008年第2期

[摘　要] 从目前国内期刊上发表的口译研究类文章来看，不少文章仍以主观推测和实践经验总结为主，尤其是研究方法不够科学，存在以下几个方面的问题：文献综述不够全面系统、研究问题不够典型深入、研究方法不够清晰明确、研究设计不够严谨科学、研究结果往往未经系统的理论推演进行证明或基于数据的实证分析进行验证。

本文首先在回顾西方口译研究二十世纪五十年代中至今的发展阶段及主要研究范式的基础上，总结了口译研究主要的研究课题及发展成就。然后分析近年来口译研究发展所面对的困难，提出口译研究的跨学科发展路径。进而提出口译研究方法的若干原则，并总结了口译研究方法设计的若干途径。

通过对西方口译研究路径与方法的回顾与前瞻，可以看出：口译研究的总体发展路径正在向跨学科的多元式研究扩展；口译研究的方法由原来的主观推测和实践经验总结向以数据为基础的客观描写和实证分析转变。

口译研究的方法论已经引起众多口译研究者的关注，近年来部分口译研究成果在实证研究方面已有与笔译研究并驾齐驱的趋势。假以时日，在科学的研究方法论引导下，在相关学科理念和方法的支持下，中国的口译研究可望产生出更多优秀的成果。

关　键　词　口译研究；路径与方法；回顾与前瞻
作者联系地址　School of Languages, Cultures & Societies, University of Leeds, Leeds LS2 9JT, U.K.
电子邮箱　wangbinhua@hotmail.com

6

Author: WANG Binhua & MU Lei
Title: Approaches and Methods of Interpreting Studies: Retrospect and Prospect
Published in: *Foreign Languages in China*, 2008 (2).

[Abstract] As seen from the papers on interpreting published in Chinese academic journals, quite some papers are heavily based on personal speculation or summary of practical experience, which call for more scientific methodology. Methodological problems are evident in the following aspects: incomprehensive literature review, poorly-defined research questions, inadequately outlined research methods, and (as a result) research findings without a solid base of theoretical deduction or data-based empirical examination.

Based on a retrospect of the history of interpreting studies in the west since mid-1950s, this paper reviews the major approaches and methods of interpreting studies. Major themes of researches are summarised and the achievements of interpreting studies are evaluated. With an awareness of the major difficulties faced by interpreting researchers, the paper proposed a prospective outline of research design and research methods for interpreting studies.

From the retrospect we can see that interpreting studies are developing towards interdisciplinarity and the research methodology is evolving from subjective speculation based on experience to objective description and empirical analysis based on data. The retrospect and prospect may provide valuable guidance to interpreting researchers in China.

Key words: interpreting studies; approaches and methods; retrospect and prospect

7

作　　者　穆　雷、王斌华

标　　题　国内口译研究的发展及研究走向——基于三十年期刊论文、著作和历届口译大会论文的分析

发表刊物　《中国翻译》2009年第4期

［摘　要］　与近年国内口译实践和教学蓬勃兴起的现状形成对比的是，作为一门新兴子学科的口译研究尚缺乏坚实的理论基础和系统的研究方法，因此有必要对其发展历史和研究路向加以厘清。本文以过去三十年的期刊口译论文、著作以及历届全国口译大会上的提交论文等为数据，考察国内口译研究的发展概况，分析国内口译研究的研究数量、研究主题和研究方法。以此呈现口译研究在国内的发展态势，探讨存在的问题、研究的走向和提升的路径。

通过分析发现，国内口译研究呈现研究主题多样化、研究内容具体化、研究路径跨学科、研究取向市场化，及研究交流国际化的特点。主要存在的问题为学科理论意识薄弱、研究方法缺乏科学性、研究者身份单一。

研究提出，国内口译研究可通过拓展口译研究主题、改进研究方法、提倡口译跨学科研究等方法提升广度和深度。

关 键 词　国内口译研究；考察；发展；研究走向
作者联系地址　广东省广州市白云区白云大道北 2 号，广东外语外贸大学
电子邮箱　mulei2002@139.com

7

Author: MU Lei & WANG Binhua
Title: Interpreting Studies in China: A Journal Articles-based Analytical Survey
Published in: *China Translators Journal*, 2009 (4).

[Abstract]　The boom of interpreting practice and pedagogy in China makes it even more urgent for interpreting studies, a newly emerging subdiscipline lacking in a theoretical foundation and a systematic methodology, to look back and reflect on its own development history. Responding to the call, this paper surveys the journal articles on interpreting published over the past three decades. Analyzing these articles in terms of the central concern addressed, the theme developed and the research method adopted, the co-authors identify the existing problems and the developmental trends, and explore the approaches to improve interpreting studies in China.

Analysis shows that interpreting studies in China are getting more and more diverse in terms of research topics, more specific in research content, and with inter-disciplinary, market-oriented and internationalized characteristics. The main problems mostly lie the lack of theoretical analysis, scientific research methods and the homogeneous background of the researchers.

The study suggests that interpreting studies in China can be improved by expanding research subjects, research methods, and promoting interdisciplinary research.

Key words: interpreting studies in China; survey; development; trend

8

作　　者　王建华
标　　题　同声传译中的视译记忆实验研究
发表刊物　《中国翻译》2009年第6期
[摘　要]　同传及带稿视译对译员的同步性口译要求是一个挑战。本文意图为译者提供一种针对常见口译文本信息的快速记忆型摘要模式，以求提升同传译员应对此挑战的能力。在面对同传任务时，如果译员是在口译现场拿到口译任务的书面材料或拿到材料的时间很仓促，同传译员会快速浏览文稿，快速提取同传关键信息，以求提升同传质量。本文从解决同传记忆问题入手，通过心理实验的方法，研究提高同传视译记忆效果的摘要记忆模式。本研究共做三组实验，每组实验考察的同传信息提取文本题材不同，第一组考察经济类题材的文章视译摘要提取方式比较，第二组考察文化类，第三组考察政治类。研究发现，在视译不同题材的文本时，快速信息提取的摘要式加工有不同的应对策略。同传译员高效获取文本的关键信息模式：对于经济类文章，译员需要快速记忆首句和关键词，关键词为文中出现频率较高的词，从而快速抓取全文重要信息，进行高效同传；对于文化类题材的文章，译员在完成同传任务之前应速记题目和关键词，从而确保快速掌握全文的核心信息；对于政治类题材的文章，同传译员要快速记文章的题目、首句和关键词，以确保高效率同传。总之，对于同传中的视译加工，同传译员需要按题材分类处理，采用不同的摘要式信息提取策略，才可以最大限度地确保口译过程的快、准和顺，从而使口译结果最大化地忠实于原文信息，同时快速顺畅地完成口译任务，这对于保证口译质量至关重要。

关 键 词　同声传译；摘要模式；视译
作者联系地址　北京市海淀区中关村大街59号，中国人民大学（邮编：100872）
　　　　　　　　山西省临汾市尧都区贡院街1号，山西师范大学（邮编：

041004）

电子邮箱　wjhsfl@ruc.edu.cn

8

Author: WANG Jianhua

Title: Empirical Study on Summarization Memory Models for Simul-or-Sight-interpreters

Published in: *Chinese Translators Journal*, 2009 (6).

[Abstract]　Keeping pace always forms a great challenge for simul-or-sight-interpreters. This study targets at providing a summarization memory model to improve simul-or-sight-interpreter's performance to keep pace better during conferences. Three sets of experiments are conducted on summarization extraction models for three styles of texts of economic texts, political ones and cultural ones. Experimental results prove that topic sentence + key words summarization model can best convey the general meaning of economic texts, title+key words for cultural ones and title+topic sentence + key words for political ones.

Key words: empirical study; summarization memory model; simul-or-sight-interpreting

9

作　　者　李　婧、李德超

标　　题　基于语料库的口译研究：回顾与展望

发表刊物　《中国外语》2010 年第 5 期

[摘　要] 过去十五年来，基于语料库的翻译研究影响日增。但由于口译语料库的缺乏，基于语料库的口译研究仍不多见。本文在评价当今较具代表性的国内外三个口译语料库的基础上，归纳口译语料库的特点和基本的建立方法。具体而言，如要建立口译语料库，一般要遵循以下步骤：1）根据研究目的决定建立口译语料库的类型：对应、类比，还是两者兼具。2）录音/影：录音分为现场录音和实验室录音。3）录音/影资料数字化。4）影音资料文字转写。5）文本标注和对齐。随着时间和技术的发展，语料库口译研究也开始显示出自身不同于语料库笔译研究的特点，如：1）语料收集：收集难度较大。录制、分类以及声音处理都极大的依赖各种尤其以电脑技术和软件功能为主的科技手段，收集程序比较繁复。此外，语料来源相对较少，真实场景的口译语料更是难得。2）语料库的建立：口译语料库建立的过程要比笔译语料库复杂，主要在于数据搜集、文字转写、标注以及对齐等过程。其中文字转写要根据一定转写依据进行，以及根据需要增加的笔译文本语料库。3）语音特征：口译语料库的基础在于口语资料，与笔译语料库的文本资料最大的不同是能够凸显口语的特征。这对研究语音学，音韵学相关问题差等提供重要依据。4) 教学价值：口译语料库能为教学提供宝贵的材料。真实场景的语料可以为学生提供实用的口译练习环境，职业译员的口译更能为学生提供参考和标准。对于外语学习者而言，不同的口译语料库对于听力以及口音训练也能起到对比，认知和改进作用。基于语料库进行的错误分析，也可为教学分析和纠正学生问题找到更有效的途径。

关 键 词　语料库；语料库翻译研究；口译研究

第二作者联系地址　香港九龙红磡育才道 11 号，香港理工大学中文及双语学系

电子邮箱　ctdechao@polyu.edu.hk

9

Author: LI Jing & LI Dechao

Title: Corpus-based Interpreting Studies: The State of the Art

Published in: *Foreign Languages in China,* 2010 (5).

[Abstract] Corpus-based translation studies as a discipline has been gaining ground over the past 15 years. While there are abundant corpus-driven studies on written translation today, few similar studies are conducted in the field of interpreting studies largely due to the dearth of rigorously-built interpreting corpora. Based on the review of three existing interpreting corpora in the world, the paper summarizes the features and the necessary steps in building interpreting corpora. Specifically, the development of an interpreting corpus includes the following procedures: 1) deciding on the type of the corpus (i.e. parallel or comparable one) in accordance with the research purpose of the investigator; 2) recording/ videotaping, which includes live or lab recording/ videotaping; 3) digitalization of recording/ videotaping; 4) transcription of audios and videos; 5) tagging and alignment of transcriptions. It is generally agreed that it is more difficult and time-consuming to build an interpreting corpus than a translation corpus, as the former involves more procedures (such as recording, taping and transcription etc) than the latter. The paper concludes by pointing out the prospects and pitfalls of corpus-based interpreting studies.

Key words: corpus; corpus-based translation studies; interpreting studies

10

作　　者　莫爱屏
标　　题　口译中译员主体性意识的语用研究
发表刊物　《中国外语》2010年第3期

［摘　要］译者作为主体在翻译研究中的地位十分重要，其主体性意识则又是该研究领域中的关键问题之一。本文从语用的角度探讨口译过程中译员的主体性意识。文章认为译员主体性意识的主要表现方式之一就是译员能动性地对目的语话语选择的顺应，包括：1）译员自觉地顺应原语话题；

2）译员能动地顺应话语的信息结构；3）译员超越因语境模糊所引起的话语意义不确定性。文章得出：由于译员主观能动性的作用，译员对语言的选择是主动的选择；译员对语言选择的顺应因而也就是主动的顺应；译员能动性地选择语言并顺应这种语言的选择是译员主体性意识的产物。

关 键 词 主体性；语言选择；顺应性；语用研究

作者联系地址 广东省广州市白云区白云大道北 2 号，广东外语外贸大学

邮 编 510420

电子邮箱 moaiping@gdufs.edu.cn

10

Author: MO Aiping

Title: The Pragmatics of the Interpreter's Subjective Awareness in Interpreting

Published in: *Foreign Languages in China*, 2010 (3).

[Abstract] Translator/interpreter as a focal subject has a crucial role to play in translation studies therein the translator/interpreter's subjective awareness can never be neglected. This paper deals with the interpreter's subjective awareness in the interpretation process from a pragmatic perspective. It proposes that one way to represent such awareness is the interpreter's motile adaptation to the making of linguistic choices in the target discourse. And such an adaptation includes his/her adaptation to the topic consciously and to the information structure of discourse creatively, transcending indeterminacy of meaning in discourse caused by the contextual vagueness. It can therefore be concluded that the interpreter's linguistic choice making and his/her adaptation to it are subjective in terms of his/her creativity (i.e. subjective motility), which in turn is the product of his/her own subjective awareness.

Key words: subjective awareness; linguistic choice; adaptation; pragmatics

翻译研究专著

1.《文学翻译与文化参与:晚清小说翻译的文化研究》 胡翠娥
2.《功能语言学与翻译研究:翻译质量评估模式建构》 司显柱
3.《翻译批评:从理论到实践》 温秀颖
4.《〈道德经〉在英语世界:文本行旅与世界想象》 辛红娟
5.《翻译方法论》 黄忠廉、田传茂、刘 丽、魏家海、余承法、胡远兵
6.《中西翻译简史》 谢天振等
7.《译学新论:从翻译的间性到海德格尔的翻译思想》 蔡新乐
8.《生成与接受:中国儿童文学翻译研究1898—1949》 李 丽
9.《翻译地理学》 许建忠

Monographs on Translation Studies

1. *Literary Translation and Cultural Engagement: A Cultural Study on Late Qing Fiction Translations*   **HU Cui'e**
2. *A Text-based Translation Quality Assessment Model: A Functional Linguistics Approach*   **SI Xianzhu**
3. *Translation Criticism: From Theory to Practice*   **WEN Xiuying**
4. *Tao-te-ching in the English World—Text Traveling and the Accepted Imagery*   **XIN Hongjuan**
5. *The Methodology of Translation*   **HUANG Zhonglian, TIAN Chuanmao, LIU Li, WEI Jiahai, YU Chengfa & HU Yuanbing**
6. *A Brief History of Translation in China and the West*   **XIE Tianzhen, et al.**
7. *A New Collection of Essays in Translatology: From the Inbetweenness of Translation to the Translational Thought of Heidegger*   **CAI Xinle**
8. *Production and Reception: A Study of Translated Children's Literature in China 1898-1949*   **LI Li**
9. *Translation Geography*   **XU Jianzhong**

1

作　　者　胡翠娥
标　　题　《文学翻译与文化参与：晚清小说翻译的文化研究》
出版单位　上海外语教育出版社（2007）
[摘　　要]　研究方法：该书对晚清小说翻译进行的研究不是传统的以语言分析和文本对照为主的批评式研究，而是运用文化研究和翻译的社会学方法论，对晚清小说翻译活动进行历史的、功能的和文化的描写和解释，把晚清的翻译小说复原到产生它的社会历史背景中，着重于分析翻译策略的形成过程，观察翻译作为主体文化产品在主体文化和文学演进中所扮演的角色和所起的功能。

研究内容：第一是晚清小说翻译产生的社会历史文化背景以及时人对翻译活动的理论认识，包括对它的文化定位（即译以致用的工具主义）和概念化（即翻译为实业）。第二是晚清小说翻译的翻译策略和翻译准则。第三晚清的翻译评论准则及其和明清之际小说评点话语之间的关系。第四则探讨晚清小说翻译活动和中国现代化的关系。

主要观点和结论：晚清文人翻译群体通过选择特定的翻译策略和参与翻译批评，通过个人在文本上的经营和操作，最大限度地进行文化参与和建设，使翻译活动成为一种中西文化协调活动，把一项原则上属于客观的透明的知识输入活动转化成个人参与和干预文化的有效媒介。

主要创新：1）打破了迄今为止多数翻译批评所采取的以文本对照为主体、以理想译本为指归的单一模式；2）对"伪译"与"伪著"等长期为翻译界、文学界所忽视乃至轻视的"两不管"地带进行了深入而恰如其分的分析，肯定了其社会学与文化学意义，不仅具有翻译史的意义，而且具有文学史的价值；3）按照中国的实际情况对文化学派理论作了修正和补充，丰富和发展了多元系统的翻译学说。

关 键 词　晚清小说翻译；文化参与；文化研究；翻译的社会学方法
作者联系地址　天津市南开区卫津路94号，南开大学外国语学院

邮　　编　300071
电子邮箱　hce1970@126.com

1

Author: HU Cui'e

Title: *Literary Translation and Cultural Engagement: A Cultural Study on Late Qing Fiction Translations*

Publisher: *Shanghai Foreign Language Education Press*

[Abstract]　This research adopts a cultural and sociological approach instead of traditional normative one. The main task is to offer a historical description and explanation of late Qing fiction translation and translating by bringing it back into its contemporary social setting. Focus is put on the shaping of translation strategies and translation norms. The role and function of translations as products in evolution of receptive literature and culture are examined. The research argues that the intellectual translators group in late Qing delve into cultural engagement and construction by means of translating. The translation strategies manifested in translated texts and translation discourse serve as the best instrument for cultural participation. In this way, translating as an originally objective and transparent knowledge introduction is transformed into a subjective and evaluative milieu for cultural participation. This dissertation falls into four major parts. Part One introduces contemporary social and historical milieu in which fiction translation and translating take place as well as the way translation is perceived, conceptualized and theorized. Part Two looks into the translation strategies and translation norms. Part Three concentrates on contemporary translation criticism discourse and its relation to traditional fiction commentary discourse. Part Four makes a tentative examination on relation of fiction translation and translating to the progress of Chinese modernization.

The major values of the research are that it is among the first attempts of Chinese scholars to deviate from traditional normative translation approach, and focus on translation products as such in their cultural and societal context.

Key words: late Qing fiction translations; cultural engagement; cultural study; translation sociology

2

作　　者　司显柱
标　　题　《功能语言学与翻译研究：翻译质量评估模式建构》
出版单位　北京大学出版社（2007年）
［摘　要］ 翻译批评是翻译应用理论研究的中心内容，翻译评估是翻译批评的核心，翻译质量评估模式的研究是本领域最具本原性的课题之一。目前国内研究成果有限，缺乏一个完整、科学并具有操作性的评估模式；国际上较为成熟的豪斯《翻译质量评估模式》以系统功能语言学、语篇分析等为理论指导，以八种类型的英德翻译文本语料做实证，拥有比较完整的参数体系和遵循一定的程序，但参数设置不够合理，运行步骤过于简化，整个框架基本上是单向度的"自下而上"等不足，因而无法有效应用在英汉两种语言文化差异极大的英汉翻译文本质量评估上。

鉴于此，本书从系统功能语言学视角对翻译的本质认识和翻译质量概念等的认知基础上，根据篇章语言学关于语篇属性，功能语言学关于语言研究的语篇视角以及言语行为框架及其形式（语言）、功能和情景三个系统及其辩证关系的阐述出发，提出和论证面向语篇的翻译质量评估模式。然后，根据赖斯的翻译类型学理论，分别以反映前述三类语篇（即信息类、表情类和感染类）的汉英、英汉文本为语料，检验并修正该模式。本研究的创新在于建构了一种基于语篇、文本并具有系统性、完整性、可操作性和较少主观特征的翻译质量评估模式，在中国与世界关系愈加紧密、翻译活动影响愈大的背景下，该课题愈显重要和迫切。

关 键 词 系统功能语言学；翻译质量评估模式；语篇
作者联系地址 北京第二外国语学院高级翻译学院
电子邮箱 20160026@bisu.edu.cn

2

Author: SI Xianzhu

Title: *A Text-based Translation Quality Assessment Model: A Functional Linguistics Approach*

Publisher: *Beijing University Press*, 2007.

[Abstract] Translation criticism is the body of Applied Translation Studies, while translation assessment constitutes the core of translation criticism. Thus the position of translation assessment within the hierarchy of translation criticism, applied translation studies, and, ultimately, translation studies, clearly speaks of its theoretical significance of the research. This book aims to study the translation quality assessment model — the core issue of applied translation studies.

Based on the review of the statue quo and the literature, particularly the analysis of House's translation quality assessment model, a text-based translation quality assessment model is proposed in the light of Systemic Functional Linguistics views on the issues such as the translation nature, the translation quality, the dialectic correlation among form, function, and context within the verbal behavioral framework, and the text-oriented study of language. To validate the model, in the part of empirical study of the project, C-E and E-C translations of three types of text categorized by Buhler's theory of typology of text and translation typology proposed by Reiss, are used as the data to which the said translation model is applied for the double purposes: evaluation of the translations and the verification of the model proper. The final part of this book is devoted to the revision of the model based on the defects which appear in the application. The ultimate model finalized in this book is characteristic of being systematic, comprehensive, operative, and less subjective in application. As the exchanges between China and the world are happening at an unprecedented level, aided by countless translation activities in all spheres of the society, the need for such a model and further studies on this topic is urgent and definite.

Key words: Systemic Functional Linguistics; translation assessment model; text

3

作　　者　温秀颖
标　　题　《翻译批评：从理论到实践》
出版单位　南开大学出版社（2007年）

[摘　要] 改革开放后的中国，各领域都呈现出一派欣欣向荣的景象，翻译也不例外。然而，随着翻译实践的繁荣，翻译领域也不可避免地出现了鱼龙混杂、泥沙俱下的乱象。从二十世纪九十年代起，翻译界呼吁翻译批评介入翻译实践和翻译理论研究之声便不绝于耳。在此背景下，一些中外学者开始将目光投向翻译批评理论和实践研究，并陆续有相关论文和专著发表、出版。《翻译批评：从理论到实践》也正是在这样的背景下成书的，着重探讨了如下问题：翻译批评在中国究竟有着怎样的历史沿革？在翻译研究中到底处于何种地位、起着怎样的作用？改革开放以来的翻译批评研究取得了哪些具体成就？还存有哪些问题？当前的翻译批评家和翻译研究工作者还需要做哪些工作？未来的翻译批评会呈现出何种样态？具有怎样的特征？

带着这些问题，本书通过文献考察、案例比较、定量定性分析、理论思辨等方法，在国内首次从历时和共时的角度，对中国翻译批评实践的历史演进，特别是翻译批评理论研究的发生、发展和现状进行了详细的梳理与考察，并对梳理和考察的结果进行了系统的分析，归纳了翻译批评研究所取得的成绩和存在的问题，提出了认识和解决问题的途径；在此基础上，本书对翻译批评的本质、功能、主客体、标准、方法等基本理论问题进行了较为深入的探讨，并通过具体翻译批评实践案例对理论的应用进行了分析考察；最后，本书对未来的翻译批评进行了瞻望，本书认为，未来的翻译批评将是一种"圆形"的批评，它必须具有多元性的开放视野、民族性的传统意识、建构性的学术追求，唯其如此，翻译批评才能以自身的存在，对当代翻译事业乃至中国社会发挥重要而独特的文化影响，才能在新世纪成为翻译研究的一个分支学科——翻译批评学。

关 键 词 翻译批评；理论；实践

作者联系地址 天津市河西区珠江道 25 号，天津财经大学人文学院

电子邮箱 wen.xiuying@163.com

3

Author: WEN Xiuying

Title: *Translation Criticism: From Theory to Practice*

Publisher: *Nankai University Press,* 2007

[Abstract] After the reform and opening up, China has shown a thriving scene in various fields, and translation is of no exception. However, with the prosperity of translation practice, this field inevitably became chaos with dragons and fishes jumbled together and the bad became mixed with the good. Since 1990s, the translation circles have called for the involvement of translation criticism in translation practice and translation theory. In this context, some Chinese and foreign scholars began to focus on translation criticism theory and practice research, and have published related papers and monographs. It is in this context that the book *Translation Criticism: From theory to practice*, came into being, focusing on the following questions: what is the historical evolution of translation criticism in China? What position and role does it play in translation studies? What specific achievements have been made in translation criticism research since the reform and opening up? What are the problems? What do contemporary translation critics and translation researchers need to do? What will the future translation criticism be like? What are the characteristics?

With these questions, this book, through literature review, case study, quantitative analysis and qualitative analysis, theoretical analysis and other methods, explores for the first time in China from the diachronic and synchronic perspective the historical evolution of Chinese translation criticism practice, especially the theory of translation criticism on its occurrence, development and the present status in detail. On this basis, it discusses the basic theory of translation criticism, its nature, function, object, standard, methods and so on. The application of the theory is also analyzed through the practice cases of translation criticism. Finally, the book looks forward to future translation criticism, in which it believes, in the future, the translation criticism will be a "Circular" criticism, with diverse open vision, national consciousness, and academic pursuit. Only in this way can translation criticism with its own existence, have an important and unique cultural influence on translation study and China society, and become a branch of translation studies in the new century.

Key words: translation criticism; theory; practice

4

作　者　辛红娟
标　题　《〈道德经〉在英语世界：文本行旅与世界想象》
发表刊物　上海译文出版社（2008年）
［摘　要］《道德经》自问世以来，历代注疏极丰，它不仅是中华古文明的结晶，也是全人类共有的文化财富。十九世纪末期，《道德经》进入英

语世界，新译本频出，成为发行量仅次于《圣经》和《薄伽梵歌》的典籍，是被翻译得最频繁的中国古代文献。作为翻译起始点的《道德经》文本的理解，由于各章之间并无明显的逻辑联系，书中语言简洁到语义模糊的地步，整部文本看似格言语录的碎片，常令译者陷入绝望的境地，文章指出，正是给读者带来阅读障碍的语言的简洁性和各章节之间的逻辑松散成就了《道德经》在西方被频繁翻译、广泛阅读的命运。词义的浑圆、语法的意合和修辞的空灵赋予《道德经》文本巨大的阐释空间，召唤读者的积极建构。西方读者出于历史的需求和各自的学术前见，建构着形态各异的《道德经》：作为宗教比附的《道德经》、作为世界未来哲学的《道德经》、作为智慧源头的《道德经》和作为汉学研究成果的《道德经》。

本文从文化语境下的旅行文化研究入手，分析旅行与文学翻译实践的相似性，借助钱钟书的"翻译距离说"和赛义德的"旅行理论"，对《道德经》文本在西方英语世界的旅行过程进行细致描述，运用阐释学和接受美学以及比较文学形象学理论，剖析《道德经》在英语世界的形象变迁，分析道家学说在移入异域后产生的变形、翻译在其间起到的作用，以及译者主体和意识形态在文学传播的世界想象中的干预和操纵。在当今世界经济全球化、文化多元化的语境下，本文期待通过具有典型意义的个案研究，为弘扬民族文化及其在本土的正确回应提供学理上的分析。

关 键 词 《道德经》；旅行理论；翻译研究
作者联系地址 浙江省宁波市江北区风华路818号，宁波大学外国语学院
邮 编 315211
电子邮箱 xinhongjuan@126.com

4

Author: XIN Hongjuan

Title: *Tao-te-ching in the English World—Text Traveling and the Accepted Imagery*

Publisher: *Shanghai Translation Publishing House*, 2008

[Abstract] The *Tao-te-ching* is a book of Chinese philosophical poetry. With its simplicity and awesome profundity, it is like a "White Dwarf" of classical literature, so weighty, so compact, and so suggestive of a mind radiating thought at a white heat. The *Tao-te-ching* is widely read in China, with numerous commentaries. And it is no less known to the West through a long line of translators. The *Tao-te-ching* has acquired a widespread and diverse Western audience, and it appeals to readers on a variety of levels. The Westerners have read something new into the text and have produced many a *Tao-te-ching* text. Next to the *Bible* and *Bhagavad Gīta,* the *Tao-te-ching* is the most translated book in the world.

The vital part of translation is, of course, the transition between two different linguistic systems. This survey analyses the domesticating rendition, foreignizing rendition, modernizing rendition, deconstructing rendition and interpretative rendition in the history of the *Tao-te-ching* translation. The early missionary translation tended to domesticate the text out of their religious and political pursuit. Foreignizing rendition shows higher respect and tolerance of the "otherness", yet it would be better to come along with compensatory efforts. Still some translators make special efforts to bring the *Tao-te-ching* into the modern world. Due to the denial of the theological meaning of the Author-God, many translators take the option of improvisation to combat the extreme hardship of translating the *Tao-te-ching*, so as to cling to the tenet of Lao-Tzu's thought. Yet this deconstructing expediency can not be used too immodestly or too frequently. Scholar translations have always been trying to put lengthy and highly complex clarifying expansions to offer a genuine Chinese prototype, yet these renditions seem unlikely to have an immediate impact on popular understandings of the text.

The *Tao-te-ching* has put a magic spell on sinologists and amateurs as well to derive intoxicating qualities of it. As for the early missionaries, they caught meanings in their net, but prosily, letting the beauty slip through. With the development of sinology, increasing number of translators have begun to realize that poetic beauty is no ornament for the *Tao-te-ching*, it is the meaning and the truth. Thus, many have tried to recreate much of the terse diction and staccato rhythm of the text by printing the translation of the rhyming passages in separate lines and with indention.

Key words: *Tao-te-ching*; travelling theory; translation studies

5

作　　　者　黄忠廉、田传茂、刘　丽、魏家海、余承法、胡远兵
标　　　题　《翻译方法论》
出版单位　中国社会科学出版社（2009年）

[摘　要]《翻译方法论》共分四章。第一章为翻译求似律；第二章为全译方法论；第三章为变译方法论；第四章为研究方法论。

翻译方法论包括翻译实践方法论和翻译研究方法论。实践方法论包括全译方法论和变译方法论，全译方法论可分为增译、减译、转译、换译、分译和合译。变译方法论可分为摘译、编译、译述、缩译、综述、述评、译评、译写、改译、阐译、参译、仿作。

翻译研究方法论指的是"三个充分"（观察充分、描写充分和解释充分）的研究要求、"两个三角"研究方法论和从方法到学科的研究路径。两个三角的"小三角"为表-里-值，即语表形式-语里意义-语用价值，这是微观研究方法；两个三角的"大三角"为语-思-文，即语言比较-思维转换-文化交流，这是宏观研究方法。翻译方法得以总结，翻译史也就开始了。翻译方法和翻译史丰富、发展到一定程度，导致系统化的理论产生。理论体系的进一步系统化，可以形成一门学科。方法-历史-理论-学科，是翻译方法逐步从实践上升为学科的一般研究历程。

关　键　词　方法论；全译；变译；翻译研究

作者联系地址　广东省广州市白云区白云大道北2号，广东外语外贸大

学六教 A302 翻译学研究中心
邮　　编　510420
电子邮箱　zlhuang1604@163.com

5

Author: HUANG Zhonglian, TIAN Chuanmao, LIU Li, WEI Jiahai, YU Chengfa & HU Yuanbing

Title: *The Methodology of Translation*

Publisher: *China Social Sciences Press*, 2009

[Abstract] *The Methodology of Translation* consists of four chapters: Chapter 1 touches upon the translation principle of achieving similarity; Chapter 2 discusses the methodology of complete translation; Chapter 3 the methodology of translation variation; and Chapter 4 the methodology of translation studies.

　　The methodology of translation includes the methodology of translation practice and translation studies. The former consists of methods of complete translation, which are subdivided into correspondence, addition, omission, transference, conversion, division and combination, and methods of translation variation, which are subdivided into selective translation, editing translation, translation plus report, condensing translation, summarizing translation, translation plus review, translation plus comment, translation plus writing, explanatory translation, reference translation, and imitating translation. The latter constitutes an innovative paradigm of conducting translation studies, including a tri-sufficiency research requirement (sufficiency of observation, description and explanation), a two-triangle research approach and a quadri-chain research process from method summarization to discipline construction. A two-triangle research approach includes a "small" three-part approach of linguistic form, semantic meaning and pragmatic value at a microscopic level and a "large" three-part approach of language comparison, transformation of thinking modes and cultural exchange at a macroscopic level. Translation history begins in the company of the summarization of translation methods. The enrichment of translation methods and development of translation history bring about systematized theories, which finally lead to the construction of a discipline. A logical growth of methods, history, theories and discipline is the general research process of translation methods from practice to an independent discipline.

Key words: methodology; complete translation; translation variation; translation studies

6

作　　者　谢天振等
标　　题　《中西翻译简史》
发表刊物　外语教学与研究出版社（2009年）
［摘　要］ 本书为中国大陆翻译硕士专业学位（MTI）专业必修课教材，同时也是一部翻译史研究专著。全书共十五章，既有对中西翻译史三大发展阶段的宏观描述，又有对中西翻译史上重大翻译事件、主要代表人物的翻译思想及其相应翻译活动的具体阐释。通过对本书的阅读和训练，读者不仅可较快地掌握中西翻译史的发展脉络，同时还能对中西译学观念的演变、建立翻译学学科的历史必然性等问题有深刻的认识。本书主要特点为：一、首次明确提出了中西翻译发展史的整体观，以"翻译与宗教""翻译与知识传播""翻译与民族语""翻译与文化价值的传递"和"翻译与当代各国的文化交流"五个主题为切入点，对中西翻译史进行了有机地整合，既有历时的梳理，又有共时的比较，是中西翻译史类教材编写领域的一个全新的、有意义的探索和尝试；二、首次把人类译学观念（翻译思想和理论）的演变与人类翻译史上特定历史时期的主流翻译对象联系起来，提出

特定历史阶段的主流翻译对象是形成该历史阶段的主流译学观念的重要制约因素,并从这一立场出发,把中西翻译史划分为"宗教文献翻译阶段、文学翻译阶段和非文学(实用文献)翻译阶段"三个阶段,深刻地揭示了人类译学观念演变的历史轨迹;三、结合"二战"以后世界各国翻译的职业化趋势,对当今国内乃至国外的翻译现状进行了介绍,并从这一大背景出发,分析了翻译专业教学的特点以及翻译学科建立的历史必然性,把翻译市场问题、网络翻译等当下现实生活中的翻译事件和翻译现象编入翻译史教材,拉近了教材与现实生活的距离,体现出鲜明的时代特征。

关 键 词 中西翻译史;翻译史分期;中西翻译史整体观

作者联系地址 上海市虹口区大连西路 550 号,上海外国语大学高级翻译学院

电子邮箱 swgfxtz@163.com

6

Author: XIE Tianzhen, et al.

Title: *A Brief History of Translation in China and the West*

Publisher: *Foreign Language Teaching and Research Press*, 2009

[Abstract] As a textbook for compulsory courses of MTI in mainland China, the book is also a monograph of translation history. Within its fifteen chapters are detailed accounts about how translation history develops through three stages in China and the West, and specific interpretation of significant translation events, translation thoughts by key thinkers and their translation activities in the history. Reading the book and doing the corresponding drills will help readers to have a fast and good command of the historical development of translation in China and the West, and also a deep understanding of questions such as the evolution of views of translation in China and the West, and the historical necessity of establishing a discipline of translation studies. This book attempts to make some innovations from the following three aspects: Firstly, a holistic view of translation history in China and the West is advocated for the first time. Focusing on five topics of "translation and religion", "translation and knowledge transmission", "translation and the development of national languages", "translation and the transmission of cultural values" and "translation and cultural exchange in modern times", the book makes its debut attempts at an organic and holistic view of translation history in China and the West, along the lines of diachronic description and synchronic comparison, which is a novel and meaningful exploration and experiment in textbook compilation of translation history in China and the West. Secondly, it is a first attempt to think of how people's views of translation (that is, translation thoughts and theories) develop in history in relation with what types of texts are mostly translated in a specific period of human's translation history. It is proposed that in a specific historical period, the mostly translated texts are one of the significant restraints to influence how dominant views of translation take their forms. Based upon this proposition, the book tries to divide the translation history in China and the West into three stages of religious texts translation, literary translation and non-literary or practical texts translation, thus clearly mapping out how people's views of translation develop through the course of history. Thirdly, the status quo of translation both at home and broad is introduced after a consideration of the trend that translation has been undergoing professionalization after the Second World War across the globe. Starting from the background, the book analyzes the features of teaching of translation-as-a-major, and the historical necessity of establishing translation studies as a discipline. To include translation events and phenomena from our daily life in the textbook such as issues of translation market and network translation will definitely reflect the features of the time via drawing close the distance between the textbooks and the real life.

Key words: Translation history in China and the West; periodization of translation history; holistic view of translation history in China and the West

7

作　　者　蔡新乐
标　　题　《译学新论：从翻译的间性到海德格尔的翻译思想》
出版单位　人民文学出版社（2010年）

[摘　要]　本书是对目前的翻译研究批判性思考的一个结集，收有《居间的翻译：以〈红楼梦〉片段英译为例》、《情与世界：〈红楼梦〉的两个世界与三个世界及其在英文中的再现》、《本雅明：翻译的终结于灵韵的在场》《同一的神话与翻译的缺席：论想象力在翻译之中的作用》《基督教〈圣经〉中"我是"的意义与翻译问题初探》《海德格尔指导"你是谁"认识论翻译观》《海德格尔〈荷尔德林的赞美诗《伊斯特河》〉中的本体论翻译思想》《海德格尔〈荷尔德林的赞美诗《伊斯特河》〉中的翻译认识论问题》《翻译：在海德格尔与钱锺书之外》《自我翻译：行走在翻译"间性"之上的思想家苏格拉底简论》及《彼此彼此》等论文十一篇。文中指出，二项对立已形成将复杂的世界一分为二的定势，因而诗也就成为哲学化的对象，这种形而上学的作为危及到了我们的翻译研究，甚至已将之推向拒绝他者思维的境地；而雅各布森的翻译三分法及其"语际翻译"等概念，由于执着于结构主义的同一思想而背离了跨文化交流的倾向；本雅明的"来世翻译"，因为渲染基督教的末世主义意味，而不能归入提倡全面颠覆形而上学的"解构"思想，而他提出的"灵韵"却因为迎合浪漫主义的历史走向，而特别值得重视；海德格尔的翻译思想不能归结为他在《存在与时间》出版之后就不再使用的那种"阐释学"，而是应从他并未从中走出的认识论加以探究，尽管这种自我认识往往会形成特定的自我中心主义而需要重新检讨。因而，西方理性主义的实效，或已为日常的、非系统的思想留下生存空间，我们的翻译研究似乎也就有了另一片生发的场地。全书的基调是，如何走出"西方思想"。

关　键　词　间性；海德格尔；想象力；二项对立
作者联系地址　江苏南京市栖霞区仙林大道163号，南京大学外国语学院
电子邮箱　xinlecai@163.com

7

Author: CAI Xinle

Title: *A New Collection of Essays in Translatology: From the Inbetweenness of Translation to the Translational Thought of Heidegger*

Publisher: *People's Literature Publishing House*, 2010

[Abstract] As a collection of critical essays on current problems in translation studies, the book consists of eleven papers, mainly discussing the following issues: 1) Binary opposition, in its inclination to split the world rooted in its complexity into two and to philosophicalize poetry, has become a threat to translation studies, in its ever-strong resistance to the exotic and foreign ways of thinking as embodied in the Other; 2) The classification of translation by Jakobson and his notion of the interlingual translation deviate from what is needed in cross-cultural communication, sticking to the identity from structuralism; 3) Benjamin's "afterlife", advocating eschatologism, has nothing to do with Deconstruction that intends to subvert metaphysics, while his view of Aura should be taken into account in its affinity with the tendency of Romantic poets; and 4) Hidegger's translation thought is not to be attributed to hermeneutics, instead it should be studied from his epistemology, though the self-centrism therein asks for an examination. The studies carried out in the book are attempted to illustrate the point that the failure of western rationalism has left a room for translation studies in its daily and unsystematic dimension, and a new realm then could hopefully be ushered in, though how to go out of western thought remains a serious problem in the field.

Key words: inbetweenness; Heidegger; imagination; binary opposition

8

作　　者　李　丽

标　　题　《生成与接受：中国儿童文学翻译研究 1898—1949》

出版单位　湖北人民出版社（2010 年）

[摘　要]　以儿童为中心的现代中国儿童文学是在外国儿童文学作品和理论的译介中催生的。中国儿童文学翻译研究，不仅对儿童文学研究很重要，而且对中国翻译史也是一个不可或缺的部分。目前儿童文学翻译研究在国内外都处于边缘的位置，尤其在中国，对中国儿童文学翻译的研究，不仅数量不多，而且质量也欠佳。

　　本书吸纳描述性翻译研究、儿童文学研究和比较文学的一些研究方法，对儿童文学翻译活动的生成、接受与影响进行考察。具体来讲，以笔者编制的《清末民初（1898—1919）儿童文学翻译编目》和《民国时期（1911—1949）儿童文学翻译编目》为基础，首先对 1898-1949 研究时段内的儿童文学概貌展开描述。然后从诗学、赞助者、语言和译者性情等四个视角对儿童文学翻译活动的生成过程进行描述与分析。接受部分则以谢弗莱尔的比较文学接受学的研究模式为基础，选取了夏丏尊译的《爱的教育》、鲁迅译的《表》和"俄罗斯／苏联儿童文学在中国"等三个具体的个案，对儿童文学翻译作品在中国的接受进行考察。影响部分则利用比较文学影响研究中的渊源学和流传学，从技巧影响、内容影响、形象影响等三个方面具体考察儿童文学翻译作品对中国儿童文学创作所产生的影响。本书还对今后中国儿童文学翻译研究进行了展望。

关 键 词　翻译研究；儿童文学翻译；诗学；赞助者；语言因素；性情；影响研究；接受

作者联系地址　澳门高美士街，澳门理工学院语言暨翻译学校

电子邮箱　lili@ipm.edu.mo

8

Author: LI Li

Title: *Production and Reception: A Study of Translated Children's Literature in China 1898-1949*

Publisher: *Hubei People's Press*, 2010

[Abstract] Child-oriented Chinese indigenous children's literature was created with the translation of western children's works and theories on children's literature. The study on translated children's literature in China is significant not only to the research on Chinese children's literature, but also to Chinese translation history. At present the study on translated children's literature both at home and aboard occupies a marginalized position. Particularly in China, the limited research that has been done on the subject is of poor quality.

This book combines the methods taken from descriptive translation studies, children's literature research and comparative literature to describe and analyze the production, reception and influence of translated children's literature in China during the period of 1898-1949. Based on two catalogues compiled by the author, this book pictures the translated children's literature in China during the period of 1898-1949. The production of translated children's work is analyzed from four perspectives: poetics, patronage, linguistic elements and personality of translators. The reception part, based on the reception models by Yves Chevrel, adopts three case studies to examine the reception of translated children's literature in the Chinese context. The influence part adopts the methodology of chronology and doxologie to prove and conduct the influence of translated children's literature upon indigenous Chinese children's literature. The book ends with an outlook for future research on translated children's literature in China.

Key words: translation studies; translated children's literature; poetics;

patronage; linguistic elements; personality; influence study; reception

9

作　　者　许建忠
标　　题　《翻译地理学》
出版单位　黑龙江人民出版社（2010 年）

[**摘　要**]　翻译地理学是翻译学和地理学交叉研究的硕果，是依据地理学原理，特别是协调发展论、人地关系论、文化理论、可持续发展论等原理与机制，研究各种翻译现象及其成因，进而掌握翻译发展的规律，解释翻译的发展趋势和方向。概括地说，翻译地理学是研究翻译与其地理环境之间相互作用的规律和机制的。具体地说，是将地理学的研究成果引入翻译研究，将翻译及其地理环境相联系，并以其相互关系及其机理为研究对象进行探究，从而从地理学角度审视翻译、研究翻译，力求对翻译中的多种现象进行剖析和阐释。它不但从理论上揭示翻译地理的客观规律，而且注意密切结合我国的实际，立足于阐明翻译实践中的种种问题。

翻译地理学共分为十二章，主要论及地理翻译论的定义、研究方法及研究意义；翻译自然地理论，主要论及自然地理环境对语言及语言传播的影响、地理环境与种族、民族特征的形成、从自然地理环境解析中西思维模式的形成等论题；翻译人文地理总论，论及人文地理学的四大理论，重点放在翻译理论中的人地关系系统和翻译实践中的人地关系协调上；翻译人文地理分论，如城市地理翻译论、旅游地理翻译论、政治地理翻译论、文化地理翻译论、经济地理翻译论、民族地理翻译论、宗教地理翻译论、行为地理翻译论等；翻译与全球化地理发展，主要论及全球化对翻译以及翻译研究的启示，提醒人们要注意做好东西方文化交流中的逆差平衡工作，并以此为契机，积极同世界接轨，引进和创新相结合，创造繁荣和谐的世界翻译新局面。

作为一个新兴的交叉学科，翻译地理学主要借鉴这两个学科的研究方法，把翻译放置在自然地理和人文地理环境中，研究这两种地理环境以及人的生理、心理、行为环境的各种地理因子与翻译的相互关系，通过较系统的研究，初步构建地理翻译论的研究体系。

关 键 词 翻译学；地理学；交叉研究；天人合一；和谐共荣
作者联系地址 天津市西青区宾水西道391号，天津理工大学外国语学院
邮 编 300384
电子邮箱 jianzhong_xu@163.com

9

Author: XU Jianzhong

Title: *Translation Geography*

Publisher: *Heilongjiang People's Publishing House*, 2010

[Abstract] Translation Geography is the result of cross-study of translatology and geography. It studies various translation phenomena and their origins based on the principles and mechanism of geography, especially the principles and mechanism of the coordinated development concept, the man-land relation, the culture theory and the sustainable development. Generally speaking, it deals with the laws and mechanism of translation interacting with its surroundings. To be specific, it means to introduce the achievements of geography studies to translation studies, to associate translation with its geographical environment, and to study their interrelations and their mechanism for the purpose of examining and studying translation, and of trying to analyze and explain the various translation phenomena. It not only reveals the objective law of translation geography theoretically but also focuses on its combination with the translation reality in China, trying to expound various problems encountered in translation practice.

The book comprises twelve chapters, including the definition, approach and significance of Translation Geography, translation and its physical geography, translation and its human geography which contains urban geography, tourism geography, political geography, cultural geography, economic geography, ethnic geography, religious geography, behavioral geography, and globalized geography. It attempts to fill the gap of the absence that there is no systematic study of translation and geography.

As a newly-established interdiscipline, Translation Geography tries to build an initial system based on the research methods of translatology and geography by putting translation in its natural and human circumstances, which studies the correlation of translation and its surroundings or the human physiological, psychosocial and behavioral circumstances.

Key words: translatology; geography; cross-study; unity of heaven and man